Puritan Village

Puritan Village

The Formation of
a New England Town

By

SUMNER CHILTON POWELL

Wesleyan University Press
MIDDLETOWN, CONNECTICUT

ce

760590

Copyright © 1963 by Wesleyan University
ISBN: 0-8195-6014-6
Library of Congress Catalog Card Number: 63-8862
Manufactured in the United States of America
First Wesleyan paperback edition, 1970; second printing, 1975

In loving memory of my father
CHILTON L. POWELL
and my grandfather
ARTHUR C. POWELL

Table of Contents

$\mathcal{L}$ist of $\it{Illustrations}$

Preface

THIS book is the culmination of a six-year detective hunt among local records, archives, and private collections in England and in Massachusetts. I do not recommend a similar study to any student who has a faint heart, lack of patience, inability to travel, or poor eyesight. Such a study demands the development of various specialized skills. A knowledge of the mysteries of genealogy is essential, and these can be both complex and frustrating. One must also learn about paleography and know how to decipher the different court hands, the shorthand Latin used by clerks, and seventeenth-century handwriting in general. A note of warning: many of the church documents make the formal manorial court rolls look like works of art, as they are. Single pages, or paragraphs of entries, in Church Court Deposition Books or Churchwardens' Accounts have cost me many hours of exasperation, to say nothing of long weeks at the typewriter.

Another important ability which must be cultivated is the use of a portable photostat machine, such as the Contura, under every kind of difficulty, including the differences in types of electric current in foreign countries and the caution of archivists who fear any damage to their documents. In addition to the skill of handling a photostat machine, one should know about photographic processes in general and a certain amount about cartography, particularly for the period studied. Naturally, the technical legal language used by court clerks must be mastered.

My original scheme — to trace all of the most important settlers of Sudbury, even though their descendants knew little or nothing about them — was a considerable gamble, and I simply had to take it. But lest this project sound as if it were a singlehanded feat, let me quickly add that no study of this type can possibly be done without the generous co-operation of the many archivists, local historians, and antiquarians who know, administer, or process the specific documents involved. I have literally hundreds of letters in my files, and I am aware that I have asked many people impossible lists of questions which I blush to read over, now that the work is done. But somehow I was able to instill in these most helpful men and women the faith that I would put all the pieces together into a meaningful whole, and I hope that this book meets with their expectations. I can say truthfully that we worked rather long hours over a great deal of this.

First, I wish to express my thanks for the constant co-operation and interest of the former Town Clerk of Sudbury, Massachusetts, Mr. Forrest D. Bradshaw. He made available not only the original Sudbury Town Records, but his own research as well, including his reconstructed map and a whole store of information. I should like to think that a Sudbury student would continue the edited transcription of the Town Books which Mr. Bradshaw and I started together in 1951. Next, I owe a deep debt of gratitude to Mrs. Winifred Dodge, who taught me much about genealogy and allowed me to use her own research on Edmund Rice and on other Sudbury settlers. Any young historian would do well to appreciate the precision and careful handling of documents, which are the *sine qua non* of any professional genealogist. One must learn painfully that the "John Parmenter" on an early document may not be the same "John Parmenter" whose activities one wants to know about.

Next, I wish to thank Miss Hilda Grieve, of the Essex Record Office, for teaching me what little paleography I know at present. But more than this, her warmth of encouragement, stemming from her own dedication to careful local history, was invaluable, particularly in the early stages of the study, though she has read the final draft as well. Dr. Norman Tyack, author of an unpublished thesis for the University of London, "The Emigration from East Anglia to New England, 1630–1660," was more than generous in assisting me with the knowledge gained from his own research, and we have become good friends through this mutual interest and work.

Perhaps it would be best to proceed by geographic areas in acknowledging my gratitude to the many archivists and antiquarians in the many counties, boroughs, and record offices which I visited in England. The rector of Weyhill, Cyril B. Williams, has made the first chapter possible and contributed a whole file of letters on historical details of his parish. His brother-in-law, Edward Keep, built a portable photostat machine, which permitted us to make a successful invasion of the almost inaccessible Arundel collection of manuscripts. The three of us appreciated the co-operation of John Arundel in opening up this ancient family muniment room. Frederick Sparrow and Edmund Parsons were very helpful in regard to Andover borough records, and Mrs. Cottrill, archivist of the Hampshire Record Office, was most helpful.

Chapter II was greatly aided by Mr. Percy Birtchnell of Berkhamsted; and Mr. W. E. Tate, the expert on parish documents, checked my research on these and read the whole study as well. Mr. R. Coates, the former Town Clerk of the Borough of Sudbury, has been enormously helpful in regard to documents relating to Chapter III, as have been Mr. Grimwood and Mr. Kay of the same borough. John Booth and I worked in harmonious co-operation on old Framlingham. I discovered the old Nicholas Danforth deed, and John located the actual farm and reconstructed the map, Figure 4. Both of us are grateful to Mr. James M. Martin for the use of the Golty Account Book, to Mr. Derek Charman, archivist of the East Suffolk County Council, and to his assistant Miss D. M. White, for loan of the Churchwardens' Accounts. Mr. M. G. Rathbone, archivist of the Wiltshire Record Office, and his assistant, Miss Bell, Registrar of the Wilts Diocesan Registry, Mr. Faithful and Mr. Gardner at the Winchester Diocesan Registry, all gave valuable assistance on county and church documents. Mr. Bales helped me at the Cambridge County Archives, Miss Redstone at the Bury and West Suffolk Record Office, and Miss Honor Thomas did some valuable transcription of Essex documents.

The usefulness of this study has been greatly enhanced by the drawings and the maps. Both Kenneth Conant, a professor of Harvard University, and Charles Strickland, an architect of Boston, were very helpful in consultations on the sketches. Since 1952, when some of these drawings appeared in *The Journal of the Society of Architectural Historians,* no one has questioned the reconstructions. Miss Esmée Cromie worked many hours on the large map of Sudbury in 1650, and I am greatly indebted to her.

There are several people to whom I owe deep thanks for their constant encouragement and criticism. Mr. Walter Whitehill, Secretary of the Massachusetts Colonial Society, and Professor Mark Howe of the Harvard Law School were always ready to give advice and assistance. Professor Samuel E. Morison and Professor John Gaus, of Harvard, guided the thesis in its initial stages, and Professor Oscar Handlin, Professor Bernard Bailyn, Professor George Homans of Harvard, and Professor Edmund Morgan of Yale have added helpful comments. Mr. John Powers, one of the most active citizens of Sudbury today, has read the manuscript closely. He has been principally responsible for the founding of the Sudbury Historical Society, Inc., which is using our sketch of the Second Meeting House as its symbol. Mr. Ross Parmenter, a descendant of the original John Parmenter and an editor on *The New York Times,* has given me much valuable assistance and encouragement. My good friend Professor Walter A. Sedlow Jr., of the System Development Corporation, has contributed his incisive criticism and stimulating enthusiasm ever since the start of the study. And my mother, Mrs. Edward T. Hall, has given both her warmth of interest and her long experience as a teacher of English, while she watched the study grow from a hope to the final draft.

Just as the original town of Sudbury was a co-operative venture of many devoted townsmen, so this story of Sudbury owes its being to the loyalty and generosity of those who still honor the spirit of these free townsmen of early New England.

S. C. P.

Introduction

FOR more than seventy years a scholarly debate has been simmering over the origin of the New England town. Herbert Baxter Adams first proposed a thorough investigation of the origin and development of village communities in Germany, England, and America, and Charles Andrews and Edward Channing accepted the challenge.[1] John Sly has recently come to the conclusion that town governments in Massachusetts grew up by trial and error in each distinct town, but the concept of a typical seventeenth-century New England town is still accepted in many texts.

Historians who have been combing through the welter of English local records, however, have been forced to abandon many generalizations about both the seventeenth-century English parish and the township, and it is apparent that there was as much variety in village and borough institutions as there was uniformity.[2] Since emigrants from these English towns tended to form new social groups once they had landed in New England, and to live in settlements considerably apart from one another, it is difficult to believe that they lost their tendency to be individualistic in attitude and behavior.

The best approach to a study either of the origins of a set of social institutions or the transition of these from England to New England is a careful examination of those emigrants who comprised and administered these institutions when they were living in England and again when they had gathered to form a new town. The generalization that these inhabitants were "English" or were "Puritans" may blind us to the realization that there were at least three distinct types of English experience in the seventeenth century which had molded these settlers: the open-field manorial village; the incorporated borough; and the enclosed-farm East Anglian village. All of these entities, of course, had some relation to the English parish, but there were many types of intricate social structure.

It is necessary to understand that a seventeenth-century London businessman considered his experience quite different from that of an open-field farmer and that this farmer, in turn, had habits which differed from those of the East Anglian farmers and those of any citizen of a borough. Only when we realize that each type of man had a distinct framework of reference, as well as a distinct realm of felt experience, do we begin to grasp the tensions of the first New England towns. As representatives of different local cultures moved from areas in England to become leaders of early town groups, they were forced to adjust to each other's different habits as they attempted modifications of basic English institutions and customs.

These early town leaders had a type of challenge exciting to idealists. Each early town was, in a real sense, a little commonwealth. Legally it was able to select its members and to exclude "such whose dispositions do not suit us, whose society will be hurtful to us."[3] Furthermore, each town was free to make as many laws as it considered necessary and to operate with considerable flexibility in relation to "The Governor and Company of the Massachusetts Bay." While a town needed the general government in times of crisis and emergency and recognized the Massachusetts General Court as the source of authority, it often admitted local prerogatives which did not agree, point by point, with every law made for the good of the commonwealth. For the early years, then, each town could make an attempt to form as much of an ideal state as its leaders could conceive and find agreement on.

Edward Winslow, in Plymouth, made a revealing statement when he wrote, "We came here to avoid the hierarchy, the holy days, the Book of Common Prayer, etc."[4] Despite the fact that Plymouth was a very different settlement, operating apart from the Bay Colony, many Massachusetts town leaders acted in accordance with Winslow's words and expanded the implications of his "etc." Two major questions arise: what types of hierarchy did such town leaders wish to avoid, and what did they hope to substitute to give meaningful form to their growing social structures?

There were, depending on the local area, many types of hierarchies in England: manorial, with lord, steward, tenants; parish, with vicar, churchwardens, overseers of the poor, constables; county, with lord lieutenant, justices of the peace, sheriff; borough, with mayor, aldermen, and burgesses; established church, with archbishop, bishops, deans, canons, and visitors; national government, with the King, the Privy Council, Parliament, and the courts; Inns of Court, with judges, lawyers; trade, with corporations, guilds, masters, journeymen, and apprentices; universities, with officers, colleges, professors, and students; and grammar schools, with masters and students.

If all this social structure was to be "avoided," what substitutions did New

England town leaders intend in order to provide form, spirit, and leadership to their new idealistic small commonwealths? How successful were any of these town leaders, and how did they measure their successes?

Although each early Massachusetts, or New England, town might well provide distinct and fascinating answers, the historian is limited by his documents. Furthermore, he should not attempt to crowd his stage too much, lest the dramatis personae overwhelm his audience.

One town, well documented in relation to its specific origins, can serve as a representative study for most early New England towns until further investigation takes place. The dynamic qualities of many towns can be surmised, once we know the detailed attempts and retreats of the leaders and townsmen of one early community.

The term "well documented," however, in this age of intense analysis is a romantic one. It would be fairer to admit that one can, at best, find fragments of legal records and then make reasonable assumptions about the growth of any community, leaving many vital questions involving motivations and feelings unanswered. Most early townsmen were far too busy to sit back each evening and write journals or diaries.

It is possible, however, to find at least one Massachusetts town whose clerk dutifully recorded resolutions from its beginning in 1638 up to the 1650's, when another town clerk took the job and carried on the tradition until a member of the third generation seized the pen and the duties involved. Furthermore, in the town of Sudbury, sixteen men were consistently elected as leaders of the town in the period 1638–1660, and it has been possible to find documents relating to the activities of thirteen of these first selectmen during the period 1600–1638, when they were living in England. It has also been possible to trace the genealogical origins of 79 per cent of the first land grantees of Sudbury.

Of intense interest is the fact that the early Sudbury leaders represented the three types of English local background, seven of them having lived in open-field villages, six having lived in five English boroughs, and several others having been inhabitants of East Anglian villages.

Furthermore, a violent dispute broke out in Sudbury, Massachusetts, in 1655–1657, essentially a clash of the younger second generation against the restrictions imposed by the founders of the town. The church, General Court, and the town documents relating to this dispute give vivid clues as to the human behavior involved, and they indicate serious stresses and strains in the new ideal state of Sudbury. Although the early leaders of the town had laid down certain common land "forever," they realized painfully that they had been far too optimistic. Very reluctantly they had to permit another group to split off, in order that these younger men, with some older leaders, might attempt to establish another society called Marlborough.

The crucial split in the town of Sudbury illustrates the grave difficulties which the early leaders and inhabitants experienced in substituting a new social structure and a new spirit for the old "hierarchy, holy days, etc." which they undoubtedly hoped would be absent in the New England commonwealth.

One might even see the story of early Sudbury as a type of local morality play, replete with Devil, Greed, and Ambition, opposed by both Faith and Prudence. But personal Sudbury documents are lacking, and we must leave this drama to the novelist. We can, however, study the remarkable transition of culture and do our best to comprehend the hopeful spirit which kindled these free townsmen. It is a spirit which no New England generation would willingly lose.

Puritan Village

CHAPTER I

The Web of Open-field Life

O N THE twenty-sixth of March, 1638, Peter Noyes, yeoman of the parish of Weyhill, Hampshire, gave his land back to the Lord of the Manor. No longer would he help his Hampshire neighbors erect fences around the common fields in the spring or watch the plow teams turn furrows in the rich loam. Noyes had decided. He was taking his eldest son to visit New England in the expectation of moving his family from Weyhill forever.

As he stood before his fellow tenants in the courtroom of Ramridge Hall, perhaps Noyes felt a touch of sadness. His fields were just waiting for care. This was the season when the winter-sown wheat was starting to sprout, the time for spring sowing. Doubtless, the buds of the beech on Juniper Down were showing their spring red. And perhaps out of the window of the courtroom Noyes could see a stray spring lamb, nibbling on forbidden grass.

Not one of the villagers in the court could have predicted Noyes's destiny. They could hardly have conceived the responsibilities involved. They might not have been surprised later to learn that Noyes was being chosen, year after year, to every major post in his new town. After all, the Noyes family had built up a distinguished reputation in Weyhill. Only a few years previously Peter's uncle, William, had run Ramridge Hall, while Robert Noyes, a second uncle, had managed the next largest property in the village, Blissimore Hall. The Noyes family was considered one of the leading families in the parish.

But what villager could have foreseen that their neighbor was to be commissioner for the government of Massachusetts, church elder, town selectman, judge of small causes, and town deputy to the Massachusetts legislature? The people of Weyhill, who had seen Peter Noyes serve as juryman in their manorial court and churchwarden of their church on the hill, could have predicted that he would do well as land surveyor, road building director, grantor of timber, and fence viewer. They would have been amazed, however, and so would Noyes himself, if someone had told him, in 1638, that during the next twenty years he was to attend one hundred and twenty-nine separate official meetings in his town, to say nothing of the informal church gatherings, church services, and sessions of the Massachusetts legislature.

Noyes was destined to be a founder of a New England town, a leader of men in every sense of the word. As such, he was to be responsible for over six hundred and fifty separate "orders," carrying the weight of law and often the power of life and death over his townsmen. For a yeoman from a small West Country village, this was an awesome challenge.

Peter Noyes chose this role deliberately. He was not "harried out of the land." Far from it. He took his steps cautiously but firmly; he had courage, and he had vision. He could easily have remained with the Tarrants and the other members of his own family, none of whom favored the activities of Archbishop Laud and his "popish" ceremonies.

Noyes did not rush away impetuously either. Members of another Noyes family, undoubtedly related to Peter, had been deeply involved in the religious controversies of the period and had left five years previously, in 1633. Since this branch of the family lived only six miles from Weyhill in Cholderton, Wiltshire, their activities must have been well known to Peter.

The Cholderton Noyes family had been in the midst of the struggle over church reformation. The Reverend William Noyes, an Oxford graduate, had died in 1622, and the rectorship of the village church had gone to his son Nathan, also an Oxford Bachelor of Arts. Nathan's uncle, Robert, was a prominent yeoman in the town, as was his older brother Ephraim. But the two younger brothers had drunk deep of the Nonconformist brew, despite the fact that James had followed his father and elder brother to Oxford. Perhaps their cousin, the Reverend Thomas Parker, had fanned their rebellious spirits, for James, aged twenty-five, and Nicholas, aged eighteen, had decided to forsake Cholderton for Massachusetts.

The records do not say whether these members of the family had visited Peter Noyes in Weyhill or had passed through the village on their way to their port of embarkation, London. They do state, however, that the families knew one another.[1]

By 1638, then, Peter Noyes had heard news about New England. But however impressed, Peter displayed the shrewdness which characterized many of his later actions. During the year 1637–1638, he rented two of his four properties in Weyhill to his sister Dorothy, wife of John Waterman in Tangley, Southampton, probably to gain money for his passage and expenses. Then taking £80 from a Mrs. Agnes Bent in Weyhill, who wished to accompany Peter in due time, Noyes sailed from Southampton in April, 1638, in the ship *Confidence,* taking three servants, his eldest son and daughter, and his neighbor, John Bent. Noyes had not forgotten, however, to retain some excellent property near Andover, which paid him a yearly rent of about £20.[2]

On arrival in Watertown in 1638, Noyes was granted plowland, meadow, upland, and an outlying lot of seventy acres. Impressed by the possibilities of the area, Noyes returned to Weyhill to dispose of all business. He gathered his family, old Mrs. Bent, and a few others, then headed back to New England.

At this point one might ask whether Peter Noyes was prepared for the responsibilities of developing an institution which was to last for hundreds of years. Men like Noyes were the essential strength of the early New England towns, and every one of their decisions was open to question. The Massachusetts government in the 1630's was not ready to define "town" with much rigidity. Each town, each leader, was on his own. In what ways, then, was Noyes prepared to form a new community, whose spirit was to be so distinctly different from that in the village he had known?

The clearest method of comparison is to analyze the major social problems which Noyes argued over, discussed, and finally decided upon in his new town. Many English habits of living, of course, were continued without great modification. But enough disagreements arose in Noyes's new community to demand over 132 town meetings and the formation of about 650 orders during Noyes's lifetime in Sudbury, 1638–1657. These town laws, written carefully in the Sudbury Town Book, and often signed by the men bearing the responsibility of enforcing the laws, indicate the numerous compromises to which Noyes's townsmen had to agree.

These 650 orders can be classified into the following categories and degrees of importance, in terms of frequency of appearance in the Town Book: land distribution, appointment of town officers, economic regulations and taxes, church affairs, farming, personal quarrels in the community, relations with neighboring towns, relations with Indians, and relations with the Massachusetts government.[3]

The generalizations of scholars who have attempted to make analogies be-

tween the New England town and the English parish, or any other English social institution, tend to ignore the actual struggles of any leader of any particular town. Peter Noyes had to make two sets of important compromises. The
first set involved the relations of his vision of a new town with the actual community formed in the area chosen. The second set involved the differences between his own experiences and those of Englishmen who had been living in
distinctly different types of English towns. Perhaps it is best to examine the
various categories of administrative decisions one by one.

Land Distribution

The Massachusetts legislature gave Noyes authority to help decide how
much land, of what type, and with what boundaries, to give to almost every
male adult in his New England town. This certainly took his best judgment.
If he had been merely asked to continue the land system he had known in
Weyhill, he could have had enough problems assigning each person his "due
proportion." But Noyes and his selectmen had a problem which perhaps they
did not fully anticipate before leaving England. Their new Sudbury settlers,
far from coming from the same village, or even the same area, came from a be-
wildering variety of English parishes, towns, and boroughs. Probably the specific English land system of each new townsman of Sudbury was quite different from that of his neighbor. Noyes and his committee had to satisfy them all!

It would be fascinating if there were a document which actually described
the thoughts of a town officer suddenly given the power to "order the town" —
that is, to distribute the land. If any selectman of the 1630's used his imagina-
tion, he realized that he had as much power as the King and his legal attorneys
put together, with none of their assurance. In fact, it is still arguable whether,
under English law, these town officers could legally make such grants.

Men like Noyes, however, had an even greater responsibility than those
drawing up a royal grant. When the officers of Sudbury marked out a mere
four or five acres for a single family, they were not only asserting the power of
economic life and death over that family, but they were also assigning a type
of social status, which each settler doubtless reacted to in a very human way.
Noyes did not take the easy way of assigning equal lots to every adult male. He
and his Sudbury selectmen granted such precise amounts as "5¾ acres of
meadow," or "1½ acres of upland," or no acres of either meadow or upland.[4]
Imagine the feelings of a settler who received 1½ acres of arable land near a

swamp away from the house lots, while a neighbor received 50 or 60 acres of fat, black land adjacent to his new house.

The fact that Noyes helped to impose a complex land pattern in early Sudbury, when the selectmen of other towns such as Watertown were granting land in a very different manner, and the additional fact that the Sudbury settlers agreed to their system, is clear evidence of the strength of habits and an indication of a spirit of compromise in the early community.

Noyes was able to draw up a very distinct pattern of grants and allotments in his wilderness New England settlement probably because almost half his settlers were open-field men, as he was. To appreciate the land pattern of such early towns as Sudbury, Massachusetts, one must plunge into the complexities of Weyhill, manor and parish.

It is futile to ask if Weyhill was "typical" or not. It was obviously not. Every open-field village had unique characteristics, habits, and traditions, going back to the Saxons and the Celts.[5] But since Noyes and other open-field men like the Goodnows and the Haineses were repeatedly elected by the Sudbury townsmen to distribute and to stake out the land allotments, obviously these settlers trusted Noyes's concepts and habits concerning the land and the community.

If one examines the reconstructed map of Weyhill about 1635 (Figure 1),[6] one must recognize that the villagers knew it as a complete community, each field, each furlong, each cottage, each family fitting into a traditional set of relationships which had been handed down, generation to generation, without serious question. Noyes changed some of these relationships, but not many. The land map of Sudbury, Massachusetts, about 1640 (Figure 9), is that of an open-field English village, despite any Nonconformist spirit that might have hovered above the fields of rye or barley.

Each man's land was part of a whole fabric of tradition and community life, which included the Lord of the Manor, the annual fairs, the nearby market town, the village church, the clusters of cottages, and both common and enclosed fields. This does not mean that there were no younger sons or landless men anxious to increase their holdings. On the contrary, ample documentation in the Weyhill church manuscripts supports the general statement of scholars that Englishmen of the Stuart period were seized with an ever-increasing appetite for land.[7]

The aggressive reformer, nevertheless, was deeply resented in Weyhill, and his actions stirred up bitterness. The villagers refused to change their

land system until a Parliamentary Act of 1812 forced them to accept a different idea of community activity and farming. Even today there is a nostalgia in
the village for the traditional pattern and values of community life.[8]

The seventeenth-century Weyhill yeoman did not think of the various
landholdings in terms of statistics, tables, charts, and maps. With the exception of one church rate, or tax, in 1693, not a single villager — not even the
Lord of the Manor — had precise written documents on the total land system
in 1635. Each tenant who appeared at a yearly court to acknowledge his landholdings to the lord's steward carried this complex set of relationships in his
head. He knew who owned the strips of land next to his in every furlong, and
he knew who would inherit them. But only Peter Noyes had to write out this
system, away from home, and in so doing he instituted fundamental changes.

We have been able to reconstruct a Weyhill table of land acreage, both for
the period from 1610 to 1640 and for the year 1693 (Appendix II). The fact
that the total acreage of arable is approximately thirteen hundred acres in
both tables, a total which corresponds closely to the accurate surveys made in
the early twentieth century, means that the seventeenth-century documents
have revealed the names and holdings of almost every adult male or landholding widow in Weyhill during the period Peter Noyes, John Bent, and other
emigrants lived in the village.[9]

Two essential facts are at once apparent from a study of these two tables:
that Peter Noyes, with 61 copyhold acres of arable, and John Bent, who inherited his father's 45 copyhold acres of arable, stood fourth and fifth, respectively, in the total list of 44 landholders; further, that there were about 40
landless men, whose ages are not known, who also lived in the community.[10]

Peter certainly could not be called poor in land in terms of his parish. In
actual fact, he had control of three cottages in Weyhill, four separate parcels
of land, and freehold ownership of 55 acres in the neighboring tithing of Foxcott, worth £300 in 1652. This brought his total acreage to 116 acres of arable
land, one acre of meadow, with rights to downland, pasture, and woodland
and the use of three cottages. One of these cottages was very similar in appearance to the charming Cook cottage, still occupied today. To leave such holdings, Peter Noyes and John Bent were ambitious men and undoubtedly had
visions above and beyond the farming of land.

Since Noyes, once in New England, immediately changed the type of landholding title, the traditional and legal habits toward the possession of land in
Weyhill should be examined. Noyes, like every other landholder in Weyhill,
held land from the Lord of the Manor, in this case a legal fiction. No haughty

aristocratic lord dominated the Weyhill landscape, as, for instance, might have been true in the English home of another Sudbury emigrant, Edmund Kerley, in the parish of Ashmore, Dorset. (Figure 2.*) Instead, Queen's College, Oxford, collected yearly rents in the name of the legal "lord," Ewelme Hospital, one of the college's properties.

But even the fictional lord, acting through a representative, demanded traditional rights and heavy fees. All the land in the parish was rented, and whenever a tenant wished to transfer, bequeath, or sublet his property, he paid his fines. The existing court rolls state just how much the lord gained as Peter Noyes sublet his property to his sister and then finally conveyed it back to the lord, prior to his departure for Massachusetts:

1637:	Fine to sublet half of P. Noyes's property: (pieces 1 & 2)	2/00/00
1638:	Fine to take back piece 1	0/10/00
	Rent from piece 1 for one year:	0/06/08
	Rent from piece 2 for one year:	0/11/07
	"Admission Fee" from new tenant: pieces 1 & 2:	10/00/00
	Heriot from new tenant ("best animal"):	5/00/00
	Fine P. Noyes to take back piece 3:	0/30/00
	Rent from piece 3 for one year (new tenant):	0/07/01
	"Admission Fee" (new tenant) piece 3:	20/00/00
	Fine P. Noyes to take back piece 4:	0/10/00
	Rent from piece 4 for one year (new tenant):	0/04/00
	"Admission Fee" (new tenant) piece 4:	10/00/00
	Permission for new tenant to sublet all 4 pieces	2/00/00
		£52/19/04

Thus in a single session of the Ramridge court-baron the lord received over £52, which was a substantial yeoman's yearly income![11] Noyes had paid £4/10 just to be permitted to rent, and then give back, his property, while Thomas Barwick, a clothier from the neighboring borough of Andover, had paid over £48 to gain the new property in Weyhill and permission to sublet it. The court roll also indicates that the lord expected "works and services" for each piece of land, in addition to an oath of "fealty" to the lord.[12]

Noyes must have objected to these feudal fines, taxes, and practices, because his allotments of land in his New England town were outright grants to individuals, with practically no conditions stated in the grants. Some land was rented, and many "works and services" were expected in the town, but the

* Note the overwhelming number of lord's fields, downs, woods in contrast to the three arable fields and other common property of the tenants.

deeds, or entries of land grants in the Sudbury Town Book, attached no feudal terms to any allotment.

But despite his desire to ignore feudal habits of landholding, Noyes was not prepared to abandon the system of rights and apportionments of types of land that he knew so well in Weyhill. The medieval concept in such a community regarded the advantages of the area as communal property, to be shared by all. No one was to exclude a neighbor from such a necessity as good meadow, or the down, or the woods. And if anyone practiced such exclusion, or attempted to increase the amount of his holding at the expense of his neighbors, all villagers reacted instantly to restore their "rights."[13]

These rights consisted loosely of the full use of the manor property, from the meadow grass which grew along the little stream, the Anton, to the nuts in Chute Forest to the north. As far as one can tell from the documents, there were about ten distinct fields, or types of arable and pasture, and two areas of woodlands, and each tenant was brought up in the belief that the following practices were the rights which accompanied his holding:

He had the right to plant crops according to group agreement in the common fields of the manor, North Field, Great Field, Gorriers Field, Far Penton Field, South Field, Nudle Field, Ridge Field, and Gore Ridge Field. He also had the right to pasture sheep and other animals on the following downs: Clanville Down, Fore Down, Chalkcroft Down, Great Down, Weyhill Down, Penham Down, and the Heath.

Furthermore, every thirty acres of arable ground had the following specific rights: pasturage of twenty sheep on Weyhill Down; pasturage of four cattle on the commons; the privilege of cutting hay from three acres of meadow grass; the pasturage of animals on four acres of Ramridge Woods; the pasturage of animals in Chute Forest; the privilege of cutting wood in Ramridge Copse; the right to take chalk from the common pit; and the right to set up a booth or a pen at the Weyhill Fair.

In short, an accurate deed of a holding was a complicated affair, and an accurate map of an open-field manor a very complex document.[14] One lovely open-field map survives today in the Hampshire Record Office, an intricate design involving hundreds of strips and scores of furlongs.

Although every tenant and his close neighbors living in the stable society of Weyhill knew the boundaries of his own strips of arable, the strips were divided by mounds or fences, according to local documents. When all of the strips in one field, however, were sprouting with wheat, only an air view could have given a visitor the awareness that the fields represented the holdings of forty or fifty families.

The land that was so divided and shared, furthermore, was good land. In strictly economic terms, Peter Noyes valued his land in the adjacent parish of Foxcott at about £6 an acre; and the Rector of Weyhill sold his half-acre in Far Penton Field in 1699 for £3/05/00 or over £6 an acre. But each holding had important relationships to the total complex of land management. When the aggressive young owner of Ramridge Hall farm used a legal suit in 1651 to gain exclusive control of "The Heath" and "Ridenge," the tenants agreed to "part with the rights of commons" only after a stubborn battle and a detailed statement of all rights, including additional land for each tenant to compensate for "their loss," rights of the fair, rights of Ramridge Forest, right of digging chalk in the chalk pit, and demands that Mr. Thomas Drake swear to these conditions before all tenants at the next meeting of the court-baron.[15]

Peter Noyes was leaving a tightly knit, strong-spirited community of tenants, farmers, and parishioners, and it is not surprising that he helped to reconstruct many of the same relationships in his new town in a wild river valley in New England.

Appointment of Town Officers

One skill which Noyes had to develop almost immediately in New England was that of becoming a strong leader. During his nineteen years as one of the chief town officers of Sudbury, Noyes was responsible for 209 appointments, and he participated in 16 town elections. As far as records can reveal, this was a new experience for him, particularly in that the appointments were not made to well-defined posts but were special authorizations of power to meet distinct, often new, social problems.

Not enough Weyhill records remain to tell us all the detailed experience Noyes had in institutions of local government before emigration. Without any question he understood the functions of the English court-baron, although this court was not transplanted to New England's soil. But he served on the court-baron jury in 1629, 1631, 1632, and 1637, and he was bailiff of the court in 1637, training which prepared him to be a judge of small causes in New England a few years later.

The Ramridge court-baron was a penal court and a court of record, not a meeting of villagers to discuss new ways of solving social problems. It was principally a court for the benefit of the Lord of the Manor, held only once a year, usually near Easter. English custom required that a lord cause a public proclamation to be made either a week or two weeks before the court session, normally in church, and that it was expected that every tenant would appear.[16] On the day of the court the villagers assembled in the Ramridge Hall courtroom, and fines were levied on those who failed to appear.

Three important facts must be noted: the major business was the recording of land transfers; the atmosphere was that of a court; and the court relied on the fact that every tenant understood the traditional bylaws of the community. Thus the court was not a meeting to discuss any problems except those caused by misdemeanors on manorial property. It filled the coffers of the lord by assessing tenants for land fees and by fining them for committing petty offenses on the lord's property.

The ten Ramridge court rolls which exist for a forty-year period show only eighty-six cases, 70 per cent of which involved surrender, transfer, or rent of manorial property — all at a handsome profit to the lord.[17] The rest of the cases fall into two categories: fines for infractions of manorial rules, and repetitions of well-known bylaws.

Tenants were fined for allowing their property to fall "into disrepair," for keeping rabbit warrens illegally, for failure to repair restraining hedges around the common fields, and for tolerating unringed, unruly pigs. The jury, from eleven to fourteen men in number, annually reminded all the tenants to put up their "haya," the high, woven, restraining barriers around the common fields by a certain date in the spring, or told them that only four cattle per thirty acres (arable) were allowed on the common pasture, or instructed them to ring their pigs. Other than these petty orders and fines, the court records reveal nothing about local "self-government."

The Andover out-hundred court was a court for the area to the west of Andover, whose fines constituted income for the treasury of the borough of Andover. Although there are no records indicating that Peter Noyes himself was appointed to serve on the jury of this court, his uncle William, while running Ramridge Hall, served repeatedly. Surely the business of the court was common knowledge, for it sat in Weyhill for its semi-annual sessions.

Few men enjoyed carrying out the functions of this court. The jury at each session appointed tithingmen in each of the eleven adjacent villages, and these men were expected to appear twice a year, at April and October, at their own time and expense, to report infractions of bylaws to the court. Weyhill's tithingmen changed each year during the twenty years 1604–1624, and only a few men could be persuaded to repeat their jobs after they had served one term.

The range of business which the jury, numbering from thirteen to twenty-four men, heard was very limited. Fines were levied over a twenty-year period for the following offenses: boundary posts in disrepair; "nuisances" in the common roads; stocks, pounds, or field "haya" in disrepair; stray animals; and bridges "in decay."[18]

As other scholars have pointed out, most of the important local orders were made by the justices of the peace during their frequent sessions.[19] But since Peter Noyes was never a justice of the peace, it is not known how much he understood these functions or the authority involved.

It is clear, particularly since the Sudbury, Massachusetts, town meetings during Noyes's lifetime have left no records of sitting as a formal court, that Noyes did not carry to Massachusetts the traditions of a manorial court or those of an out-hundred court.[20] One of the most obvious reasons, of course, was that there was no lord or lord's property in his new town. Furthermore, the settlers of Sudbury came from many different areas, each with a different set of bylaws, thus making impossible a commonly understood pattern of social behavior. What, then, prepared Noyes so that his townsmen wanted him, year after year, to choose leaders among them and to assign them specific tasks?

Undoubtedly Noyes's family background prepared him, as well as his open-field farming experience. In Weyhill Noyes's two uncles, William and Robert, managed the two largest individual farms in the village — Ramridge Hall and Blissimore Hall. William Noyes took his economic position seriously and served repeatedly in all possible local government posts, from juryman to churchwarden, even if these jobs were onerous and brought little financial return. Noyes's activities in Sudbury were an extension of his uncle's tradition of responsible community leadership.

It is possible also that the Noyes family in the borough of Andover was related to Peter Noyes in Weyhill, and local genealogists are quite sure of some linkage. Probably, then, he knew Robert Noyes, who was a burgess and member of the town council, or a namesake, Peter, who was a burgess, the steward of the borough, and the town clerk as well.[21] Any one of them could have given the emigrant valuable information on running corporation government and on delegating authority.

In addition to benefiting from the influence of his relatives, Peter Noyes probably learned much as an open-field farmer. Any co-operative farming activity of this nature, where each man had to rely on the skill and conscientiousness of his neighbors, taught a person much about human behavior. For at least forty years Peter had functioned in the complex business of co-operative farming in Weyhill. Obviously he learned to know men, to pick out the leaders from the followers, and to compromise — essential talents in any early New England town.

Economic Regulations and Taxes

Apparently Noyes had little specific training to prepare him for the problems of taxation and general economic regulation in his new town. On fifty-three separate occasions in Sudbury he had to draw up tax lists, assess land, levy taxes, gather taxes, set salaries, and build up a town treasury. His parish of Weyhill had never dealt with such a volume of economic regulation.

The records of Weyhill indicate that the court fines and the land rents were fixed by custom and were not the product of group discussion or arbitrary fiat. Despite the English Poor Law, little or no money seems to have been expended for relief, unless the records pertaining to this have been lost.

Church Affairs

Weyhill parish, as run by Dr. Thomas Mason and his curate, Mr. William Woodward, had little relation to Noyes's Nonconformist church in Sudbury, except to serve as a contrast. The records of the forty-year period 1600–1640 show that the vestry, the churchwardens, and even the minister were apathetic about parish social problems, as compared with some English parishes at the time.

The manuscripts still remaining speak of 36 communicants in 1656, out of a male population of at least 90 and a total population of 450, using the low average of five members per family to compute total population. Only 35 church members contributed to pay for the churchyard fence in 1636, and the minister often had great difficulty in gathering his meager tithes.[22]

The Churchwardens' Accounts clearly indicate a minimum of activity, a complete lack of parish funds, and a great reluctance on the part of nearly all the parishioners to serve as parish officers. There is not a single church rate (or tax) recorded for the period 1600–1640, and at least sixty-five different men had to be urged to serve the single-year term of churchwarden, overseer of the poor, or surveyor of the highways. Even though the wealthy landholder, Peter

Gale, Sr., together with Robert Bendall, Samuel Tarrant, and Thomas Wale appeared on the 1636 church list, not one of these men served as church-warden or overseer during the entire forty years. Only eight or nine men were willing to take any post more than once, and only three men served about ten years each in this period.[23]

By English law the overseers of the poor were supposed to purchase material to provide work for the unemployed and then give general aid as needed. The surveyors of the highway were to require each parishioner to contribute six days' labor on the public roads per year, supervised by the justice of the peace.[24] But in the period 1601–1640, there are no surviving Wey-hill records showing expenditure for the poor or any records of any highway work accomplished.

In parishes in active boroughs, or in the East Anglian areas, the church-wardens were often busy men. Since Peter Noyes served in this post in 1625 and again in 1627, as did John Bent in 1635, and since Noyes was overseer of the poor in 1631, one might expect that he received some training. Perhaps he did, but the records indicate that even the churchwardens did a minimum of work. The entries record only two things: payment or nonpayment for church candles, and election of new officers for the coming year. It would be impossible to say with certainty that more than eight or nine people showed up in the little church at the annual Easter meeting of the minister and the parish.

The diocesan records show that occasionally the minister did not appear to meet his bishop at visitations and that no unusual presentments were ever made by the officers of the Weyhill church. The visitation books show meet-ings in 1606, 1607, 1609, 1611, 1617, 1633, and 1636, but the churchwardens in their own Weyhill records ignore these visitations completely. The year 1633, in which the church was enforcing the King's desire that the Book of Sports be publicly read and obeyed, is an example of general Weyhill indif-ference. While parishes in East Anglia had violent reactions, and churchward-ens elsewhere had many meetings, the Bishop of Winchester found the Wey-hill minister absent at his visitation and the churchwardens with very little to say. The Bishop apparently made so little impression on the Weyhill repre-sentatives that they recorded neither the visitation nor the Bishop's order in their annual notes.[25]

Such inactivity does not mean that Weyhill parish was necessarily repre-sentative of its area. But an examination of the Hampshire diocesan manu-scripts shows none of the violent reactions or intense parish activity of some

of the East Anglian churches. It is very probable that the small open-field parishes did not operate like those in crowded, busy areas, and that scholars' generalizations comparing New England town meetings to those of the English
parish are much too sweeping.[26] Peter Noyes left an inactive parish to establish a community which was active, militant, and demanding on its members.

Farming

Noyes faced a real dilemma in attempting to apply his open-field habits to
the Massachusetts wilderness. Many of his settlers had never practiced this
type of group farming and preferred to run their own individual farms. But
they still elected Noyes to lead them, and his Weyhill farming experience prepared him to be an administrator of the open fields in early Sudbury.

For at least forty years, or from the time he had been required to assist his
own father in doing farm chores, Noyes had gained experience in co-operative
farming in the open-field tradition. This meant that all the farmers of Weyhill, perhaps ninety in number, had had to form certain essential bylaws each
year in regard to crop and animal management and had had to see that these
orders were carried out to the letter. Since every family's food supply and live-
lihood depended on careful agricultural management, the imposition of these
bylaws probably constituted the core of Weyhill's self-government.

Neither the justice of the peace for the area, nor any other English governmental officer, had any say in what crop went into each of Weyhill's fields each
season. A justice might be called upon to judge disputes which became too
difficult for any community to settle itself, but there are no such cases for the
Weyhill area during Noyes's presence there. Consequently, there may well
have been a strong climate of agreement and co-operation among the tenants
of Ramridge.[27]

Professor Warren Ault has pointed to the "self-directing activities of village communities in mediaeval England" as a vital element in the "early origin and continued existence of the English township."[28] Using fragments of
records, he has described a whole pattern of agricultural bylaws, from those
defining the rights of pasture to decisions on crops, and there is ample proof
that farmers, particularly in open-field villages, met to discuss and to decide on
farming problems by common consent.

Most of these agreements seem to have been verbal — so traditional, so ordinary that they did not have to be written down. This was probably true in

Weyhill, where there are only one or two orders in the court rolls setting dates by which certain farm work had to be done. But the absence of written records does not mean that the Weyhill farmers made no group agreements. On the contrary, such agreements were absolutely necessary each season, at each time of sowing and harvesting. In the first place, since all the landholders had some arable strips in the four common fields, with the possible exception of the proprietors of Ramridge and Blissimore Halls, the men met to decide which fields were to be sown with what crops, which field (or fields) were to be left fallow, and what men would gather together to do the various jobs.

Other studies have described English medieval farming practices in great detail. In most open-field villages the juries at the manorial court administered agricultural bylaws and elected such officers as viewers, haywards, the shepherd, and the cowherd.[29] Since there are few specific agricultural bylaws left for Weyhill, one can only assume that the farmers, in periodic meetings, made extensive regulations for harrowing, sowing, weeding, and harvesting, as well as for pasturing and for general care of the animals. Few of the farmers could write, and the absence of a clerk to record such agreements seems only natural.

On English soil Noyes's farming caused few major social problems. Weyhill was in the midst of fine sheep-raising country, and farmers came from many adjacent areas to attend Weyhill's two annual summer fairs and to exchange animals and crops.[30] The arable soil, the pasture grounds, the sheep downs, and even the small amount of river meadow have always been considered excellent for farming, and the Weyhill villagers have always had Andover as a nearby market town.

One wonders if Noyes's Cholderton relatives ever wrote him of the farming conditions he would have to face in the new land. They might have said, as Francis Higginson wrote his friends in Leicester, "You shall meet neither with taverns, nor alehouses, nor butchers' nor grocers' nor apothecaries' shops, to help what things you need . . . here are yet neither markets nor fairs to buy what you want. Therefore be sure to furnish yourselves with things fitting to be had before you come."[31] Noyes had many surprises in store for him.

Personal Quarrels in the Community

Despite the surprises ahead, Noyes possessed sound habits of local administration, for the government of Massachusetts appointed him on four separate occasions to be judge of small causes, giving him the authority for one year to decide personal quarrels which involved no more than £1. More significant, the townsmen of Sudbury continued to elect him as judge.

Neither the citizens nor the Massachusetts government expected such a judge to have formal training. Except for his own reading in England, Noyes probably knew little English common law, and his Sudbury library did not contain the familiar Dalton's manual of the justices of the peace.[32] He had served on a manorial court jury, but there is no record of his appearing at the Hampshire quarter sessions, for Weyhill had a minimum of cases before these justices.

Relations with Other Towns and Institutions

Noyes was quite inexperienced when he was forced to make agreements with neighboring New England towns or with the Indians, and when required to serve in the legislature of the Massachusetts government. He had not served on the one institution in the Weyhill area which judged interparish problems, the Andover out-hundred court, and he certainly had never had to make critical judgments about members of a different culture who could not even speak his language. It is an indication of Noyes's strength of character that his Massachusetts townsmen preferred him as their representative to the central government, rather than more experienced men of the town.

Weyhill seems to have run its institutions from 1600 to 1640 almost completely oblivious to questions which disturbed people in other areas of England, particularly those living in the big cities. But, as Professor Willcox has pointed out, local and county government, at least in the open-field country, operated quite independently of Parliament and of national problems.[33] Certainly the Weyhill Churchwardens' Accounts give no indication that prices were increasing, that rents were rising, that famine struck hard in 1629–1630, or even that the King was levying special taxes called "ship money."

It is quite possible, of course, that Peter Noyes had read about and discussed many of these national events, despite the fact that King Charles was incensed when any commoner questioned his decisions or the problems of state. But when Noyes appeared in Boston as Sudbury's delegate to the Massachusetts legislature, he was totally lacking in governmental experience in English national institutions.

Perhaps the very fact that Noyes was willing to leave his land in Sudbury to argue the many questions and reforms brought up in the Massachusetts legislature is an important clue to his decision to leave Weyhill. It is very possible that he realized that none of the social institutions in his home area would permit him to discuss his ideals or allow him to test various possible reforms.

The court-baron's yearly meetings might have entertained proposals for planting rye on Far Penton Field instead of barley, but the court rolls give no indication that broad social reforms were discussed. Noyes apparently was never in a position to be appointed a justice of the peace, and he had no training as a Nonconformist lecturer. His parish sent churchwardens to church court sessions, but practically nothing seems to have been accomplished at these gatherings, and Noyes did not expect to change the attitude of a bishop or archdeacon once Archbishop Laud had started to apply conformist pressures from above. And Weyhill parish meetings were dull affairs, attended by only a handful of men who merely went through perfunctory motions.

Expressions of dissent in Weyhill in the 1630's were confined to strong words and a few resignations from parish offices. George Tarrant expressed his Nonconformist views by resigning as curate in 1633 when the King's Book of Sports was ordered to be read in the church.[34] And someone, perhaps Peter Noyes himself, wrote one biting comment in the Churchwardens' Account Book.

The incident occurred in 1629, when Noyes was senior churchwarden. For years the parishioners had contributed money, or wax, to provide candles as altar lights, as lights on the rood loft, and as tapers in front of the images of a few saints. But for a decade before 1630, there had been growing resentment against this practice, since leading citizens such as Gregory Tarrant and William Grace had absorbed the Nonconformist arguments that altar lights were "popish" and superstitious and therefore evil. Finally, these two men began to refuse to contribute for the lights. In 1629, a churchwarden wrote, "William Grace hath not paid his wax." Someone added in the margin at a later date, "W. Grace is a fool to pay, but some have no sence. But here it is for all this."[35] Could these have been the words of Peter Noyes?

The tone of resignation to tradition in the final sentence of this brief comment tells a great deal. It was impossible to gain even limited satisfaction in Weyhill if one was a dissenter. Either the rigid pattern of community life, or the force of tradition, or perhaps an apathy toward questions involving the Nonconformist ideals, stifled activity and expression.

But Peter Noyes's determination broke through this web of tradition and probably surprised his entire village. Returning in the spring of 1639 from his inspection tour of Watertown, Massachusetts, and the nearby area, he paid to transport eleven residents of Weyhill and their goods toward a dramatic future. By good fortune, the bill of the carriers who carted Noyes and his party to the wharfs of London and to the ship *Jonathan* has been preserved:[36]

Mr. Noyes	£05/00/00	William Stret	05/00/00
J. Waterman	05/00/00	Peter Noyes	02/10/00
Nicholas Noyes	05/00/00	Anis Bent	05/00/00
Doreyti Noyes	05/00/00	Elizabeth Plemten	05/00/00
Abigale Noyes	05/00/00	Richard Barnes	02/10/00
		Agnis Blanchet	05/00/00
			£50/00/00

R'cd in pt for the fraught of goods for J. Waterman			02/10/00
4 hds frayght	03/00/00	2 chests	01/00/00
4 Ferkins	00/10/00	mele	10/19/00
4 kelderkines	01/00/00	Butter	04/19/00
1 barrell	00/10/00	Licores	01/00/00
3 packes & 3 barrilles	01/10/00		£17/18/00

R'cd this 12th of Aprill 1639 of Mr. Peter Noyes the sum of Fifty pounds for his one and Fameleys passage to New England:	50/00/00
R'cd more for Fraught of goods	08/10/00
R'cd more for mele and 4 ferkins of Buter and 2 cases of licores	17/18/00
	£76/08/00

Noyes was investing more than a year's income for freight, food, and the passage of eleven people to distant shores. He was taking the first steps to prove that he was prepared to do more than speak about reforms. He had convinced his family and his neighbors. And he had a whole town waiting for his voice as well as for his vision.

CHAPTER II

Land Hunger, Borough Rights, and the Power to Tax

EDMUND RICE, like Peter Noyes, had a vision which involved both leadership and ambition for the acquisition of land. Not only did Rice become the largest individual landholder in Sudbury, but he represented his new town in the Massachusetts legislature for five years and devoted at least eleven out of the first fifteen years to serving as selectman and judge of small causes.

Rice remained a dissenter all his life. He moved from Suffolk, in England, to Hertfordshire; from Hertfordshire to Watertown, Massachusetts; and from Watertown to Sudbury. Not content with the land policy of Noyes and his followers, Rice helped lead a younger faction out of Sudbury to establish still another New England town with differing social policies.[1]

Two generations of Sudbury men selected Edmund Rice repeatedly as one of their leaders, with full realization that they were ignoring men of far more English governmental experience who had come with him. Robert Darvell, a chief burgess of the borough of Berkhamsted, who had spent years helping to administer both town and church, left England with Rice, as did Thomas Axtell, the young son of the mayor of the borough.[2] And yet neither of these two men was ever elected to any major town post in their new town of Sudbury.

Perhaps the explanation lies in their attitudes toward land. There are very complete records concerning the availability of land in Berkhamsted, as well as the activities of the parish officers, and when these are compared with similar records in Sudbury, Massachusetts, it can be seen that Edmund Rice seems to have put more energy into the acquisition of land and the administration of his new community than either of the two Berkhamsted neighbors who emigrated with him.

The Berkhamsted documents present a vivid contrast to the situation in Weyhill and make clear the truth that some sections, as well as certain institutions, differed widely within England itself. It was the triumph of men like Rice and Noyes to be able to blend these contrasting backgrounds into a new whole, called a New England town.

Land and Land Policy

Rice's experience in Berkhamsted, and that of his neighbors, is excellent documentation for the general study of the land hunger of New England's first settlers. Personal ambition and ideals must be given due weight. For the records of Berkhamsted make it clear that not only was good English land available in one of the centers of emigration to New England, but that nearly every adult male in the parish was increasing his landholdings year by year.

The summaries of the parish rates (or taxes) on individual holdings of land over the period 1613–1637 are startling. Over one thousand acres were opened up, bought, or traded, in countless individual transactions. If the men of Berkhamsted were doing nothing else, they were trading land. Three adjacent parishes were included in the general rate of Berkhamsted, and it is easy to see that the farmers in each area were adding to their holdings.[3]

These summaries indicate that over a twenty-year period, more than three hundred farmers in the parish of Berkhamsted were able to add land to their holdings, or gain land where they had had none previously. This huge amount of land trading was greatly aided, of course, when the grounds of Berkhamsted Castle were "disparked," allowing at least 96 men to gain small holdings from the 756 acres thus made available.[4]

A close examination of the rate lists for the years 1613, 1617, 1622, 1632, and 1637, drawn up in Appendix III, is revealing. Where the churchwardens listed 65 landless men in the parish in 1613, 51 in 1617, and 50 in 1622, no men were designated "landless" in the rate lists of 1632 or 1637. Of course this could mean that the churchwardens wanted to avoid the difficulty of making arbitrary assessments, small in amount, on those men without land. But since the rates were not popular, and since several men took legal action against the churchwardens for being overtaxed during these years, it is likely that the churchwardens took special pains to spread the rate over all available adult men or landholders in the parish.

Berkhamsted

Date	Gained Land*	Lost Land*
1617	28 men	5 men
1622	25	12
1627	20	9
1632	109	17
1637	64	40

Northchurch

1617	9	4
1622	7	2
1627	3	2
1632	6	5
1637	3	1

Fresden

1617	5	9
1622	14	4
1627	12	3
1632	6	5
1637	2	1
Totals:	313	119

* "Gained land": the number of men who gained land during the period between the previous church rate (tax) and the date listed.

"Lost Land": the number of men who decreased their holdings according to the acreage on the church rate list, or who died or disappeared from the lists.

Obviously young men were getting their hold on the land, once the castle's park was broken up and put under the plow. The Percival family, the Benning family, the How and Adams families, all began to have numerous representatives on the rate lists after 1627. And 33 additional names appeared in 1637, some from old families, some representing new families. Most of the allotments were small, from one to eight acres in size, with the majority two to three acres, and undoubtedly younger men were starting their landholding careers, aware of the general rise of prices and rents in England at the time.[5]

Those considering emigration to New England were right in the midst of this busy buying and selling of land. Robert Darvell was rated at no land in 1617, but had gained 22 acres by 1622, sold 7 of these by 1632, and was listed with 19 acres in 1637. William Axtell, father of the emigrant Thomas, had 2 acres of arable and 1 acre of meadow in 1613, 7 acres of arable and 3 of meadow in 1617, and a total of 24 acres in 1632 and 1637. Edmund Rice had come to join the rush for land. Having left Bury St. Edmunds, Suffolk, he had arrived in Berkhamsted by 1626, acquired 3 acres within a year, and was rated at 15 acres in 1637.

The great fluctuation of holdings makes a vivid contrast to the land situation in the small villages of the open-field country such as Weyhill. Since the court rolls of the Manor of Berkhamsted and Northchurch have not survived, one cannot be sure of the type of holdings which these 200 taxpayers enjoyed. But there are extracts of the rolls which give a very significant entry about 1636: "The jury answers and presents all the names of the freeholders, with lands and rents" — and the partial list has 71 names, including that of William Axtell.[6]

It is probable, then, that the 200 taxpayers in 1637 were considered freeholders of the Manor of Berkhamsted and were paying rents for their portions of the total of over 2000 acres of arable and pasture.[7] Almost all of them increased or decreased the size of their holdings in the period 1620–1640.

The lack of court rolls also makes it impossible to describe completely the land system, if indeed there was one system during such land fluctuations. Many men did hold enclosed tracts of arable and pasture, ranging from the tenant of the manor (240 acres in 1637) to Robert Speed's 10 acres of arable with 1 acre of meadow. One can assume that they managed some of these enclosures individually, but there is a brief note in the Churchwardens' Account Book that in 1639 John Surman was "paying 30/00 for 3 acres of land in Greeneway Field — renting this at 26/08 per year."

It is probable, then, that some general fields were in operation about 1637, containing perhaps all the many small strips listed in the tax rates.* If so, the fields were managed in the same way that the farmers of Weyhill ran their general fields, by bylaws composed and enforced by all farmers concerned.

It is also evident that although the Manor of Berkhamsted, through its great court and view of frankpledge, technically had jurisdiction over the area, most of the farmers were shifting as fast as they could to individual management of their own plots or farms.[8] The rate lists indicate that the men with large holdings were buying up the land from those with small holdings. Certainly the emigrants, Rice, Darvell, and Axtell, while they tolerated the open-field farming system in Sudbury, Massachusetts, for fifteen years, all wanted to run their own freehold farms as independent managers. Rice continued his practice of buying up lots of land and emerged with the largest single farm in Sudbury.

* The use of the term "Greeneway Field" proves this. As Tate has pointed out, any "field" meant an open field. A "close" was the term for the enclosed, individually managed plot of land. *The Parish Chest*, p. 250.

Local Government

This general desire to manage local affairs independently was quite apparent in the two major institutions in Berkhamsted, the borough government and the church government. Berkhamsted was known as a market town, a seat of wool-trading and manufacture, and a chartered borough as well. It represented the transition from manorial management to that of "one body corporate and politic," and the operations of its institutions were excellent training for all those men who later established New England towns.

For although the townsmen of Sudbury preferred Rice as a leader to Darvell or to Axtell, men like the latter were welcome in all the Sudbury town meetings and free to raise their voices whenever they wished. Undoubtedly they must have made suggestions from their own experience in town and parish government.

Robert Darvell and Thomas Axtell had seen a far more active local government than that which had functioned in Noyes's parish. Thomas's father, William, had served once as stonewarden (supervising road repair), twice as churchwarden, and three times as sideman (reporting church offenses). After being appointed a lifetime chief burgess of the borough, he served a year as mayor and then was elected town clerk in 1639. Darvell also had been made a chief burgess, which office gave him a permanent place on the town council and a voice in all borough affairs. Apparently Edmund Rice had not been in the borough long enough to be considered as an officer before he decided to leave for New England.

Improvements in the structure of borough government in England were difficult to make. Tradition dominated, the charter defined all "rights and privileges," and the function of a burgess was simply to impose ancient customs and demands on the populace. One thing was certain. Borough government flourished when there was trade and languished when business declined. For English borough government consisted in a set of rights rented from the King, and these rights allowed the governing council to levy fines and to rent property, all in the name of keeping peace and order. The rights were rented, not given. If the bailiff failed to pay the annual sum of £1/00/00 to "his Highness's particular Farmer for his Highness's use" within twenty-eight days of the stated time, the whole borough of Berkhamsted would "cease and be void."[9]

Although the Berkhamsted Borough Court Book covering the period 1600–1640 has disappeared, the charter, rewritten and reaffirmed by James I in 1619, clearly defines the concept of town government which Darvell, Rice, and Axtell had known. The charter, issued under the great seal of England, "incorporated the inhabitants of the borough into one body corporate and politic, by the name of Bailiff (Mayor) and Burgesses of the Borough of Berkhamsted, Hertfordshire."[10] The expressed aim was an economic one: the body politic was granted the power to buy goods and chattels, to purchase lands and houses, to grant and rent the same, and to hold courts.

The government consisted in the following set of rights and privileges, rented yearly from the King:

1. The right to have a seal.
2. One bailiff, to be chosen by the burgesses, for a term of one year.
3. Twelve chief burgesses, "of the best and most honest burgesses" to constitute, with the mayor, the common council. They were to serve for life, "as long as they are well behaved."
4. Bailiff and burgesses might purchase a council house (guildhall), where they could hold court, make laws and ordinances for the borough, and impose fines, penalties, and imprisonments, provided that such laws were not repugnant to the laws of England.
5. One recorder, learned in law, to be elected by the bailiff and burgesses.
6. One common clerk, to be elected yearly.
7. Yearly elections: bailiff to be selected by outgoing bailiff and chief burgesses; two sergeants of the mace, empowered to execute all processes and warrants, to be selected by bailiff and chief burgesses.
8. Bailiff, chief burgesses, and recorder given the power of justice of peace, without authority to order the death sentence or loss of limb without permission from the King.
9. Courts:
   A. Court of Records: to be held monthly before the bailiff and recorder and to listen to all manner of pleas, actions, and suits, or offenses against the laws and liberties of the borough.
   B. Court of the Market: to listen to petty offenses occurring during market days and held by the bailiff as coroner.
   C. Court of Pie Poudre: to be held before the bailiff to settle petty offenses occurring during the three yearly fairs.
10. Markets, allowed every Monday and Thursday, with the right of the borough to collect all tolls and rents of stalls.
11. Three yearly fairs: Shrove Tuesday, Whitsun Monday, St. James's Day.
12. The right to maintain a jail, with a keeper.
13. The privilege of buying and possessing any or all manors, lands, or rents not to exceed forty marks yearly.
14. The privilege of returning all writs of the King within the borough and retaining the fines.
    The privilege of taking waifs, strays, goods of felons, fugitives, and outlaws.
    The privilege of being free from all tolls within England.

15. The charter to be valid for thirty-one years, at £1 per year, paid in two installments.

Despite the fact that the mayor and burgesses had gained a charter which gave them the right to rent properties and collect tolls, they seem to have handed a substantial amount of this income over to the churchwardens. Lacking the mayors' accounts, one can conclude that the officers of the local Church of St. Peter's had more control over the economic flow of the town than did the burgesses. It was the churchwardens who received yearly rent from the Town House, the Butter Market, and the lofts and stalls in these properties. The churchwardens, from 1602 to 1640, not only received rents from this and other markets, but they also gathered the "toll corn" and sold it to the poor at "reasonable prices."[11]

There are at least two possible explanations for this unusual state of affairs. From an economic point of view, the Berkhamsted market suffered heavily from the competition of three markets, set up within a few miles of the borough, which "took most of the trade," dropping the receipts in quarters of grain from possibly 250 to 300 per day to a mere 10 per day in the period of 1618 to 1632.[12] Perhaps the burgesses, despairing of a rise in tolls, simply let the churchwardens do what they could in absorbing a declining income from corn market sales.

But since the chief burgesses were themselves the principal body of the church vestry and served in all the church posts, another explanation is more likely. The vestry, prompted by orders from the bishop, had decided that the parish church needed extensive repairs and that this should be the major expense of the parish. In contrast to the relative inactivity of the churchwardens of Weyhill, the officers of St. Peter's Church were levying rates almost yearly to pay a host of carpenters, bricklayers, tinners, and glaziers. The following summary table of expenses for church repair makes this clearly evident:[13]

Year	Rate	Year	Rate
1602	£12	1627	£5
1603	1	1628	35
1605	10	1629	17
1613	32	1630	4
1614	34	1631	8
1615	5	1637	44 (4000 bricks
1617	16		bought)
1619	19	1638	18
1622	9	1639	66
1623	16	Total	£385

Since it appears that the parish, not the borough, held the vital power to tax, the flexibility of Berkhamsted's local government is apparent. The burgesses were receiving less and less income from the market and probably had relatively few borough expenses. But since the church and parish needed vital expenditures, the "chief men" met as a vestry, levied at least fourteen separate rates between 1602 and 1640, and spent an estimated total of £1300 on their parish needs.

In other words, the parish vestry was the one institution of local government in Berkhamsted which, because it was in a position to tax a growing population, could meet and solve various social problems. Perhaps if so many men in Berkhamsted had not been increasing their landholdings, and presumably their incomes as well, the vestry could not have accomplished so much in this period of rising grain prices. Other churchwardens' accounts from small towns do not indicate anywhere near the amount and range of expenditure which the Berkhamsted churchwardens exercised.

In contrast to Darvell's and Rice's subsequent powers of government in Sudbury, Massachusetts, the Berkhamsted churchwardens acted virtually unopposed by their community. The philosophy of a merchant oligarchy, inherent in the corporation charter, was carried over into parish government.* All the chief burgesses were active vestrymen. Gentlemen like William Pitkin, Oliver Haines, and Samuel Besouth were repeatedly elected to various church posts, served as mayors of the borough, and had substantial plots of land the crops from which probably supplemented their owners' incomes.[14] This close parish-borough government relationship is well illustrated by the fact that the minister, the Reverend Thomas Newman, a staunch Anglican, not only conducted most of the vestry meetings but also served as chief burgess and even mayor of the borough in 1631.†

Whether Mr. Newman called a meeting of the borough council in the Guildhall or a vestry meeting in the church, he faced the same small governing body of merchants and yeomen, and he operated on the same principles. Occasional vestry orders were signed "by general consent," but only a fraction of the communicants actually attended. In all the recorded meetings between 1600 and 1640, the maximum attendance seems to have been 15 men (7.5 per cent of the ratepayers in 1638) and the minimum number 4 (2 per cent of the

* Control of a parish by a "select vestry" seems to have been common throughout England at this time: W. E. Tate, *The Parish Chest,* p. 18.

† He was cited in the charter of 1619 as "one of the best and most honest burgesses, Bachelor of Divinity and Rector of the Church of Berkhamsted." He was a top landholder, possessing ninety-four acres in 1627.

ratepayers in 1638). Nonetheless, 128 different ratepayers, or 64 per cent of the total number listed in 1638, took their turns in serving for at least one year as church officers in the period 1600–1640.*

The churchwardens, during their yearly terms, had extensive and rather ill-defined powers, but they were somewhat checked by the diocesan visitations, the wishes of the parishioners, and occasional orders from county justices of the peace. The two Berkhamsted churchwardens felt obligated to submit their table of expenses only once during the year, at the annual vestry meeting at Easter, and they were restrained in church administration only by the two visitations of the archdeacon, once at Easter and once at Michaelmas. The bishop often made a visitation, but how often and when seem to have been unpredictable.

A churchwarden in Berkhamsted, after his election in April, could count on at least £10 income from rents and fees of town property, could draw up a rate list at his own discretion, and could spend sums relatively freely.† The annual receipts in Berkhamsted were drawn from the rent of the Town House and the Butter Market and their lofts, the toll of the market, and various benevolences, such as annual gifts to maintain the master and usher of the free school of Berkhamsted.

The annual expenses were much more flexible. Fixed payments consisted of wages of the sexton, the wages of the men who gathered the "toll corn," the charges at the annual church courts, and the fee to the high constable of the area. But beyond these expenses, the churchwardens and overseers of the poor simply had to meet contingencies. The poor needed constant attention; stray travelers and children had a penchant for seeking out generous churchwardens; sudden emergencies called on all the resources of the parish officers. In short, a few terms as churchwarden or overseer of the poor, in a busy and relatively wealthy parish such as Berkhamsted, was excellent training for any man destined to meet even greater social demands in the new role of selectman of a New England town.

A close examination of the Berkhamsted vestry book gives an excellent idea of the response of an active parish to "national events" and to emergencies within the area. While Peter Noyes seems to have been buried in Weyhill's atmosphere of slow-moving country life, Robert Darvell and Edmund

* Service by rotation among all householders in a parish was quite common: Tate, *op. cit.*, p. 84.

† Parliament had passed very few definitions of churchwardens' powers: Tate, *op. cit.*, pp. 26–27.

Rice were closely linked to great personalities and to the fluctuations of the wool trade. Berkhamsted's castle was known as the home of young Prince Charles, the town was not very far to the northeast of London, and the parish reflected the turbulences which arose in both government and trade at large.

The churchwardens early in the seventeenth century fulfilled their obligations as defined by Parliament and by canon law. They paid the annual fee for maintenance of maimed soldiers and for the court of the king's bench, and they paid the expenses of the two visitations of the archdeacon, as well as those of the occasional visitation of their bishop. In addition, they paid to clothe the poor in the parish, to maintain "a girl," and to buy food for poor families on relief. Since their ringers were instructed to toll the church bells at any event of national importance, naturally the Berkhamsted churchwardens had to provide beer and fees to their ringers when they celebrated the coronation of James I. But the churchwardens could also stretch their funds to cover the construction of a "ducking stool," to be used in ducking unreasonably talkative parishioners who had sharp tongues, and they paid a fee to the man who rang the school bell for the few young Berkhamsted "scholars."[15]

This pattern of expense continued through the final decades of the seventeenth century but was added to by various unexpected problems. When the bishop began issuing yearly specific Articles of Inquiry, the churchwardens started to buy these documents annually. The Articles made it clear that the office of a churchwarden, assisted by the labors of the sidemen, when properly fulfilled, was an extremely demanding one. These officers had three areas of responsibility, as defined by their church superiors: the habits and attitudes of all the parishioners, the activities of the minister, and the state of the church's property. The churchwardens were on oath to "present" at the archdeacon's or the bishop's court any of the following offenses: disagreement with the minister, adultery, whoredom, incest, drunkenness, swearing, ribaldry, usury, any uncleanness or wickedness, hindrance of any sermons, defending Catholic or "false doctrines," disturbing divine services in any way, or not attending church on Sunday or on the holy days.

The churchwardens had to repel loiterers during the services, note whether the parishioners took Communion regularly, repel strangers from the parish lest they become public burdens, report any arguments among preachers, prevent any profane use of the church, and present any parishioner who asked to have his child baptized by nonpreaching ministers.[16]

Furthermore, the churchwardens had to note whether their parson was irregular in his conduct of divine services, neglected his parochial duties, or was guilty of any immorality. And as a third area of responsibility, the church-wardens were expected to collect the alms, furnish the bread and wine for Communions, maintain the Book of Common Prayer, and take complete supervision of church property. They had to maintain the church in good repair, arrange for the distribution of seats in the church, and keep close watch of the sacred vessels and objects in the church.

All these principles were explicitly set forth in a book of Articles, revised every two or three years, and the Berkhamsted churchwardens apparently bought a new book almost every year from 1604 onward. The Articles listed by the Bishop of Winchester for this period enumerate over one hundred separate questions to be asked churchwardens and sidemen during visitation, an exhaustive inquiry into all phases of parish life.[17] It is doubtful that a seventeenth-century New England congregation could be any more "prying" into the habits and attitudes of their brethren than was an English churchwarden who fulfilled all of his canonical duties.

The churchwardens of Berkhamsted were assisted in their tasks by two sidemen, who were supposed to present any unorthodox habits of any parishioner, but they have left no surviving records, and such records are indeed rare.[18] Four other parish officers in Berkhamsted, elected annually, helped the churchwardens spend their money — two overseers of the poor and two stonewardens or surveyors of the highways. By the terms of the famous Poor Law of 1601, the overseers had to support and to direct all the poor families and children in their parish. And the highway statute of 1555 had instructed each surveyor of the ways (or stonewarden) to remember that each parishioner was expected to contribute about six days per year to the maintenance of all the roads in the parish.[19]

Characteristically, the functions of all four types of church officers were collectively recorded in the Berkhamsted Churchwardens' Accounts of the seventeenth century. The vestry kept a running record rather than four different books. For example, not only was parish money spent in 1608 to buy the latest book of Articles, but parish officers took £10 from Sir Alexander Cary to "set the poor on work" and thus prevent these unfortunate people from being vagrants in the parish.

By 1614, the churchwardens showed that they could spend their income rather freely. Not only did they pay laborers to build tables and benches in the town's courthouse, but they also gave alms to certain "poor Irish and Venetians" who appeared within the parish bounds and whom they undoubtedly shoved on to the next parish.

In the year 1617 the churchwardens paid due respect to the royal family, and yet they were not immune from criticism from their superiors. Although they gave beer and fees to the ringers to celebrate the visit of Prince Charles to his old tutor living at the castle of Berkhamsted, the churchwardens were cited at the archdeacon's court for their neglect of their church building. When the archdeacon pointed out that St. Peter's needed both a cross and a weathercock, the churchwardens were quick to respond and to hire laborers to put these important symbols back in their respective places.

The churchwardens were businessmen as well as borough representatives at the court of their archdeacon. In 1621 they rented a house and an orchard to one William Oxley for thirty years at the annual rent of £3, with instructions to Oxley that he had to add two bays to the building rented. In the following years the churchwardens of Berkhamsted were affected by the wars in Europe. They were willing to make gifts to a man "taken prisoner by the Turks" and to one who had "fought in the wars in Bohemia." One year later they gave alms both to some "poor Irish" going through their town, as well as to "some soldiers from Turkey." A market town producing wool for European trade had a wide variety of visitors.

Within four years they had another type of responsibility. The King gave £100 of wood to the poor of the parish and expected the churchwardens to distribute it with justice. The parish officers sent fifty-eight loads to seventy-two families, and apportioned the wood with such success that they had no complaints — at least none that were serious enough to be recorded.

William Axtell, father of the emigrant Thomas, was an officer in Berkhamsted on two occasions when some very serious thinking had to be done by the vestry as they faced two rather unfamiliar social problems. The first one, the maintenance of an abandoned child, was not very difficult to solve; but the second one, the calamitous effects of drought, created a crisis in the parish.

In 1628 the overseers met with the vestry to present two cases of bastardy. One Robert Orive, living in the nearby parish of Whitchurch, wished to resolve his guilt and shame by giving the Berkhamsted overseers of the poor £5 to "maintair" his illegitimate child in Berkhamsted. Both the vestry and the overseers agreed to accept the responsibility and undoubtedly began searching for a family willing to adopt the poor youngster. The actions of the overseers were even more explicit in dealing with little Alice Chappel, "an abandoned child . . . left upon the parish by her grandfather." One of the overseers, Robert Partridge, agreed to take Alice as an apprentice — perhaps he was engaged in the manufacture of woolen cloth — but he needed financial assistance. Consequently, the vestry drew up a list of "contributors," the chief men of the parish, including William Axtell and Robert Darvell, and £2 was raised by these "voluntary gifts" to aid Partridge.

Two years later, however, in the winter of 1630–1631, the parish of Berkhamsted was in the midst of a severe crisis. William Axtell and his friends were not alone. A combination of bad weather, drought, and decline in the wool trade had sent a flood of anguished pleas and cries to the Privy Council. The scarcity of wheat had sent the prices of bread soaring, and the poor, particularly in the boroughs, suddenly faced starvation and the cruelty of an economic system over which they had no control. The Privy Council ordered the justices of the peace all over England to control the price of wheat and bread as best they could and sent many specific orders to the justices in the coastal towns to aid them in facing angry, desperate mobs.[20]

The chief men in Berkhamsted, however, have left no record of any attempt at price control, a very difficult operation in a seventeenth-century market town. They met as a vestry and tried to handle the emergency in another way. Their description of the problem is characteristic of that period: "Forasmuch as the heavy hand of God hath been upon this whole land this summer and harvest last, which is sensibly known and tasted by the most, but especially by the poor, who therefore are compelled, and do make daily complaints to the overseers for relief; who, although they pity their want, yet cannot well tell in what manner and measure to supply them without further and better advice than their own . . . have therefore called together the parish to pray for their desire and direction therein."[21]

The vestry, suddenly thrown on its own resources, clearly exercised powers of orderly self-government. First, one member recalled a "law made for such purpose 43 Elizabeth" that provided for local bylaws, if confirmed by the justices of the peace of the borough. Next, the vestry acknowledged the fact that "the prices of corn and grain are double the price which they are wont to be" and accepted the responsibility of caring for those people in the parish who might suffer, or possibly starve, as a result. Accordingly, the following "orders" were passed:

1. The overseers should give to every old, lame, sick, or impotent person, in their monthly distribution, as much as "the largest allowance" ever given before. Tradition ruled, even in a crisis. The overseers could not give grain freely but could donate only the largest amount they could ever remember having given before.
2. Children of poor families who were six years old and under and therefore

unable to maintain themselves should be given similar large amounts of "distribution" by the overseers.

3. Children of poor families between the ages of six and twelve, if their families were unable to assist them, even though they were "set to some honest labor and diligently holding to it," should be entitled to certain relief. Overseers were instructed to give 8d. per month to each such child "during these hard times" until either the child "has grown up to more dexterity" or the conditions improved.

4. No extra allowance was given to "such healthy women or children above twelve years." The churchwardens added, "Nature intended, as well as God and law of man, that they who have bodies of years and health, may and ought to provide for their own necessities."

5. Overseers were instructed to visit and take notice of all who were lame or sick or in great distress, and to relieve them monthly, "but not by diminishing the stock of the poor without public and general consent."

6. To defray expenses a larger rate was necessary, and the overseers could distrain any person in the parish or borough who refused to pay the parish tax.

Before this unusual order became effective, it had to be signed by twelve "chief men" of the vestry, six of them chief burgesses; it was then countersigned by the mayor, William Axtell, and the rector, Thomas Newman, a principal burgess. The order sanctioned the largest rate in the entire period 1600–1640, 5s. per acre, and up to £1 for a man's "ability," as decided by the churchwardens. This was from ten to thirty times the normal church rate and was designed to bring in as much as £600.

The vestry had to fight in the courts of England for the legality of this order, but the overseers apparently collected and distributed this relief tax. The vestry was strengthening their powers of self-government, even inserting a number of long notes and orders into the Account Book during 1630–1640. With the exception of the actual accounts, the book looks somewhat similar to the Town Book of Sudbury, Massachusetts, 1638–1656.

For instance, the Berkhamsted vestry made an order in January, 1631, "That warning be given at some convenient time before the next Communion . . . that the meaner sort of people do not press into that seat in the chancel where the minister doth usually begin to distribute the holy bread and cup, but leave it free for the Bailiff and such others as are fit to sit with him and next after him." The vestry insisted on a "comliness and order" as "commanded by God," which meant that the local aristocratic hierarchy had to be held in respect and deferred to, both in the borough and in the parish church.

The vestry had even more ingenious solutions to the "unseemliness amongst the communicants at the Lord's supper." The parish clerk was not only supposed to command the "meaner sort" to keep their place, but he was also instructed to read loudly from the Psalm Book to instill an atmosphere of reverence. The vestry, well aware that "many, through lack of devotion, are idle beholders" and that the actions of these annoying skeptics disturbed others' "holy meditations," ordered the clerk to "read some fit Psalm" until order and a spirit of meditation were restored within the church.

Some of the parish began to take action. In April 1631 John Davey, a mere three-acre holder but the tenant of the "Churchouse," came to the vestry to complain that the "widow Burr refused to admit him to sit in the seat set up for her husband when he was tenant in the same Churchouse." Both the minister and the vestry agreed on the principle of apportionment of fixed places in the parish pews and ordered widow Burr to admit John Davey and his wife into the pew traditionally reserved for tenants of the "Churchouse."

In June Edward Scott expressed his outrage at being presented at the archdeacon's visitation for not paying his "dues for poor people," but he was flatly informed that where there were poor in the parish "who have not means to bury themselves decently," the overseers had the power to tax the other more fortunate parishioners to provide a suitable burial for the poor.

In the same year a very unusual entry appears in the book: "the rule for stonewardens is this: the beginning [of work on the roads] is at both sides of the Town and so to come on into the market of the Town." If the two stonewardens, William Glaniser and John Davey (tenant of the Churchouse), carried this out, the parishioners of Berkhamsted must have done considerable work on their roads, an impressive achievement at that time.*

More and more phrases implying a sense of self-government appear in the Berkhamsted records. The church rate of 1631 was "agreed upon and granted by the general voice." And in April 1632 a solemn agreement was written down: "For the effectual and final agreement between the Corporation and the rest of the townsmen, it is agreed that the Bailiff and Capital Burgesses shall pay the rent of the Churchouse to the Churchwardens yearly, and the Churchwardens shall pay for the toll yearly to the Bailiff and Burgesses and discharge the King's rent which is 7s/8d." Thus it appears that the churchwardens were making the important orders for the town, levying rates, paying for the privileges of the borough charter, and letting the rest of the chief burgesses administer the courts.

Perhaps both emigrants, Robert Darvell and Edmund Rice, as they left

* Tate finds very few entries of expenses for any road repair: *The Parish Chest,* pp. 242–247.

the borough for New England about 1638, were aware that an active vestry was beginning to talk in terms of a town rather than solely in terms of a parish. Even more important, both men were well versed in a somewhat regular tax system, parts of which they definitely helped to institute in their new town of Sudbury, Massachusetts. Since the orders in the Sudbury Town Book relating to tax procedure are not at all detailed and do not even include lists of tax assessments, the system in Rice's old parish needs close examination.

The Tax System

The Berkhamsted churchwardens levied far more church rates on their parishioners than seems normal for an English parish at this period. The records for all the other emigrants to Sudbury show only occasional rates on special occasions, and the churchwardens' records for Weyhill indicate no real tax system whatever. It is now impossible even to guess whether Rice and Darvell had more tax experience than other Sudbury officers, but it is significant that the Sudbury citizens elected Rice as their representative to the Massachusetts legislature, where the principles of taxation and representation were hotly debated.

Robert Darvell, as ratepayer, landholder, churchwarden, and chief burgess in Berkhamsted had experienced the following rates:

Date	Rate	Total	Number of Ratepayers
1613	4d./acre for arable 12d./acre for meadow "Adding a proper amount for ability for such as have land." Those with no land taxed "according to their ability."	£35	143
1617	2d./acre for arable 6d./acre for meadow "The landed inhabitants at the proportion of a third part added to their land for ability." Those with no land taxed "according to honesty & discretion."	£16/19/06	108
1618	Agreed that every future rate to be levied according to the 1613 assessment.		

Date	Rate	Total	Number of Ratepayers
1620	2d./acre for arable 6d./acre for meadow With an ability rate added.	£18/15/01	110
1622	1d./acre and "ability with discretion."	£9/07/04	134
1627	½ penny/acre and ability.	£5/10/02	106
1629	"A new and lower assessment." [No further definition recorded.]	£17/00/01	81
1630	5s./acre and "for ability each man shall be rated as he has been up to £1."	est. £600	no list
1631	Those with no land "rated arbitrarily" up to £1 each.	£05/05/01	130
1632	2d./acre for "all landholders." "All others as were formerly assessed."	£22/14/07	186
	[Churchwardens' Accounts for 1633–1636 missing.]		
1637	3d./acre "and ability with discretion."	£33/19/00	210
1638	3d./acre "and all other persons at a fourth penny more than last year."	no data	no data

Whereas a tax in any other parish was a very special "rate" for a special occasion, the parishioners of Berkhamsted had come to expect a rate almost every year, and there are records of fourteen rates in twenty-three years, even with five years of accounts missing.* They could never really predict their assessment, even on their land, and the decision on "ability" was admittedly arbitrary.

This system of determining a man's ability became very important to those men settling in New England. Often the Massachusetts legislature left the heavy responsibility of granting land to the selectmen, with the warning that they should maintain "due order and proportion." The officers of Sudbury developed an assessment system which seems fairer than that in Berkhamsted,

* As W. E. Tate comments, "There grew up the inconvenient and wasteful practice of levying a whole host of special rates, some of which were so small as to amount to only a fraction of a farthing in the pound, so that the cost of collection absorbed most of the sum received." (*The Parish Chest,* p. 28.)

because they redefined the problem of "ability" in their town taxes. Perhaps Rice and Darvell gave advice on this matter.

Both men had seen a completely arbitrary system at work, imposed by a ruling oligarchy, with little chance of successful opposition by the ratepayers. Some examination of the "ability rate" can make this evident. In the 1613 rate, for example, the following parishioners were rated as follows:

Ratepayer	Acreage	Ability Rate
Mr. Barker	48 acres arable	20 s.
	4 acres meadow	
Mr. Blount	91 acres arable	20 s.
	5 acres meadow	
W. Hill	3 acres arable	none
	1 acre meadow	
W. Axtell	2 acres arable	5 s.
	1 acre meadow	
H. Axtell	10 acres arable	6s. 8d.
	1 acre meadow	
"All outlyers"		6d. each

But in 1617 the situation and the rate changed as follows:

Mr. Wethered	100 acres arable	5 s.
	no meadow	
Mr. Barker	92 acres arable	9 s.
	4 acres meadow	
Mr. Blount	100 acres arable	7 s.
	6 acres meadow	
W. Hill	3 acres arable	2 s.
	1 acre meadow	
W. Axtell	7 acres arable	2 s.
	3 acres meadow	
H. Axtell	12 acres arable	4 s.
	1 acre meadow	
"All outlyers"		From 3d. to 12d. each

One wonders how much debate, or objection, was caused by the changes in this ability rate. The over-all rate was half that of the 1613 one, and yet Barker, who had doubled his property, showing management ability, received more than half a cut in his ability rate, while at the same time W. Hill had his ability rate raised from nothing to two shillings.

A similar account of arbitrary assessment can be seen in the 1622 rate, which was one fourth the assessment of the 1613 rate:

Mr. Wethered	100 acres arable	4s. 4d.
	2 acres meadow	
Mr. Barker	92 acres arable	3s. 10d.
	4 acres meadow	
Mr. Blount	119 acres arable	4s. 9d.
W. Hill	14 acres arable	10d.
W. Axtell	7 acres arable	3d.
H. Axtell	19 acres arable	17d.
R. Darvell	22 acres arable	2 s.

Why, for instance, when William Hill had the ability to increase his holding from ten acres in 1617 to fourteen acres in 1622, did his ability tax decrease? This could be asked about the rates of the Axtells, as well. And why did Robert Darvell get assessed eight times the rate of W. Axtell when he had only three times the acreage? Was this "according to honesty and discretion"?

The 1627 rate proves that the amount of acreage did not necessarily imply an "ability." Robert Darvell and Mr. Kellet both had fifteen acres of land, and yet their ability rates were 9d. and 2s. 4d. respectively. Perhaps the "Mr." recorded for Kellet was, to the churchwardens, their way of saying that he should have been twice as able as Darvell in paying for town expenses.

The various assessments by the churchwardens did not go completely unchallenged. Propertied landholders, angered by a rate assessment, and knowing that the chief burgesses were both vestrymen and justices of the peace, could appeal to the justices at the county courts. As a result of the 1628 rate several landholders in Berkhamsted complained to the justices at the quarter sessions that they were "overrated in the poor rate and demanded that a new vestry be called and a new rate made." Further, they wanted a check on their vestry and asked the county justice to "judge if the rate is fit." Since the rate was not changed in the accounts and the vestry remained the same, apparently the plea was either turned down, or the churchwardens were able to defend their assessment system convincingly.[22]

On the other hand, when Mr. Francis Wethered, one of the top landholders and a chief burgess as well, complained of the 1630 rate, Berkhamsted's vestry had real troubles. The records show how deeply involved such an argument could become. Wethered, perhaps skeptical of the power of a county sessions court, started a suit against the Berkhamsted vestry in the appropriate church court, claiming that he had been overrated. According to the rate, his assessment was £25, one of the largest in the parish. The vestry spent £8 defending their position, and, upon losing the case, called a special meeting for further counsel.

The vestry decided to "speed the cause to sentence" and £2 more of the ratepayers' money was spent to appeal the case, perhaps to the archbishop's provincial court. Apparently the vestry lost, however, for a brief note was entered about "payment to Mr. Wethered" in later accounts.[23]

The rates and assessments of the vestry in Berkhamsted, then, were subject to review by higher courts, despite such phrases as "this levy made by general consent." A citizen well aware of English and canonical law could force his parish officers to alter, or to repudiate, orders or bylaws which did not conform to English law in general.

In reverse fashion, a justice of the peace could prosecute a parishioner for breaking the law. One Thomas Redwood of Berkhamsted was convicted of drunkenness in 1627 and fined; the same Mr. Francis Wethered, "yeoman," was fined for erecting a cottage without four acres of land attached to it; Mr. Young, yeoman of Berkhamsted, was prosecuted and fined for allowing his hedges and fences, bordering the land of Mr. Halsey, to get in such a state of "disrepair" that Halsey's sheep escaped and were lost.[24]

Even the mayor and burgesses were held up to a higher authority. The justices of the peace for Herts ordered that the borough officers appear in 1638 to explain about certain money raised by the sale of a house of correction. But these county justices recognized that even their decisions were subject to review. They were, after all, but part of the whole intricate system of English courts and English common law. Thus, when the poor of Berkhamsted petitioned the Herts justices in 1638 for relief, thereby expressing their discontent with their churchwardens' administration of the Poor Law, the justices told them to submit their petition to the court of king's bench.[25]

Only in a New England town, far away from the King's courts, could men like Rice and Darvell make local orders which for some time could not be checked by appeals to royal courts. Perhaps, in moving away from this system of English courts, these men wanted an even stronger local administration in the name of their town.

As W. E. Tate has pointed out, a parish in England was not necessarily a township.[26] Some emigrants had never lived in a parish as active in local government as that of Rice and Darvell. For many Englishmen at the time, the term "town" meant a chartered borough, a manufacturing center where the burgesses spent much time running their courts and administering their trades. For that reason it is necessary to examine the old borough of Sudbury itself.

CHAPTER III

The Secrets of the Corporation
of This Town of Sudbury

THE borough of Sudbury, Suffolk, was not only known as the stronghold of Puritanism in the Eastern Counties, but it also sent more emigrants to New England than any other town or village in East Anglia.[1] One of its ministers, Edmund Brown, was probably responsible for the fact that the Massachusetts General Court graced a wilderness settlement with a name which connoted, to the English, a thriving center of wool manufacture.

Brown, the first minister of the Massachusetts town, is a mysterious figure. Born in 1606 in Lavenham, Suffolk, just northeast of the borough of Sudbury, he had been sent to Cambridge University and had become a member of Emmanuel College at the height of the Nonconformist movement in England. Following his graduation in 1624, he returned to Suffolk to assist in one of the larger churches in the borough of Sudbury, to train himself to play the bass viol, and to continue his study. He had kinsmen in Bury St. Edmunds, in Lavenham, and in the borough itself. But despite the fact that he served in Sudbury for fourteen years, no personal documents and very few official documents naming him have survived.

The activity of Sudbury parishes during this time, however, was inextricably tied to the life of the borough. Town officers walked in procession to the churches, attended divine services and, on occasion, fined citizens either for nonattendance at church or for unseemly behavior in the pews. Burgesses and ministers knew each other well.

One other aspect of this borough is significant for the history of early New England towns in general. John and Geoffrey Ruggles, both capital burgesses, left the town in 1630 to join the Winthrop fleet and shortly thereafter became principal founders and officers of Roxbury, Massachusetts.

An examination of the operation of Sudbury's borough government in general, and John Ruggles's functions in particular, helps to clarify the concepts of town government which Edmund Brown must have carried in his head during those early years when he was a founder of the new settlement and responsible for helping to transplant the vigorous roots of English local government.

His borough of Sudbury, Suffolk, was quite different from Rice's borough of Berkhamsted. With only half the area, Sudbury had perhaps three times the population of the Herts market town, an estimated three thousand people engaged in at least forty-five different trades. Most of the sixteen hundred adult inhabitants of the town relied on some sort of industrial skill, or some type of trade to earn a living, and not more than 1 per cent or 2 per cent who appeared at the courts considered themselves "yeomen."[2] The men of Sudbury were busy in the cloth trade and not engaged in the accumulation of plots of land, so characteristic of the men of Berkhamsted.

Other scholars have had high praise for the administrative abilities of those English merchants who ran their trades and their corporate governments side by side. Professor Notestein has termed the London merchants, as well as the aggressive businessmen in exporting towns such as Sudbury, "the most knowing people in the realm."[3] And the historian of the New England merchants in this period has pointed again to the fact that the merchants of Bristol, Plymouth, and London were the first to conceive and organize workable schemes of colonization in New England.[4]

Such schemes were but extensions of corporate administration in active English boroughs. In the borough of Sudbury, where clothiers and mercers supervised the manufacture of woolen cloth and exported much of this to the Continent, the officers of the borough were very busy people with many problems to solve. While the churchwardens of the various parishes may have been faithful and conscientious, the government of the borough clearly dominated parish activity.

The framework of Sudbury's corporate government was quite different from that of Berkhamsted, owing to the fact that the chief burgesses had jurisdiction over two parishes of contrasting size, and one tenth of a third parish, the largest area of which was in the adjoining county of Essex.[5] Thus Sudbury is a clear example of Mr. Tate's warning that "a parish was not a township," and a proof that men like John Ruggles had to subordinate affairs of the parish to affairs of the town when sitting as a member of the borough council.

When John Ruggles took his oath as juryman in 1619, to "help the Mayor govern the people that they obey the orders of the borough, anciently made," he was learning the essence of corporate government: legal pressure to make all the populace conform to "ancient orders."[6] There was much to learn. In that particular session of the peace, held in the moot hall before Thomas Smith, Gent., Mayor, the sergeants of the mace were commanded to bring in thirty-seven citizens, "all to reply to various transgressions, contempts and misdeeds for which they stand separately indicted," and the jury had much to report, as well.

Ruggles and his jury made presentments against at least fifteen butchers, two clothiers, and an assortment of weavers, saymakers, curriers, bakers, and mercers. Some butchers were selling unhealthy ewe's mutton; others had sold "unbaited" bull's beef. Two men were not only keeping unlicensed alehouses but were allowing "luxurious living" in contempt of town custom and causing "great harm" to the inhabitants. Other careless inhabitants had allowed their noisome pigs to dig up and spoil the borough commons. Those twenty-four who came and threw themselves on the mercy of the court were promptly fined.

The same jury witnessed the mayor draw up bonds for thirteen citizens who wished to keep common alehouses for the following year. There were detailed rules — no playing at dice, cards, quoits, loggets, bowles, or any other unlawful game; none but ordinary household servants could stay at the inn during the time of divine service on the Sabbath or holy days. The names of anyone who stayed more than one day and one night had to be submitted to the local constable. Further, no tippling or drinking was allowed after nine o'clock at night. The innkeeper's measurements and prices were strictly limited — sealed and true measures had to be used; strong beer or ale could cost no more than a penny a quart; small beer or ale was fixed at half-penny the quart. And, above all, he could not willingly harbor any rogues, vagabonds, sturdy beggars, masterless men, or "other notorious offenders."[7]

As a juryman, Ruggles had to know a good deal about the legitimate activities of the many trades within the borough, as well as the functions of the various courts. During the period of his participation in Sudbury's government, the borough courts administered an average of 117 indictments a year, a low of 60 in 1626 and a high of 174 in 1627, a year in which the town fined a number of citizens for refusing to go to church. Members of a jury were to overlook no aspect of disorder.

Once a citizen had gained some training in the basic laws and liberties of his borough, and had both status and a reputation for responsibility, he could be arbitrarily elected to be a "Free Burgess" of the borough. And the franchises, liberties, and privileges of the same borough, according to the statutes, decrees, and customs, were given to him on payment, naturally, of a fee.[8] The responsibilities were as great as the privilege. Indeed, in some boroughs busy merchants tried to avoid being on the borough council, fearing that they would never have time to attend to their businesses.[9]

As a free burgess, or freeman, a Sudbury citizen was anything but free. He was thereby appointed to a committee of the top 110 men in Sudbury, who were expected to give lifelong service to the government of the borough on pain of being dismissed and disgraced for negligence of duty. And as a junior member of the governing hierarchy a free burgess was also eligible for yearly appointment to any one of the forty town posts, where he had to volunteer to regulate his neighbors' activities for an entire year. The Sudbury town officers were personally responsible for the administration of order, as follows:

3 constables (one for each parish)
2 surveyors of the corn market
2 surveyors of the fish market
2 surveyors of the poultry market
2 surveyors of the meat market
3 searchers of leather
7 surveyors of weaving
2 sizers and sealers of weights and measures
6 ale tasters (two for each parish)
  town crier
  hog warden(s)
  hay warden(s)

The parish constable was the pillar of order, both a spokesman for the law and an executive who had to put the law into practice, unpaid, for the year's term of office. Professor Notestein and Mr. Tate have given vivid descriptions of the functions of the office, gleaned from many sources, and the entries in the Sudbury Borough Book show nothing unusual.[10]

The corn market surveyors were sworn, in Sudbury, to see to it that there was enough grain available for sale to the inhabitants and to prevent any cor-

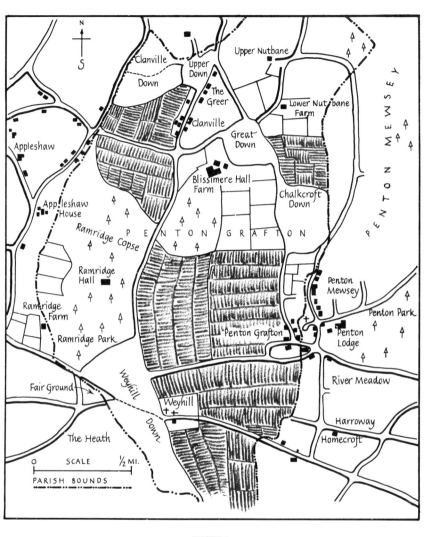

FIGURE 1

Weyhill, Hants, about 1635

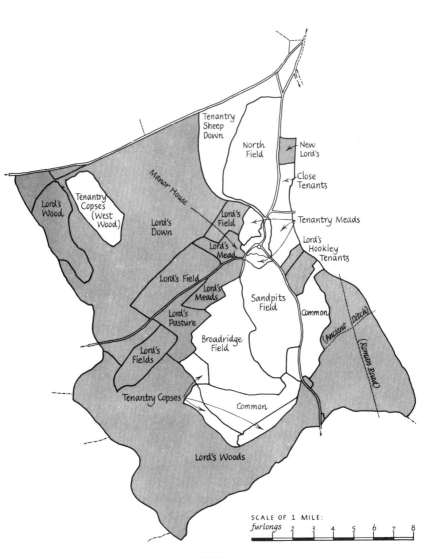

Lord's Wood

Tenantry Copses (West Wood)

Manor House

Tenantry Sheep Down

North Field

New Lord's

Close Tenants

Tenantry Meads

Lord's Down

Lord's Field

Lord's Field

Lord's Hookley Tenants

Lord's Mead

Lord's Field

Lord's Meads

Sandpits Field

Common

Lord's Pasture

(Ancient Ditch)

Broadridge Field

(Roman Road)

Lord's Fields

Tenantry Copses

Common

Lord's Woods

SCALE OF 1 MILE:
furlongs   2   3   4   5   6   7   8

FIGURE 2

Ashmore, Dorset

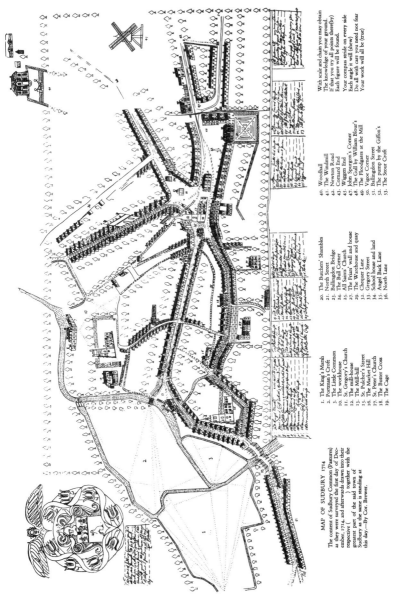

MAP OF SUDBURY 1714

The content of Sudbury Common (Pastures) as they were surveyed the first day of December, 1714, and afterwards drawn into their respective ( ) together with the greatest part of the said town of Sudbury as the same is standing at this day.—By Cor. Brewer.

1. The King's Marsh
2. Portman's Croft
3. The Little Common
10. The workhouse
11. St. Gregory's Church
12. The mill-house
13. The Mill-hill
15. St. Pulcher's Street
16. The Market Hill
17. St. Peter's Church
18. The Butter Cross
19. The Cage

20. The Butchers' Shambles
21. North Street
23. Ballingdon Bridge
24. The Bull Corner
25. All Saints' Church
27. The Friars' wall and house
29. The Warehouse and quay
31. Chequer Lane
33. St. Gregory Street
34. School house and land
35. Angel Back Lane
36. North Lane

40. Woodhall
41. The Windmill
42. Newton Road
43. Cornard End
45. Wiggen End
47. John Spurgeon's Corner
48. The Gull by William Blour's
49. The Floodgates at the Mill
50. Vigoe Corner
51. Ballingdon Street
52. The pump by the Giffon's
53. The Stour Croft

With scale and chain you may obtain
The knowledge of your ground.
If that you try all points thereby
Each figure will be found.

Your compass stride on every side
Each angle it will (shew)
Do all with care you need not fear
Your work will all be (true)

FIGURE 3

Sudbury, Suffolk, 1714

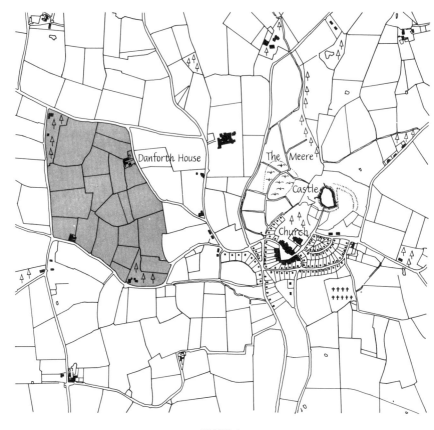

Danforth House
The Meere
Castle
Church

FIGURE 4
Property of Nicholas Danforth and Town of Framlingham, Suffolk

nering of the incoming grain to force prices up. The surveyors of the fish market had to prosecute any fishmongers who sold "by lesser measure than be not
lawful to the Standard of the Exchequer," while the flesh market surveyors
had to watch for all unwholesome forms of meat.[11] Both surveyors and jurymen in Sudbury indicted butchers who sold meat which "hadn't been chased
enough by the dogs," or was "unbaited." They were merely strengthening the
medieval practice of allowing bulls to be tormented by dogs for sport just before slaughter, which was supposed to improve the quality of the meat by mixing the fat with the lean.

The Sudbury searchers of leather were instructed to impose the English
standards on tanned, curried, or "wrought leather" and on the shoes and boots
made within the town. The surveyors of weaving, however, had even more demanding tasks, if conscientiously carried out. The borough was full of clothiers and weavers of all varieties, and the borough court indictments for the
period 1618–1640 list 11 different types of cloth trade, and at least 137 different men involved in the business, who were also presented at court. Since 37
per cent of all the cases in this period involved such men, the surveyors, and
the juries and constables, must have been busy. Technically, these town officers had to determine how many weavers or saymakers there were who kept
more than two broad looms or five say (narrow) looms in their homes. Those
who had this number of looms had to obey the legal regulations for having
apprentices. Such a boy had to be bound by the churchwardens and overseers
of the poor of his parish, with consent of the mayor, that he had agreed to
serve his master for seven years. And each clothier had to have one older jour-
neyman for each three apprentices.[12]

When the wool trade began to go into a slump, the Privy Council heaped
numerous contradictory commands on the shoulders of the borough councils
and justices of the peace. The weaving surveyors must have been at their wits'
ends in trying to compromise between the commands of the central government and the ingenious attempts to aid business made by the various independent weavers.

The Sudbury sealers of weights and measures had a difficult task in making all the merchants use honest measurements. The ale tasters were to visit
the various inns and alehouses to be sure that the food and ale offered was
"sweet and wholesome for man's body." The surveyors of the town commons
were to present "all such persons . . . who put upon the commons any farcy,
mangie, scabbied horses, or geldings or mares" and were to "distrain any cattle, hogs, or sheep as you find damaging or surcharging the commons against

the laws of this Town." As in Weyhill, and probably in Berkhamsted, each landholder was limited in the number of animals he could pasture on the commons.

The most onerous duties of the borough fell on the free burgesses who held these numerous posts, and on the mayor, as justice of the peace. Once a free burgess had completed his share of service to the borough, he was eligible for appointment as capital burgess, when a vacancy occurred. By 1619 John Ruggles, together with his relative, Geoffrey, had achieved this privileged title, which they held until they left the borough for New England in 1630. They did not have to spend many hours, however, maintaining their status.

In 1619 for example, John appeared as a capital burgess at four courts, and as a juryman at one. During the next year he turned up at only two courts and accepted fines for absences at five. He had virtually the same record in 1621 but, for reasons unknown, served at six court sessions in 1622 and missed only three.

The position of capital burgess did not prevent indictment or arrest. In 1622 John Ruggles was indicted for having one seven-pound weight "short," and he paid his sixpence fine without question. A relative, George Ruggles, was given even harsher treatment. Because he had "failed his duty many times," George was dispossessed of his privileges by Mayor Robert Howe, who replaced him, as capital burgess, by Nicholas Last. The town of Sudbury demanded that all its burgesses give some service if they expected to receive the dignity accorded an officer of the borough.

More specifically, the burgesses were expected to attend the courts which handled four areas of activity: yearly elections, borough finance, relations with the central government, and the issuance of borough orders.

Elections

The borough government really began each year in September, when the annual election and its accompanying festivities were held. The free burgesses, capital burgesses, and aldermen assembled at the moot hall, a picturesque gabled building of timber, placed at one end of the central market square, opposite St. Peter's Church. The bell in the little cupola over the high-pitched roof tolled the hour, and the town officers, all wearing distinctive gowns, climbed the stairs to the paneled council chamber, located in the overhanging second story.

The rate of attendance increased with the importance of the actual office held in the government. The seven aldermen appeared with great regularity, knowing that one of them would be chosen mayor; about 67 per cent of the capital burgesses came to what was known as "The Court of Elections," while only about twenty-four of the free burgesses showed up, a mere 31 per cent of the actual number of men raised to this position. But, then, they realized that they stood the greatest chance of being appointed to any one of the town posts for a year, unpaid jobs with little reward for the hours of service involved.

The group of free burgesses, capital burgesses, and aldermen who finally gathered in the council chamber, usually a total of about fifty-five men, elected the mayor for the coming year by indicating which of the aldermen they preferred. In the period 1600–1641, there were twenty-one different mayors, half of whom served for only one term of office, while the other ten men served two or three terms apiece. Only John Willet inspired enough confidence among his fraternal brothers to be asked to serve five times.[13]

Once the mayor had taken the silver maces and had sworn to "well and truly serve his Sovereign Lord the King, the people of this Town, and this corporation and to defend the lawful rights, liberties, privileges and charters," it was his job to "elect" the other town officials. While the old mayor automatically became the town coroner, the new mayor, with the consent of the aldermen and burgesses, appointed two capital constables, and two chamberlains (treasurers), usually from the capital burgesses. The functionary positions of bailiff, beadle, and two sergeants of the mace, men who took care of the ritual of the court and served processes, tended to be held for many years by the same men.

Either at this court of elections or at the court of the borough held the following month, the mayor appointed all the vital administrators of his authority: the constables, surveyors, searchers, supervisors, and ale tasters. These were chosen partly from the free burgesses, and partly from the list of responsible inhabitants. While 60 per cent of the grain market supervisors were free burgesses, 75 per cent of the leather searchers were chosen from the townsmen at large. Some burgesses must have taken their positions as honorary ones, for although at least one hundred twenty men enjoyed "the freedom of the borough" during 1620–1630, only about half of them were appointed to administrative posts.

The Sudbury records give no indication of any contested election, or any dispute about appointments to town posts, or petitions against the administration of any mayor or alderman. The businessmen who ran their corporation considered themselves a "select fraternity for the better government of the town and for the prevention of all disorders and confusions," and made their town steward swear that "you shall not utter or disclose any of the secrets touching the fellowship or corporation of this Town."[14]

Consequently, the yearly elections were in no sense public affairs, nor were any court sessions open to complaints of borough administration by the inhabitants. In fact, to question the mayor was a criminal offense. An older administration had clearly stated that "any person inhabiting or dwelling within the town of Sudbury who shall contend, in any cause or matter, by word or deed against the mayor of the town during his office shall from thenceforth be utterly void of all manner of freedoms, liberties and commonages and be held merely as a foreigner, until such time as he pays a fine for his offence."[15]

The mayor, aldermen, and burgesses conducted the "mystery of government" up in the moot hall, quite apart from the commoners, and only now and then appointed a particularly worthy citizen to be privy to their secrets. One of these secrets, of course, was the matter of taxation and expenditure for the town.

Borough Finance

The corporation of Sudbury, like that of Berkhamsted, rented its liberties and powers from the King and was expected to show a profit each year. The mayor received income and expended funds as did the churchwardens of Berkhamsted. He spent what seemed necessary to him, levied a tax occasionally for special purposes, and each year presented an explanation of his finances to his council.

Considering the large population and the active wool trade of the town, the borough budget seems very small. The average yearly income during the period 1618–1640 was from £5 to £20, hardly the level of expense of the churchwardens of a small rural parish in the area. These figures, incidentally, give us another proof that the Berkhamsted taxes and general flow of money was quite unusual for a town of its size.

The mayor of Sudbury could count on a fixed income from rent of the butcher stall, the bay hall, and three market stalls, and an average of £3 per year from the fines imposed by the various borough courts. He had his steady expenses, as well: the wages of the town clerk, of the sergeants of the mace, his fees to the juries, and, most important, "dinners at the Crown Inn." One might gather that each mayor thoroughly enjoyed mixing good food and discussion about borough problems, knowing well that he could entertain his guests on an expense account.

Although there are none of the specific details which filled the Berkhamsted accounts, the Sudbury records indicate that the mayor assumed that he could tax the inhabitants of the town at his discretion, merely by giving an order to the constable in each parish to "collect a rate." One does not know how the assessments were made, but the size of the taxes could not have made this a very serious problem. Except when the King of England levied his famous "ship money" tax, no inhabitant could have been taxed more than a penny in any single Sudbury town tax. The mayors imposed only eight taxes in eighteen years, as follows:

1619	Tax to repair Ballingdon Bridge	£5
	Tax to defend the borough against a Quo Warranto in the King's Courts	£4
1626	Tax to repair Ballingdon Bridge	£1
1628	Tax to pay the keeper of the House of Correction	(amount not recorded)
1632	Tax for prison charges — to pay the keeper of the House of Correction	£3/12/00
1633	Tax to repair Ballingdon Bridge	£2/13/06
1635–1636	His Majesty's Ship Money Tax	£85
1637	His Majesty's Ship Money Tax	£66

The size of the last two taxes makes it easy to see why King Charles heard so many complaints in his coastal towns. On a per capita basis the citizens of Sudbury were being forced to pay a tax, in 1635, that was twelve times their normal tax. This probably made far more difference than the fact that the tax, again on a per capita basis, was only one shilling per person.

But a shilling was a shilling, and the mayor of Sudbury did not begrudge any of them, particularly if they were income to his treasury. Each mayor kept meticulous records, listing expenses as small as a farthing, giving an excellent indication of what a borough mayor considered a proper expense.

In 1618–1619, for example, Mayor Smith repaired the bridge which led to the town's market, ordered stocks to be made for the square, and paid to have North Meadow fenced. The town armor was to be cleaned, also, and the mayor did not think it improper to give fees to the Queen's Players who had entertained the aldermen and burgesses of the town. In the following year, Mayor Willet submitted his expense account, "for going to the Assize Court," paid the King's messengers who brought a public proclamation, and paid £4 to build "the little house."

Mayor Abbot in 1622 again greeted the Queen's Players, ordered the Stour River to be cleaned, constructed a booth at the fair, built a ducking stool, and bought a new town pump. His military expenditure consisted in paying a few shillings to some soldiers when "they wore the Town Armour," and his budget for charity allowed him to give five shillings in "several payments for sick and maimed soldiers."

The following year's expenses could hardly have delighted any cold-eyed Puritan. If the accounts are accurate, Sudbury's entire town budget was devoted to festivals and fishing. Contributions were made to assist the expense of forty floats and "painting," in what must have been a fine parade through the borough. Later the mayor was careful to put down every shilling spent for "west country packthred" for fishing lines and "for chelps when we did fish."

Mayor Nichol, in 1626, charged the dinners he ate during the sessions courts, the only recompense for spending many hours listening to various misdeeds. He felt it quite proper, also, to ask the borough to pay the expense of those who had to hire horses to "go choose the Knights of the Shire."[16]

The mayor of Sudbury, in 1628, felt it proper for the borough to give a Christmas present to their own knight, Sir Robert Crane, who represented them when Parliament convened. His only other usual expense that year was to replace all the linen in Sudbury's house of correction.

Two years later, the mayor had a more serious problem: the charter was being legally questioned, but apparently a proper defense was made. The borough again had to repair its bridge, and it met the hardship of the terrible 1629–1630 drought by allowing borough expenses to buy clothes for the poor and to help "set the poor to work."

In the years 1633 and 1634, the borough was again repairing its much-used bridge, adding to the house of correction, mending the fences around the commons, and cleaning the town armor. A few "poor travellers from abroad" and an occasional "maimed soldier" reminded the inhabitants of Sudbury of wars in Europe, but most of the citizens assumed that paid professionals would continue to do all the serious fighting.

By 1636, complaints against the King's ship-money taxes and alarms about the state of the wool trade began to disturb the mayor and his council. The mayor journeyed all the way to Ipswich to confer with the high sheriff "about the ship money," and he entertained the borough M.P., Sir Robert Crane, in order to discuss the serious business of "providing work for the spinners and weavers."

Relations with the Central Government

The burgesses of Sudbury had their problems in this period. The principal trade had been the wool business ever since the weavers of the Low Country had taught the enterprising men of the borough how to manufacture the lighter, cheaper bays and says. The town government was dominated by men in the wool business. Five of the seven aldermen, at least, were either clothiers or weavers, and 50 per cent of the burgesses were managing some phase of the wool trade. But their business was international, tied to the European markets, and they turned to London and to the Privy Council for assistance in difficult times.

There had been a serious crisis in 1616–1617, when a very large foreign wool merchant named Cragg had gone into bankruptcy, forcing certain London clothiers into the same condition. The combination of the closing of many European markets owing to the Thirty Years' War, the rise of competitive wool manufacturing in the Dutch Republic, and the consequent oversupply of cloth in England had been devastating. The justices of the peace reported to the Privy Council that the Suffolk clothiers were bankrupt and pointed to lack of free trade as the fundamental cause of the business crisis.[17]

The clothiers and weavers in three eastern boroughs had immediately moved to incorporate, to be in a stronger position to bargain for a share of what was left of the foreign market. In each, the businessmen had worked closely with their borough governments to enforce the power of supervision of all the related operations. Since the various workmen were not gathered together physically in any sort of factory or shop but labored individually in their own homes, it was a difficult and complicated job to standardize methods and quality, to say nothing of wages and prices.

The clothiers in Bury St. Edmunds had been incorporated since 1607, and the borough's aldermen and burgesses chose six overseers each year who took the responsibility for imposing standards of workmanship. The clothworkers and tailors of Ipswich had formed an even more extensive corporation, embracing a third of Suffolk and containing representatives from the towns of Hadleigh, Lavenham, Glemsford, Waldringfield, Boxford, and Groton.[18] By 1618, the Privy Council had granted incorporation to a "Company of Clothiers, Clothworkers and Bay and Say Makers of Colchester," but the clothiers and weavers in Sudbury, twenty miles away, had preferred to rely on their cheaper says and on competition to battle a declining market.[19]

The whole question of whether borough governments should take on the responsibilities of appointing inspecting officers in the various trades, or whether individual corporate groups should be given such powers was much argued. The Privy Council tried to establish a set of regulations for wool and the manufacture of cloth, but found that the problem of actual regulation was almost insurmountable, as long as the workers lived and worked in such a scattered state.

By 1620, there was so much general complaint in Suffolk that a royal commission was appointed to meet at Bury St. Edmunds, to hear that cloths were piling up, that neither the Russian nor the Turkish merchants were buying, that overhead was eating up capital, and that something had to be done. The major accomplishment seems to have been the expression of the many complaints, but the principal problem of monopolistic practices in sales to foreign markets remained unsolved.[20]

When the crisis of the drought of 1629–1630 threw the Eastern Counties into a panic, the Privy Council acted immediately. The justices of the peace were ordered to control the prices as best they could. The Essex justices surveyed the amount of wheat stored in farmers' barns, the amount sown and growing, and then they allotted the amount of wheat per week each person should carry to market at Coggeshall, Colchester, and Malden. The Suffolk justices met at Bury St. Edmunds to discuss the problem and to fix wages and prices.[21]

The mayor of Sudbury did not leave any records of his response to this problem. As justice of the peace for his borough, he, too, fell under the commands of the Privy Council. But perhaps he was too busy to write down his administrative decisions. Unfortunately, none of the three parishes in Sudbury have their early seventeenth-century account books, or other records, and so one does not know whether the vestries met to levy special taxes to relieve the poor, or not.[22] Undoubtedly, they were forced to take some special action, just as every other vestry in East Anglia in the crowded towns seems to have done.

But the complaints of the Sudbury spinners and weavers make it evident that some of the governing body of the borough, as businessmen, reacted like normal businessmen in a sharply declining market: they lowered wages and refused to pay such high prices for the cloths, or the process for furnishing the cloths. The combination of low wages and high food prices was an explosive one, particularly for wage earners. When the saymakers all began to lower the wages of their spinners, weavers, and combers, bitter complaints were made to authorities outside the borough walls.

The justices of the peace in Essex were ordered by the Privy Council to investigate. They received the standard reply from the saymakers that they would agree to wage control if a national wage level were strictly imposed, but that otherwise an attempt to force them to pay high wages in a declining market was a form of unfair discrimination. The Privy Council ordered a wage level for a year for the various trades in the cloth business, but the Sudbury borough administration left no record indicating whether they tried to impose this wage level or not.[23] The number of indictments of clothiers did not rise in the Sudbury court records, and it is doubtful that the clothiers who sat on the borough council felt it fair to penalize themselves for what was so obviously a national economic slump.

It is evident, however, that both the Privy Council and Sir Robert Crane, M.P. for Sudbury, were concerned about unemployment in Sudbury. At least by 1636, if not before, the mayor and Crane were discussing how to provide work for the spinners and the weavers. Since there are no parish records for this period, one cannot tell whether the churchwardens aided those who had to go on relief, but if the Berkhamsted records are any indication, a responsible and vigorous vestry could have supplied food and clothing for the most unfortunate.

The mayor never dreamed of calling any sort of "town meeting" of the citizens to discuss the various problems. If his burgesses, that "select fraternity," could not find the solution, then the commoners had best pray to God for deliverance and search their own souls to see why the Lord might be punishing them. And the Sudbury churches had plenty of lectures to make clear the state of corruption in the world at large.

John Wilson, famous later for his opposition to the Antinomian heresy in Massachusetts and for his actions against the she-devil, Anne Hutchinson, who spread the evil doctrines, had been a lecturer in the borough of Sudbury in 1624. Just a year later, he used the London plague to sound his own trumpet in order to wake the sleepers:

> In the one thousand year of God,
>   Six hundred twenty-five,
> Was sent the Pestilential rod,
>   Our rocky hearts to rive.
> In the chief City of the Realm,
>   It had the chiefest seat;
> There like a sea to overwhelm,
>   Pride that was grown so great;
> Or like a fire to purge away,
>   The dross of hateful sin;
> Or like a trumpet thence to fray,
>   The sleep that souls were in.[24]

The citizens of Sudbury were expected to receive such wisdom from their ministers and apply it as best they could to their own lives. The average inhabitant had neither a tradition, nor a definite institution in the borough, by which he could articulate the "will of the people." Even the burgess John Ruggles was accustomed to a local government that was administrative, not legislative.

Borough Orders

Ruggles's "select fraternity," however, did make several bylaws during the period in which he was a member of this governing body. It is amusing that the first bylaw recorded in this particular period of Sudbury's history concerns the animal which caused the initial set of bylaws in early New England towns, the unruly pig.

The combination of "scoyne, in an undecent manner rooting and defiling" the market place in the center of town, and the dumping of refuse and other "noisome things" in the same area finally drove William Byatt, Gent., mayor of the borough, to action. In a very long-winded "law and ordinance," abbreviated by the town clerk on the margin as a "decree about hogges," the mayor reminded his citizens that they were breaking the ancient decrees of the town and causing "great scandal and discredit of the said Town imputed to the same by strangers passing through and coming into the same, from time to time . . . and great annoyance and inconvenience of the freemen and inhabitants thereof."

In short, the mayor forbade all the inhabitants from throwing any food, suds of wool yarn or of says, or other refuse out on any of the streets, ordered them to keep their hogs both penned up and ringed, and soundly warned the rude country folk not to "inhumanely pollute and defile the poultry cross or corn cross by making the same the place for the easement of their bodies." The town clerk was ordered to post the notice on the moot hall door and to read the order loudly in the market square. The constables were directed to drive any "hogs of diverse offenders to the common pound" until the fine of one penny to the driver and one penny to any assistant had been paid. The mayor further decreed that if only one credible witness reported to any officer of the borough any of the "aforesaid offences," the unruly offender would be brought before the mayor and fined fourpence for each offense.[25]

The bylaw made on May 13, 1622, however, was much more explicit in describing the power of the borough to make such orders. The decree was "consented and agreed to by the mayor, aldermen and chief burgesses," including John Ruggles. The burgesses defended their right to make the order, citing a previous bylaw of September 14, 22 Elizabeth, made for the same purpose by the borough council. Next, they noted that "many inhabitants of this Towne" had neglected the older law and were putting too many animals on the commons of Sudbury.

Since the Reverend Edmund Brown was later to be deeply involved in a serious dispute in the new Sudbury over just such a problem, it is important to understand the provisions of this bylaw in his borough. Custom in the borough was strongly opposed to those citizens who bought too many cattle or who pastured the cattle of "strangers dwelling without the town . . . to the great annoyance and surcharge of the commons of the town." The borough council reaffirmed the Elizabethan law which provided that "No person who is a freeman of this town, and has right to common, shall keep any more cattle in any of the town commons than has been accustomed and allowed by previous town orders."

All the cattle in the town had to be kept under the roofs of the freeman and "in his own possession." Any cattle which were "not their own but other men's possession" were to be empounded until the offender had paid the town chamberlain five shillings within two days, on pain of having his goods or cattle distrained and "the money forfeited." (See map, Figure 3. Note the relation of land and crowded row houses.)

The town council, however, did have pity on "any poor inhabitant within this town, being a freeman, with right of common, but with only one shed." Such a person, or his widow, could freely keep one milk cow, "or milk bullock" on the commons "for the sustenance of his family."[26]

John Ruggles, in the following year, was one of the burgesses who signed the only bylaw made during his period of stay in the borough which attempted to meet the problem of rising prices. The council was particularly concerned about the "poorer sort of people," the scarcity of firewood during the winter months, and the "excessive prices" for this wood.

The burgesses explicitly blamed this condition on the wasteful habits of the brewers of Sudbury: "Forasmuch as great waste and consumption of fuel and firewood has been made within our town by beer brewers, innholders, alehousekeepers and tiplers, who use common brewing of ale and beer . . ." firewood had grown expensive and scarce. The burgesses were very critical of the fact that their brewers refused to "brew with sea coal only," and they claimed that the excessive use of wood "is a principal cause of the raising of the prices of wood in the borough . . . so that the inhabitants cannot in the winter time buy wood, except at excessive prices . . . nor buy wood by the fagot, as heretofore."

The council had a definite solution: no brewer or innholder could, at any time after May 1, use any "wood or brush for fuel or firing their ale or beer," but had to use "sea coal and the like." The constables and sergeants were ordered to apprehend any such offender, bring him to court, where he would be fined 6s.8d. for every offense, or his goods taken if he refused to pay.[27]

The problem grew so serious in Sudbury by 1628 that the major refused to grant a license to any inhabitant to "keep any alehouse or victualling house and to sell beer or ale there," unless he put up a bond for £20, swearing that "He shall not brew, or cause to be brewed, any beer or ale," except using "sea coal or pit coal and not with wood, straw or broom."[28]

There were only five other borough bylaws enacted in the period 1621–1640. One dealt with the construction of a house of correction; one met the problem of those who refused to pay taxes; and three orders concerned the burgesses themselves. The order of 1624 outlined many details for the administration of the Sudbury house of correction, "for the safekeeping, punishing and setting to work of rogues, vagabonds, and sturdy beggars, and all persons not able to find themselves habitation or able to sustain themselves and their children through their own lawful usefulness." This order gives a vivid glimpse of the way in which a borough council handled such a problem at the time.

The master of the house was to be in charge of any men, women, or children from the ages of seven to sixty, "of strong body and able to work," who were "noisome or offensive to any of the inhabitants." The council defined nine classifications of such disturbers of the peace:

1. Those who broke the common hedges, or fences, or gates, or stiles, or who pulled up or carried away the same.
2. Common or silent gatherers.
3. Those who cut wood, or grain, or gathered peas or beans, when these were growing on other men's ground, without "lawful leave."
4. Robbers of orchards or fruit trees.
5. Milkers of other men's cattle, against their will.
6. Any women having a bastard, or bastards.
7. All persons, not in the Subsidy Book, judged "reputed fathers of bastards."
8. Those who would not observe order in any respect, or who refused to be apprentices in contempt of the law, or who ran away from their masters.
9. Any artificers, laborers, or apprentices who were common drunkards.

Such people, "after lawful examination and hearing, can be committed to the House, there to be whipped until their bodies be bloody; then to be set to work by the Master of the House, until the Mayor shall consent to let them depart."

But the mayor had a strong sense of social and economic rank. No one who "contributed to the poor where he or she dwells," could be committed to the house, nor "one who is rated in the Subsidy Book" (that is, on the Sudbury tax lists). Furthermore, no one who "has committed a felony" could be committed. As the mayor added, "such people [were] to be punished in another way, as the law directs."

The instructions to Francis Long, the new master, give a clear expression of Sudbury's methods of imposing order on its citizens. Long was not to keep any lame or sick people for more than five days, and was to refuse any "lunatic or any person with infectious disease." He was to maintain separate lodging for the men and the women, and to care for any child born of one of his inmates. He was to start each morning by putting his "whole company on their knees, with loud voice, having a general confession of sins and the Lord's Prayer, the Ten Commandments, a prayer for the King, and the following prayer:

> Almighty and most merciful Father, we acknowledge that the punishment wherewith we be now scourged is much less than our defects; but we humbly beseech thee that it may work in us a reformation of our former life and true obedience of His Majesty's laws, and at thy good will and pleasure, enlarge us; and enable us to live as thy servants and dutiful subjects; and in the mean season to grant us patience to undergo this punishment willingly and a little faith to apply to ourselves and all the suffering of Our Lord and Savior, Jesus Christ, with full assurance that He alone must be our only helper and redeemer to whom, with the Father, the Son, and the Holy Ghost, be ascribed all power, prayer, and thanksgiving now, and forever, Amen."

Following this, the master was to set the inmates to work, with full use of "any chains, fetters, locks or blocks on the same," and with a ready whip for those who broke any of the orders, or disturbed the others, or opposed the officers. Naturally, he could deal harshly with any who tried to escape.

The master, however, was to provide some semblance of civilized life. He was to give them "meat, drink and lodging," was to "correct them, at his discretion, for their negligence," and on Sundays he was to bring some of them to one of the borough churches. There they were to hear the morning and evening prayers and sermons for the betterment of their souls and the reformation of their hearts.[29]

The maintenance of the house of correction, however, brought a further problem to the mayor and burgesses. Their rents and fines would not cover the wages they felt they had to pay Mr. Long, the master. Consequently, in 1628–1629, by virtue of their authority as governing body of the borough, the council levied three taxes, one in May, one in October, and the third in July, 1629, to be collected by the constables of each parish.

Unexpectedly, "divers refused to pay the same rates," which were probably larger than the previous special taxes. The mayor moved swiftly. Acting on his authority both as mayor and as "The King Majesty's Justice for the Conservation of the Peace within the borough," Thomas Smith ordered the constables to start distraining the goods of any nonpayers, and to start selling the same goods if the taxes were not paid within two days of the distraint.[30]

Neither the mayor nor the aldermen would countenance disrespect for their powers and privileges. And this principle held within the council itself. The mayor was reminded that he had to give at least one day's warning to all the aldermen before he held an election to replace any of these seven officers who had died, left the town, or had been removed from his post "upon special cause." Another mayor was warned that he was expected to "keep his grand dinner or festival upon Hock Monday, according to the former orders and customs to the Borough," and that he would have to pay the chamberlain a fine for neglecting either this feast, or the election dinner, or any of the eight court dinners during the year.[31]

The borough council wanted to be sure to dispel "all disorders and confusions" within the borough. One of the ways to do this was to set a perfect example of an ordered society, each man in his proper place. Consequently, the council issued a detailed decree that each member of the governing body "shall set and go according to the seniority and choice," in the moot hall, or in walking about the town, or at any fair or market, with the heavy fine of four shillings for anyone so ill-mannered as to forget his place or his privileges.[32]

The Browns, Ruggleses, and Welds of Sudbury left a community that was well ordered, with its rights and privileges explicitly defined. One of the Reverend Edmund Brown's problems was that neither his status nor his privileges in his new society remained as clearly defined as it had been in the old borough. This was partly because he was joined by other men who came from English communities in the midst of a transition from manorial administration to that of a legally chartered town. Consequently, it is important to examine a final type of English village — an East Anglian community.

CHAPTER IV

"It Is Ordered by the Court"

ETER NOYES, Edmund Rice, and Edmund Brown were joined in New
England by men from still a different local background, those emigrants who had grown up in the rural parishes and towns of East Anglia. This area, which contributed so many town names to New England, has
generally been considered by historians to be the source of New England institutions, and a recent study has traced at least 1877 emigrants from Norfolk,
Suffolk, and Essex.[1] The names given to such early Massachusetts settlements
as Ipswich and Dedham make it evident that East Anglians wished to carry
some of their local heritage into their New Canaan.

Perhaps Noyes's and Rice's settlement of Sudbury was unusual in having a
predominantly open-field population, but Noyes's men were the first to admit
that they needed some enterprising East Anglians as well. One of their most
prominent selectmen was John Parmenter, who had left Bures St. Mary, Essex,
with other families. Furthermore, the selectmen lured their town miller,
Thomas Cakebread, away from a perfectly good house and lot in Watertown
by promising him a large lot in Sudbury and the privilege of being the only
miller for the entire town. Along with Cakebread, who had left Hatfield
Broad Oak, Essex, the Sudbury leaders granted land to at least six other families who had emigrated from Suffolk and Essex.[2]

Whether Noyes and his fellow selectmen realized it or not, they were in-
troducing a very volatile agent into their fresh brew when they welcomed the
East Anglian farmers. In time, the East Anglians came to a violent disagreement with the open-field men over land policy in Sudbury and changed a large

group of the younger generation to their way of thinking. A close study of the background of these rural folk from Essex and Suffolk will help clarify the tensions and problems which the Sudbury selectmen found impossible to resolve.

Land habits in East Anglia were quite different from those in the open-field country. Fundamentally, a farmer like Cakebread expected to manage his own land, more in competition with his neighbors than in co-operation with them. The court-baron rolls for Cakebread's Essex village of Hatfield Broad Oak are quite different from the records of landholdings in Weyhill. Farmer Martin, for instance, held freely "a messuage and about twenty-four acres of land belonging to it"; Farmer Henry Sworder held "one parcel of land called Burges, containing five acres, and three parcels of land called Greenestede, containing seven acres"; William Humerston held "one tenement and three crofts of land called Upper House containing about twelve acres, more or less."[3]

A map of 1609 for the adjoining manor of Matching indicates that the "parcels" of land, termed "crofts" or "closes," were enclosed by each individual farmer. Although often scattered somewhat around the village, they were managed by the farmer and his family according to his own schedule, sown with his own choice of crops, and worked by his own animals and equipment. There was one common pasture, but each farmer was expected to provide a balance of arable, pasture, and hay meadow for himself. He succeeded, or failed on his own farming ability.

Cakebread and the fifteen others who left this Essex village did alter the methods of landholding once they were in New England. In Essex Cakebread was a freeholder, but he, too, had to show up in the yearly manorial court and fulfill various feudal obligations. He rented his land from a landlord, as almost everyone else in his village did, paid a heavy fine of fifty shillings if he forgot his rent, and was fined sixpence for failure to appear before his lord when the court-baron was held.

One single deed, taken from the Barrington court roll, not only illustrates the position of such a tenant, but also indicates that medieval obligations of working for the lord were still imposed in Cakebread's area. In 1637, the jury of tenants of the manor reported that one tenant, James Cecil, had died. Before his daughter Elizabeth could inherit, as by Cecil's will she was entitled to, she had to pay an inheritance tax of sixpence, swear loyalty to her lord, and appear yearly in his court to pay the rent of five shillings. Furthermore, the jury reminded Elizabeth that this particular land carried the following obligations and rights: the tenant had to reap three acres of the lord's wheat and three

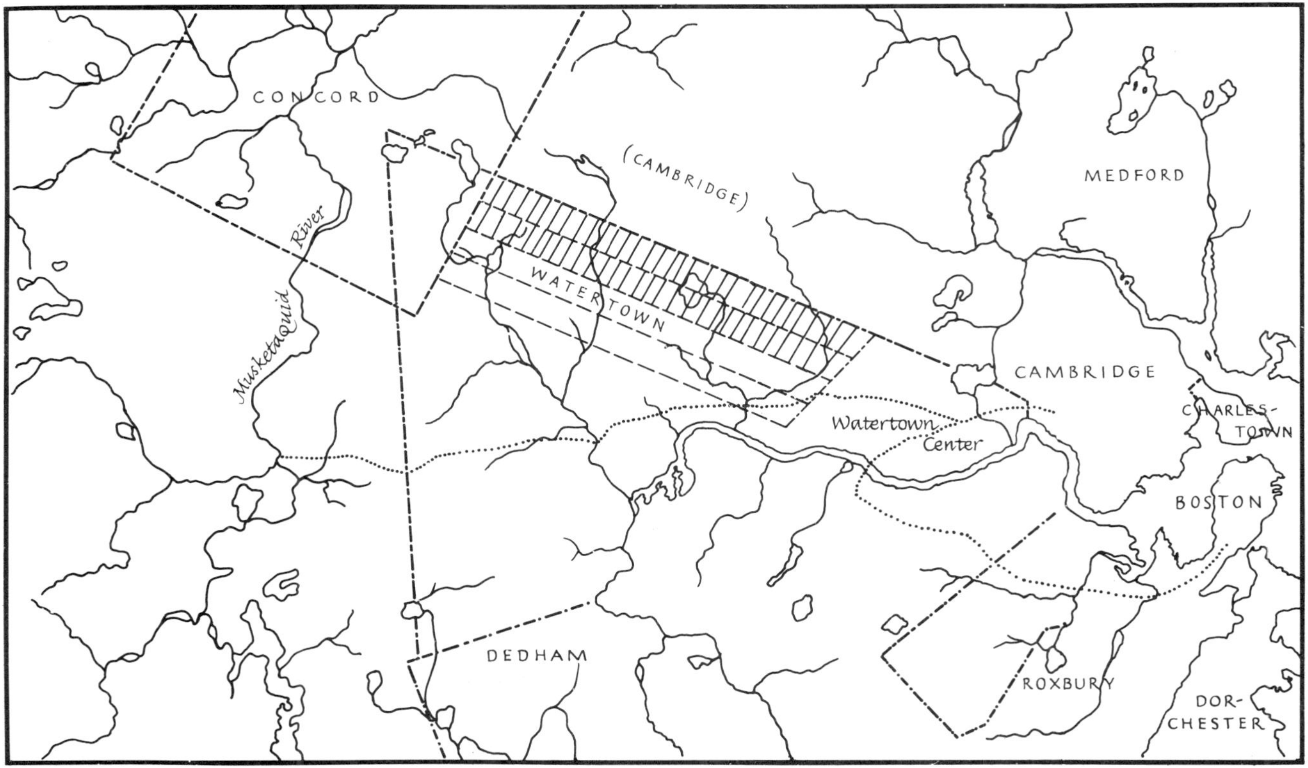

FIGURE 5
Watertown, Massachusetts, and its Neighbors, about 1638

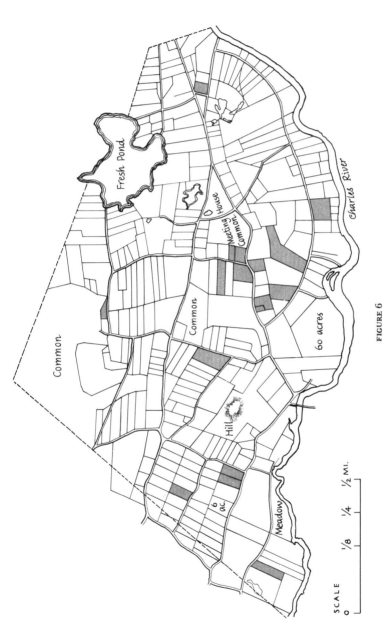

FIGURE 6

Watertown Center, about 1638

Shaded Areas: Lots granted to Sudbury men

Common

Fresh Pond

Charles River

Meeting House Common

Common

60 acres

Hill

Meadow

6 ac.

SCALE

0   1/8   1/4   1/2 MI.

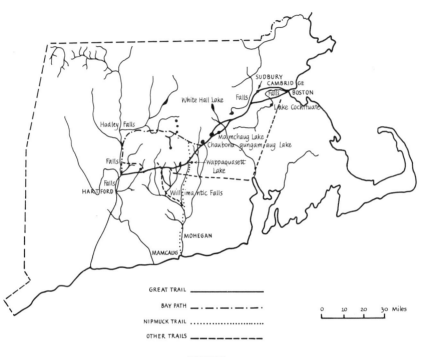

GREAT TRAIL _____

BAY PATH _ .. _ .. _ .. _ .. _ .. _ .

NIPMUCK TRAIL ....

OTHER TRAILS _ _ _ _ _ _ _ _ _ _

0   10   20   30 Miles

FIGURE 7

The Great Trail and Connecting Pathways

FIGURE 8

English Origins of Emigrants to Sudbury, Massachusetts

KEY TO MAP

Wi	– Wiltshire	C	– Cambridge
H	– Hampshire	Hr	– Hertfordshire
D	– Dorset	M	– Middlesex
W	– Warwick	L	– London
N	– Northamptonshire	S	– Suffolk
Li	– Lincoln	E	– Essex
		K	– Kent

Shaded Area: Approximate bounds of open-field system of farming.

acres of his oats, and work two days for him at harvest time; but the land also permitted the tenant to "make hay in the lord's meadow and to mow half an acre of meadow in Turrmer Marshe."[4]

Despite feudal duties and yearly rents, the farmers of this section of Essex took pride in managing their land themselves and worked to increase their holdings. The competition among such villagers bred an independent, occasionally stubborn attitude. The case of one of Cakebread's neighbors, a yeoman named John Garrard, taken from the Quarter Sessions Records of 1610, is representative. Garrard had been charged by his churchwardens for the following offenses: being away from his church on October 8; carting grain on St. Matthew's Day; and sitting with his hat on his head during divine service.

For these alleged misdeeds Garrard had been cited at his church and then excommunicated. But never the one to be slandered unjustly, Garrard went immediately to the justice of the peace for his area, told his story, and "denied the offences to be true." Furthermore, he demanded some compensation for the 18d. he had paid for appearance in his church court, the 18d. "for his excommunication and 10 shillings for other charges which he knoweth not."

Garrard had the satisfaction of having the deputy commissary of the church cited by the justice of the peace, "for extortionately, corruptly and unjustly taking, at Hatfield Broad Oak, by color of his office, John Garrard, yeoman, of the same parish." Although something went amiss in the legal proceedings, Garrard made his churchwardens and his archdeacon realize that he knew his rights and would not be charged unjustly.[5]

Garrard's spirit, multiplied in the larger villages, made for enterprising towns and ambitious townsmen. But however much the yeomen and petty tradesmen wanted their hamlets to become flourishing towns, they could never avoid the overwhelming authority of two legal institutions: courts of the common law and ecclesiastical courts of the English church.

Framlingham, Suffolk, about forty miles northeast of the borough of Sudbury, sent twenty-two emigrants to New England, one of whom, Nicholas Danforth, became a selectman of Cambridge, Massachusetts, and its deputy in the Bay Colony legislative body.[6] His activities as churchwarden of Framlingham and those of his fellow townsmen, contrasted with his actions in Massachusetts, make clear what the selectmen in early New England settlements were trying to avoid. As Danforth shifted from Suffolk to his new home on the banks of the Charles River, he took along his training as a townsman but left behind him archdeacons and all bishops.

As churchwarden, Danforth spent more time and money for his town

than he did for his church. Despite the fact that his market town and sur-
rounding farmland had over four hundred taxpayers in 1630–1640, twice the
size of Rice's town, the townsmen did not obtain the charter of a borough.
They called the cluster of perhaps one hundred houses in the center of town
"the borough," but they were still legally a town, and all were tenants of the
Lord of Framlingham, that staunch royalist, Thomas Howard, Earl of Suffolk.[7] (See map of Danforth property in relation to the town, Figure 4.)[8]

There was a borough jury in the lord's court, which defined the townsmen's obligations to their lord and filled his coffers with money from court
fines. The manorial court had expanded its functions far beyond that of a
small village in order to take care of the crowds during market and fair times.
The jury elected four constables, an ale taster, a sealer of weights and measures, a leather scaler, and a pounder.[9] But these officers reported to the lord's
bailiff, not to a mayor of their own choosing.

Consequently, the churchwardens were taking over the real administration of the town. They had land and buildings which they rented, they levied
frequent parish rates, and their expenses in the few years during which their
records remain, were from two to fifteen times those of the burgesses in Sudbury, Suffolk:

Date	Framlingham Church-wardens' Expenses[10]	Parish Rate
1629	£35	£6
1630	6	0/03/00
1631	150	66
1632	70	66
1633	112	4
(Records missing: 1634–1638)		
1639	54	none

In this ten-year period the churchwardens listed hundreds of town expenses. Under such categories as "Town Poor," and "Town Children," the
churchwardens, acting in co-operation with the overseers of the poor, paid for
the rents of at least twenty families, bought clothes for ten to twenty people
each year, distributed numerous loads of wood, and found apprenticeships for
the young sons and daughters of indigent families.[11]

Besides this, the churchwardens listed many specific town expenses. A
"town house" was constructed in 1631 to house some poor, and carpenters
were paid to cut, cart, and hew the timbers for this. The stocks were rebuilt, a
"goose house" constructed, and repairs were made to the town bridge. The

town even paid some money for work on its roads and taxed its parishioners to pay for several loads of gravel used. The churchwardens purchased a belt for the town sword in 1631, together with a set of bandoliers, and had the town armor scoured. But Framlingham's citizens never felt it necessary to turn out to any military drills. The town budget could take care of such obligations, and the churchwardens listed "soldiers' wages for carrying the town arms" more than once. They paid for a parade of professional soldiers just as the mayor of Sudbury did.

As in Berkhamsted, the drought of 1629–1630 brought a sharp crisis. But neither the citizens nor the vestry had to call any special meetings. The churchwardens simply assessed a heavy tax, at approximately the same rate as the one used by the Berkhamsted vestry, took in large receipts for rental of town land and from various legal charges, and spent their time administering to the poor. One man went to Norfolk, bought two hundred forty bushels of grain, had it carted to Framlingham, and distributed it to the poor. Another purchased a cartload in Woodbridge and had it brought to town. The two churchwardens that year expended over two hundred separate charges for their poor, ranging from buying hemp as stock to making outright gifts to the sick and unfortunate.

It was impossible, however, for the churchwardens to act alone. Their records are full of visits to the Woodbridge sessions of the peace, the Bury St. Edmunds assizes, and fees for various warrants. In 1629, for example, it was necessary to go to the justices of the peace for a warrant against "the Dinnington wench." Probably this woman had become a vagrant, or worse still, mother of an illegitimate child. The Framlingham churchwardens wanted her warned out of their town and sent back where she belonged. In the April session of the same year the churchwardens again paid a fee to the justices, this time to suppress the alehouse.

Although the town officers paid the court fees, they charged their own citizens where possible. The constable of Framlingham in 1630 handed over a ten-shilling fine to the churchwardens when he served a warrant on "goodwife Brown for suffering drinking and fighting in her house," a two-shilling fine when he caught Henry Grant in an alehouse on Sunday during church, and three shillings from Oliver Motes for "being very drunk in our town."

It was almost impossible for the churchwardens to make a legal action without the specific sanction of a warrant from the justices of the peace. In 1631–1632, one of the churchwardens, George Fishe, was forced to attend the general sessions in March, April, November, February, and the following

April to obtain a variety of warrants and to see to "certain causes for the town." In 1633, Churchwarden Wayth entered the following list of charges: "To Bury Assizes: bread and beer on the way, at Woolpit; dinner and supper at Bury, Tuesday night; dinner for nine men and justices Wednesday night; bread and beer on Thursday; bread and beer on Friday; tip to the porter at the Judge's houses; fee to move the Judge to settle Mary Woodcraft and her child; fee for the order for same; fee for warrant for same and to pay the messenger to deliver it to Mary Woodcraft."

Wayth, who had already paid for Mary's midwife and for food for the unexpected youngster, was anxious to force someone else to take care of the woman and her child. And having discharged the town of the expense of this poor family, Wayth added to his account, "and money for horse meat and the tips to the boy at the Bury Inn."

The justices, for their part, were constantly dealing with town and parish officers. A glance at the surviving records of the Suffolk justices for the year 1629 shows that the major court business consisted of attending to the complaints, desires, and the misguided actions of inhabitants in the rural towns. Of the eighty cases heard before the four or five Suffolk justices in 1639, by far the largest number consisted of the "settlement" type which Framlingham's Wayth had to contend with. The situation was clearly summed up by Justices Barker, Brook, Duke, Rivett, and Forth in their October sessions: "Whereas it appears that the inhabitants of Framlingham are so much overcharged with a multitude of poor persons inhabiting therein, that the charges have become intolerable for them to bear, and therefore have petitioned to be relieved," the judges decided that the adjacent parish should take part of the burden and ordered "some of the chief inhabitants" to appear at the next sessions to "show cause why they should not be compelled to contribute toward the said charge according to the meaning of the [Poor] Law."[12]

The justices had to decide on the merits of each parish's particular problem and pleas. The overseers of Melton, Suffolk, were ordered to raise the allowance of Elizabeth Frith, a "poor impotent" woman, to 18d. instead of 12d. On the other hand, the justices had found a relative of John Langley, "a poor, bedrid old man," and forced his son, though living in a different parish, to relieve the overseers of Baileham of the expense of maintaining the old man.

The justices, despite their fees, could be extremely helpful in parish disputes. The churchwardens of Framlingham were angered in 1630–1631, when one of their largest landowners, Edward Alpe, refused to pay his assessment. Alpe's side of the case is not recorded, except that he held over one hundred acres of land and stood to pay a large share of the unusually high tax in a year of drought.[13] Since each tax was a special and unpredictable affair, Alpe had every right to object, particularly when he was not a party to the original tax decision. The minister and Nicholas Danforth had signed the church rate, "by us, the inhabitants of the town," but obviously Alpe did not admit that they had been representing him at the time.

After Alpe had refused to pay his tax and influenced others to do the same, the churchwardens acted in two different directions. They presented Alpe and "others who refuse to pay the rates," in the church court at Ipswich in July, hoping to have all these men brought to court and possibly excommunicated. Meanwhile, they entered a suit at the quarter sessions against Alpe. By October, the church court had acted and called for various witnesses at a trial, and the churchwardens obtained the satisfaction of hearing Alpe and the other offenders condemned. But they wanted more than mere satisfaction. They wanted Alpe's money to feed their poor. They had obtained a warrant from the clerk of the peace to force Alpe to pay, but he had again refused. Advised by an attorney that this refusal constituted a contempt of court, the churchwardens went to their justice of the peace and had articles drawn up "against Alpe, J. Gooding and T. Reeve for their contemning the justices' authority."

All parties were in earnest and settled down to a long, complicated legal battle. During 1632–1633, the churchwardens went to Michaelmas, Christmas, and Easter sessions about the case and fought it up to the assize courts. Meanwhile, they paid Mr. Ireland, another large landowner and town officer, to work in London and Bury St. Edmunds on the case, and gave fees to no fewer than six other legal advisors. Finally, the churchwardens were awarded a decision in their favor, after which they held a dinner to celebrate their victory. Over the meat and the wine, they estimated that the fight had cost the town £19, plus countless hours with judges and lawyers. With ill-concealed glee, the churchwardens entered the following note under "Receipts: . . . From Edw. Alpe, forced to pay by virtue of an order made by Judge Heath for his refractory corses, nonpayment of rates and arrears of rates — £30," a sum which represented half of the whole parish tax for the critical year, 1630.

One of the most interested parties in this rate case was the Reverend Richard Golty, rector of Framlingham, for he, too, occasionally needed legal assistance against nonpaying parishioners. Unlike a lecturer, Golty had no yearly salary but had his living and his tithes to sustain him and his family. Collection of tithes was a complicated business in any English parish and one of the tax systems which New England townsmen abolished completely. But Golty's account book gives a clear indication both of his income and of the nature of his parish.

Golty wrote, "When I came, I found these tithes paid in kind, viz: corn, hemp, flax, roots, turnips, tithe calf, tithe lamb, and wool, tithe geese, and tithe pigs."[14] This meant that it was the rector's job to walk around to every farm each year or to send a clerk to collect some sort of tax on almost all the agricultural products of the village farms. It was the custom in every parish for the farmers, in harvesting their crops, to divide the bushels or bundles into tens and literally set aside the "one tenth" for the minister, or his assistant, to pick up.

Golty gives many of the actual figures for seventeenth-century Framlingham. He put down:

Tithes in Framlingham:		
For milk cows, for lactage		2d. a cow
For mowing grounds, for those cattle which paid no tithe for lactage, or tithe calf:		
	upland:	3d. an acre
	low meadow:	4d. an acre
For houseyard and orchard		2d.
For hearths [in a house or cottage]		6d. a hearth
For outdwellers refusing the above customary tithes		8d. in the noble
For those who used land for fatting and grasing cattle		8d. in the noble
For geldings and riding horses		6d. a horse
For colts		2d. a colt
For heifers		1d. a heifer
Fees: for marriages		12d. a marriage
for burials		10d. burial and churching
for mortuaries		a noble (But 10s. for those men worth £40)

Golty's account book gives many details as to the farming activities of the 235 men who lived "without the borough," and the 167 with houses in Mixt Row, Back Lane, and on other streets. In 1634, he collected tithes from 402 cows, 330 calves, 45 buds, 31 heifers, 7 horses, 8 colts, 38 sheep, pigs, geese, 9 skeps of bees, and 115 acres of meadow. Only 4 men grew wheat, while 7 grew barley, and the rest raised oats, beans, peas, and flax.

As in Hatfield Broad Oak, the farmers managed individual parcels and "closes." Golty made the following entry for 1642:

> Mr. Waldgrave:
>> 5 acres of very good wheat
>> 4 acres of barley
>> oats and peas in Little Diggons
>
> Nicholas Skeene: at the great Lodge:
>> 30 acres of excellent wheat
>> 16 acres of very good barley
>> 6 acres of flax
>> 18 acres of oats
>> 4 acres of horse beans
>
> John Butcher:
>> 1 acre of peas
>> 5 acres of barley
>> 3 acres of oats and beans
>
> Robert More: at Little Lodge
>> 8 acres of barley
>> 20 acres of very good wheat
>> 2 acres more of barley
>> $\frac{1}{2}$ acre of flax
>> 9 acres of oats and beans at the Castle
>> 1 acre more of barley
>> 2 acres more of oats[15]

Nicholas Danforth, before he left to settle in Cambridge, Massachusetts, and to gain land south of Sudbury, had about seventy-five acres of land and four groups of buildings in many different enclosures of arable, meadow, and pasture.[16] On his two houses, orchard, and land, Danforth paid his rector £1/12 in tithes, from 1628–1630, and £2/11 in 1633.[17]

Danforth, despite the fact that he paid his tithes and served as church-warden, opposed Golty's Anglicanism. He went as far as paying for a minister to lecture in Framlingham's church, and a neighboring divine, Mr. Burroughs, together with others, gave weekly sermons strongly tainted with Nonconform-ist principles.[18] But Danforth could not avoid or underestimate his minister's influence in the parish. Golty knew each family intimately, knew their lands and their animals, and he ran every vestry meeting as chairman. Furthermore,

Mr. Golty, like every other Anglican minister, was backed by his church courts
and the oaths of his two churchwardens and his two sidemen.

These oaths were not simple agreements to carry out routine functions.
When Danforth pledged his oath as churchwarden in 1629, and when other
men pledged theirs in later years, they agreed to pry into almost every unfamiliar activity in their whole parish. Those who continue to think that seventeenth-century New Englanders were excessively prudish should ponder the
detailed Churchwardens' Oath in Suffolk for 1638 (Appendix V). It is an attempt to seek out almost every possible bit of nonconformity.

These *Articles of Inquiry* could not be avoided. The Framlingham Churchwardens' Accounts and those of other East Anglian parishes record the biennial visitations, as well as the church court sessions which followed up the reports of the visitors. The Framlingham churchwardens reported, in 1629, fees
and dinners at the visitations, expenses when two church officers had to appear
at Wickham court, and in March, a call to Wickham court to certify for various
defects. This was not all. There was a general court in April, 1630, and a
bishop's court held at Ipswich.

Nor was 1629 unusual. In 1631–1632, the churchwardens entered fees and
charges which included fees and a dinner for the visitation, a trip to Wickham
court on May 23, another similar journey on July 26, a general court at Wickham on September 20, which included dinners with officers and fees, an appearance against Alpe at Wickham court on February 25, a session of the
commissary's court with fees, a general court in April, when one churchwarden made a presentment, and a synod at Ipswich on April 23. In 1632–
1633, not only were the churchwardens called by the commissary in the spring
to certify that faults had been corrected, but they were ordered the following
January to make their presentments. They stayed through two visitations and
attended at least five church courts, where they were requested to buy a new
book of Articles, a Prayer for the Queen's Safe Delivery, and a Book of Liberty
on Sabbath Days, the famous Book of Sports.

The Archdeacons' Act Book for the period and the Books of Depositions
show the types of cases which the churchwardens were likely to bring up, or to
be questioned on. There was much testamentary material, for the archdeacons' court reviewed and sanctioned wills, at a fee. But there was also a great
deal of vigorous Elizabethan language, particularly in the slander cases. Apparently there were phrases which no man or woman would tolerate, and they
were ready to go through the tortures of meticulous and detailed court exam-
inations to defend their reputations. Maria Stiles, for example, was bitterly

offended when a neighbor called her a "darci-tailed trull." There were many other taunts in the depositions which still convey a sharp sting or a crude sneer.

The deposition of William Capon, a cooper, before the archdeacons' commissary when sitting in Framlingham in 1632, was mild: "The said Alexander Smith spake these words, viz: 'I never came back from church to be naught with another man's wife.' "[19]

But on the majority of items actually listed by the bishops in their Articles of Inquiry, the churchwardens could be either silent or cleverly evasive. Lionel Cook, yeoman, was examined by the archdeacon in 1632, and "freely deposed and answered" as follows:

> To the 1st Article: that the stated Edmund Randall was parson and lawful possessor of the Church of Bareham, and of all the tithes thereunto belonging, and has quietly enjoyed the rights of his office.
> To the 2nd Article: that he had nothing to depose.
> To the 3rd Article: that he had nothing to depose.
> To the 4th Article: that he had heard that one parishioner, A. Murwell, had died without a will, but that he was not sure.
> To the 5th Article: that he had nothing to depose.
> [This entry of "nul.dep." continues down the whole list of Articles.]

Despite evasive churchwardens and parishioners, the church courts were busy in this period. The commissaries of both the archdeacons and the bishops must have worked overtime. The court of the Bishop of Salisbury, for instance, handled 134 cases in the single month of August, 1634, and the following analysis of the types and frequency of cases during this month is representative of most of the church courts of this period.[20]

Type of Case	Per Cent of Total
1. "Decay" of any part of church property: building, roofs, windows, seats, yard fences	24%
2. Incontinency before marriage	12%
3. Parishioners not going on yearly perambulation around church lands	6.5%
4. No Table of Marriage or Ten Commandments posted inside the church	6%
5. Bastardy — or fornication	6%
6. Not going to parish church services	5.5%
7. Lack of Communion cup, table, or cloth	5.5%
8. Drinking at alehouses during church services	5%
9. No list of church land ("Terrier")	4%

	Type of Case	Per Cent of Total
10.	Disturbances in church during divine services	4%
11.	Not receiving Communion	3.5%
12.	Drinking on Sunday or holy days	3.5%
13.	Working on Sunday or holy days	2%
14.	Living apart from spouse	2%
15.	Teaching (or preaching) without a license	1.3%
16.	Allowing a bastard to be born in one's house	1.3%
17.	Refusing to serve as churchwarden	.7%
18.	Opposing a minister's sermon	.7%
		100%

The archdeacons, bishops, and certainly Archbishop Laud were all working hard to increase the standard of morality in the parishes, improve the quality of the services, and, in general, establish some principles of church uniformity. The courts were crowded, but the obvious question is — how much was one parish affected over the years? Were the church officials harrying the average parishioners so that, in Thomas Shepard's words, "the power of the tyrannical Prelates [was] so great, that like a Strong Current [it] carried all down strem before it . . . [causing] a rash, heady rushing into the Wilderness out of discontent."[21]

This question has been debated, off and on, for over three hundred years, but few have looked into the records of the actual parishes concerned.[22] The records show that not many cases were brought to the church courts in a single year. For example, Great Bromley, which sent at least nineteen emigrants to New England, among them relatives of John Stone, another settler of Sudbury, can be examined.[23] Over a ten-year period, 1624–1634, the churchwardens received biennial visitations and made one or two appearances in the archdeacons' courts each year.[24]

In 1625, the churchwardens presented one woman for having an illegitimate child, one couple for incontinency before marriage, and one man for suspicion of adultery.[25] The following year they reported one parishioner for refusing to take Communion at Easter, and in 1626, they presented Robert Baker, "for pulling down and rending off the pulpit an order from the Lord Bishop of London against irreverent sitting with their hats during divine service." In 1629, they reported a "common fame" of fornication, but they made no presentments. The parish in 1630, however, had three cases; drunkenness on Sunday, adultery, and a parishioner's failure to repair a portion of the churchyard fence.

The archdeacon himself, in 1632, presented the Great Bromley church-wardens for failure to ring the church bells to celebrate the coronation of King Charles. There was also one case of "binding branches on a Sunday in the forenoon." A Nonconformist spirit was definitely noticeable in the parish, for John Daniel was presented in 1633 for "not receiving Communion at Easter last," and again "for not coming to church divers Sundays in a row."

But such men could, if they were courageous enough, or stubborn enough, flout church pressure. John Daniel and his wife were excommunicated, then excommunicated a second time, and, a year later, again censured for remaining in their unholy state.

Some men could be both amusing and stubborn. In May, 1630, John Stone was presented by the churchwardens of Ardleigh for arriving in their church so full of drink that he became sick. In June the archdeacons ordered him to appear and excommunicated him when he failed to show up. By July the pressure of community and church opinion forced Stone to come to the arch-deacons' court, swear to obey the church law, and be repentant. The commis-sary ordered the standard form of public penance — Stone had to stand on the sill of his church, dressed in a white sheet, each Sunday, "until the next court." But Stone obviously considered this too humiliating. He did not turn up with a signed certificate of his penance and was again excommunicated.

By August Stone had become cocksure in his defiance. He was reported as follows: "On the 15th of August last, Mr. Evans, the minister, took occasion in his sermon to speak of Adam and Eve's making themselves coats of fig leaves. Stone presently whispered to his neighbor, Thomas Woodward, in the church, and asked him where they had thread to sew them, and then laughed withal. Being afterwards told in the churchyard of his misdemeanor by Joseph Daniel, Stone answered, 'Let him [meaning the minister] prate what he will. He knows his wages!' And on last Easter Day, the said Stone took away the bottle with the wine, which was left after Communion, and drank it up, and after bragged."

The archdeacon, accordingly, excommunicated Stone. He did so again in October, and for a third time in November. Still Stone did not appear to ask forgiveness and to agree to penance. By February, the archdeacon had lost all patience. He issued a fourth writ of excommunication for refusal to obey. In April, the archdeacon again "warned him to appear in person" and con-demned Stone to perdition for the fifth time.

Finally, in June, 1631, Stone could not stand the repeated censures. Hav-ing had his fling, and his laugh, he did his penance and was made to contribute 5s. 8d. to the poor of his parish. Whether this was the same John Stone who turned up in Sudbury, Massachusetts, in 1639, or not is not certain.[26] But there were Sudbury emigrants who were caught in the ecclesiastical courts.

The Goodnow family, soon to be strong leaders and citizens of Sudbury, lived in an area of Wiltshire greatly disturbed by local controversies over Nonconformity. The parishes of Sutton Mandeville, Donhead St. Andrew, and Donhead St. Mary lay close together and many of the families in them were linked by kinship and by marriage. All three parishes became involved in the church courts.

In 1634, one Thomas Feltham, of Sutton Mandeville, became angered by his minister's opposition to the King's Book of Sports, which sanctioned such activities on Sundays. Even though he must have realized that he was attacking the dominant figure of his parish, Feltham made an accusation against his minister in his archdeacons' court. He claimed that "Mr. Gabriel Sanger, parson of Sutton Mandeville . . . in a sermon preached in church a little before Candlemas . . . said these words: 'That those who did allow sports and pleasure times upon the Sabbath Day were not the Children of God.' And in another sermon, he said, 'that there was a narrow way that leadeth unto heaven and that there was a broad way that leadeth into hell, and many there were that went therein; and that the papists and protestants did meet in that way and may shake hands in hell.' "[27]

These were strong words and prompted strong reactions. While the case went slowly up the ladder of church courts, Sanger continued to preach his vigorous Nonconformist doctrines. Apparently, he drew men and women from neighboring parishes. But their churchwardens and parsons resented his appeal, and a typical Puritan-Anglican controversy arose. Unfortunately, the records do not give the outcome.

In 1636, William Kerley, of Ashmore, Dorset, a parish just next to Donhead St. Mary, was cited at the archdeacons' court for "neglecting his parish church." Kerley simply replied, "that he did not do this out of contempt, but in respect that he has land at lower Donhead and has something to do there." He was dismissed with a mild warning to improve his habits.

Edmund Goodnow and Roger Strong, churchwardens of Donhead St. Andrew, were cited in the same year for similar wanderings from their parish church. They were required to do public penance and to contribute thirty shillings to the poor of their parish, a heavy fine.[28]

But Sanger, and other preachers, had an irresistible appeal. The whole Goodnow family was drawn to these vigorous sermons and to others of a similar Nonconformist variety. In February, 1637, Ralph, Simon, and Edmund Goodnow were forced to come before their archdeacon once again. They were all presented "for going to Shaftesbury to church on Sundays and Holy Days," and they quite frankly asked their superior if they could not attend other churches than their own.[29] The archdeacon cited the canon and told them to reappear the following month, with a certificate from their parish minister that they had attended morning and evening prayers in their own parish church.

All three Goodnows obeyed dutifully. They did not openly show their resentment, as had John Stone in Essex. But some had seen and heard enough. Joined by Walter Haines of Sutton Mandeville and William Kerley of Ashmore, a large Goodnow tribe headed for embarkation to New England aboard the *Confidence*.[30] Ralph and Simon remained at home. But Edmund and John and Thomas were never again to stand humbled before an archdeacon's authority. From 1638 onward they were determined to establish the true path to God, narrow though it might be.

CHAPTER V

Watertown on the Charles

WHEN the Goodnows, the Noyeses, and the Rices landed in Watertown about 1637–1638, they found, indeed, a "select society," and a vigorous spirit of dissent. There were many yeomen and artisans but no archdeacons or bishops and, most important, no landlords. Everyone hoped that there would be no poor, and Watertown had made special provisions to exclude them.

Noyes must have been one of the first to sense that he was surrounded by East Anglians. Or, at least, he knew that these were the men who were quickly obtaining large grants of land in the new town. A rough survey of those granted meadow in Watertown in June, 1637, shows that 60 per cent of the total number of grantees had come from Essex, Suffolk, and Norfolk.[1]

Even more important, all the first selectmen of Watertown but two had emigrated from East Anglia.[2] As might be expected, these men were establishing the land habits they were familiar with. The 4625 acres which had been granted to 120 men in 1636 were to be rectangular sections, laid out "successively one after another," in four "great dividends."[3] Although the town law gave the alternative, "for them to enclose or feed in common," it was obvious what these East Anglians hoped to do. (See map, Figure 5. Two dividends have been drawn in.)

Each man was obtaining from twenty-five to fifty acres of uncleared land, by a freehold grant, to be made into arable, hay ground, and pasture. Houses had been constructed around a village common, to be sure, and a few "plowlands" were being tilled in common for the first years, but each farmer was shifting to individual management as quickly as he could.[4] (See map of Watertown Center, Figure 6.)

This posed a serious dilemma for West Country men like the Goodnows, the Haineses, and others. They were not able or willing to change farming habits which went back "till the memory of man runneth not to the contrary." Few of them had brought over enough equipment to run a whole farm. Just as serious was the fact that the Watertown men were not granting any more lots after 1634–1635. The center was crowded, and Watertown was considered one of the most populous settlements in the Bay Colony. Any newcomer was ordered to obtain his land by purchase, and no one could settle in the town without the express permission of the Watertown freemen.[5]

Peter Noyes was fortunate. Although he had arrived after the cessation of the free allotments, he either bought, or wheedled, twelve acres of plowland, twelve acres of meadow, eighteen acres of upland, and lot number nineteen in the first dividend, a seventy acre piece of land.[6] But it was all distant from the town center — the plowland and the upland were on "the further plaine"; the pasture was in "the remote meadow"; and his grant lot was about five miles from the central cluster of houses in Watertown itself.

His fellow open-field men in Watertown in 1638 were in a difficult position. Unable to get free allotments, perhaps unwilling to buy land and to settle among the East Anglians, they were faced with tax assessments and the threat that anyone who "may prove chargeable to the town" could be ordered to leave.[7] The leaders of Watertown wanted to avoid the excessive charges for the poor which every one of them had known in their English parishes.

Is it any wonder that the open-field folk banded together and looked to Noyes, who had become a citizen of Watertown, to help them? They certainly did not want to become tenants, or worse still, landless laborers, in a settlement in which everyone else, if he had arrived early enough, was becoming a landlord.*

But these unhappy residents in Watertown had learned a key political fact — that the will of the people was respected, however begrudgingly, by the Massachusetts government. They learned swiftly that it had been the citizens of Watertown who, in opposition to a colony tax levied by the assistants alone a few years previously, had helped establish that basic English principle, no taxation without representation.[8] Laws were also in process to give legal sanctity to the privilege of raising one's voice in a town meeting. One did not have

---

* There were, however, at least five or six men from the open-field country who were granted meadow lots in Watertown in 1637.

to apply to a justice of the peace; one could express one's own desires and claim rights as a citizen of a town.

The problem for the landless open-field men in 1638 was clear — they needed allotments. But who constituted the source of power in Watertown? To whom did one address pleas for land? The townsmen of Watertown were not certain themselves. In 1634, "the Freemen," or members of the newly formed Watertown church, chose three men to "order the civil affairs in the Town." In the following fall the freemen chose eleven men, as a committee, to "divide to every man his proportion of meadow and upland."[9] This was fine, but what were "civil affairs," how was "every man's proportion" to be decided, and for how long did the committee have power to grant land? No one was quite sure, least of all the committee.

Two years later a different committee of eleven freemen were elected to "dispose of all the civil affairs of the Town for one year."[10] Since no definition of power existed, problems of government multiplied. In the year 1636–1637, the leading citizens of Watertown discovered a basic fact about their new town government: yearly elections, combined with a lack of a fixed social hierarchy, could lead to great fluctuations in political power.

Perhaps in the minds of a few militant leaders a body of "elect" should have run each town according to noble ideals. But for citizens of Watertown in 1636–1637, the political truth emerged that when many had a voice, few agreed on the powers of the elect. Nine men were dropped from the governing committee of eleven; only two were retained.[11] New England town politics had started in Watertown, and the men discovered that even a Saint could be voted out of office.

This new political spirit had even infected the central government. Groups of settlers, once they had town deputies or spokesmen to represent them, had learned that the Bay government, legally or illegally, had vast resources almost for the asking. Towns began haggling for meadows and new boundaries, and Thomas Hooker's emigration to Connecticut in 1636 had started a whole series of applications for town grants. A group had been voted a large tract on the Musketaquid River, called Concord, in 1635, and a dissatisfied Watertown group had been granted a plantation called Dedham about two miles above the falls of the Charles River in 1635–1636.[12]

Technically, it was still possible to obtain more land in Watertown, with enough political pressure. Although the boundaries were never very exact, it has been estimated that the original grants in the town totalled about 29,000 acres.[13] But a contemporary observer saw only about 1800 acres under tillage,

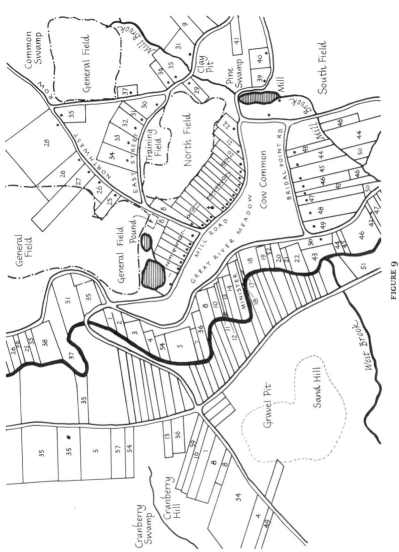

FIGURE 9

Sudbury, Massachusetts: The Village Center

FIGURE 10
Town Pound, Sudbury, about 1648

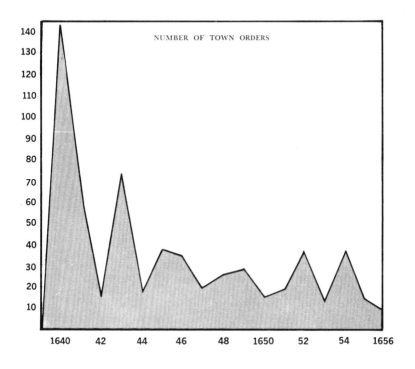

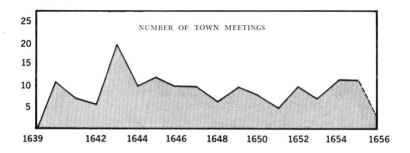

FIGURE 11

Sudbury Town Orders (above) and Town Meetings (below), 1639–1656

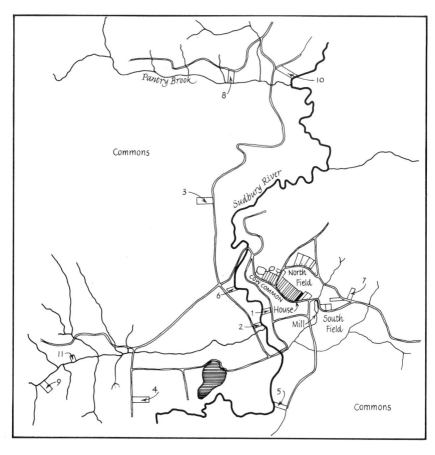

FIGURE 12

Grants of Land to John Goodnow, Sudbury

House lot

Strips in North & South Fields

Other lands as follows:

#1	4½ acres meadow		#6	6 acres meadow
#2	9½ acres meadow		#7	5 acres upland
#3	9 acres upland		#8	5 acres meadow
#4	8 acres upland		#9	20 acres upland
#5	13 acres upland		#10	6 acres meadow
			#11	5 acres meadow

and some 450 cattle grazing on the various commons.[14] Much of the really excellent land had been staked out, however, and with the central government in such a generous mood, few were content with the heavily timbered land that offered only the promise of ceaseless labor and long trips to market.

It cannot be said with any accuracy what man conceived the idea of a settlement below Concord on the Musketaquid River, but Peter Noyes was certainly one of the first men involved. He was elected so consistently to every major town post in the first years of Sudbury that he was certainly considered a major spokesman for his open-field friends.

Noyes seemed to have an instinctive flair for leadership in these new towns. A citizen and landowner in Watertown, he joined two other leaders, forming a triumvirate consisting of an administrator, a land speculator, and a minister. Noyes united with Brian Pendleton, a wealthy London man who had enjoyed power in the first few years of Watertown and then fallen out of favor, and together they added a third man, the Reverend Edmund Brown. All three petitioned the General Court of Massachusetts for a town grant below Concord.

Brown was looking for another parish. Having left old Sudbury, he arrived in Watertown in time to give the petition added support.[15] It is very likely that the General Court, full of Emmanuel and Cambridge graduates, named the new settlement in Brown's honor.

The petitioners gave as their reason for wanting a grant of land, "straitness of accommodation, and want of meadow."[16] They meant by this that while twelve of the group had been granted a substantial amount of land in Watertown, there were at least twenty-four men, or 74 per cent of the new town petitioners, who seemed to have neither land nor citizenship in the town on the banks of the Charles.* These men had suffered deprivations, but they had gone out to find land for their cattle.

It had not been necessary for the leaders to cut their way through a forest wilderness, or to paddle up rivers and streams. The great emigration of over one hundred families, following Hooker into Connecticut, had already passed through Watertown and used the Great Trail laid down by centuries of Indians.[17] (See map, Figure 7.)

Information as to possible settling places on the trail and on the inland waterway had reached the coastal towns early, as various Indian chiefs had

* Only the following petitioners had been granted Watertown land: B. Pendleton, P. Noyes, G. Munnings, W. Parker, H. Curtis, T. Cakebread, R. Darvell, J. Knight, T. King, J. Grout, J. Taintor, H. Pelham, and A. Belcher.

come up it to visit Governor Winthrop in Boston.[18] The men who had gone
out to Concord had already discovered the great stretch of green river meadow
in the Musketaquid valley, whose very Indian name meant "grassy ground."
This expanse of rich grass was the largest area of good fodder within ten miles
of Watertown, and, because of the Indian trail, the most easily available.

When Peter Noyes went out to view the site in the summer of 1638, however much he might have feared both the wilderness and the heathen, he must
have been excited about the possibilities. Just about seven miles west of the
far border of Watertown, the trail suddenly dipped down as it left the large
groves of oak and chestnut and turned to the southwest. A secondary trail continued into the valley westward, only to disappear in a great broad plain of
meadow grass, free from trees, growing as high as a man's waist and in some
places as high as his shoulders.[19] The men from Weyhill had probably never
seen such meadows. Their extent, about three thousand acres, was twice the
size of the whole Weyhill parish, and vastly greater and more luxuriant than
the small amount of meadow which bordered the little stream, the Anton,
which ran through Penton Grafton.

The river which flowed through this wilderness valley was full of salmon,
alewives, shad, pickerel, and other fish; beaver were plentiful, and the country seemed well stocked with game such as grouse, wildfowl, turkeys, bear, and
deer.[20] With several brooks rising from springs and with the sparkling Musketaquid River, the site was ideal for pasture and for hay ground. Another
factor was important: while there were many Indian settlements and camping
places in the valley to the north and south at the falls and by various ponds,
there were no major encampments in the immediate area and only one or two
Indians living on nearby hills. The main Indian trail, going eastward, had few
fordings, no large hills to cross and ran almost directly to the Bay towns over
gently rolling woodlands. It assured communication both with towns on the
east coast and with the settlements to the southwest, and within ten years it
became the highway to Watertown, particularly for the annual cattle drives in
the fall to the coastal markets.

The economic facts must have been quite clear to the men considering the
move. The Musketaquid valley contained fodder for cattle, which had quin-
tupled in value owing to a high mortality rate, partly as a result of the harsh
New England winters and the devastating attacks by wolves.[21] There were natural clearings for both pasture and tillage, and the area was well watered.

The arable land, however, had disadvantages which must have discour-
aged some of the first to glimpse its thick woods. It was a far cry from the rich

soil Noyes had known in Weyhill. Poor in nutriment and very porous in structure, it needed much fertilizing.[22] Perhaps some of the settlers may have heard comments similar to those made by a Suffolk farmer's son, William Pond, "We cannot live here long without provisions from old England . . . I may, as I will, work hard to set an acre of Indian corn, but if we set it with fish, that will cost twenty shillings. If we set it without fish, we shall have but a poor crop."[23]

There was precious little pasture that could compare to English downs. John Smith had warned many years previously, "Although [the grasses] be good and sweet in summer, they will deceive your cattle in winter; therefore be careful in the spring to mow the swamps and the low lands . . . till you can clear ground to make pasture — and unless you make this provision, if there come an extraordinary winter, you will lose many of them and hazard the rest."[24]

Farmers in other towns had found that the hard New England winters killed many of their cattle and that wolves emerged from the woods to attack and destroy an even greater number. In addition, many English cattle had become very sick eating acorns, making the task of pasturing cattle fraught with dangers.[25] The Musketaquid valley had natural clearings which had been used by Indian tribes, but the dark woods surrounded these as a foreboding menace.

Nonetheless, the new group had leaders ready and willing to face the challenges. Their spirit of dissent, hitherto frustrated in England, was being rewarded with political and economic power unknown in their old homes. In the fall of 1638, the Massachusetts General Court granted full power to Peter Noyes, Edmund Brown, and Brian Pendleton, to "go to their plantation and allot the lands."[26] The wilderness settlement could begin.

CHAPTER VI

"It Is Ordered and Agreed by This Town"

THE choice of Sudbury leaders seems an excellent one. Brian Pendleton had been repeatedly elected one of the first town officers of Watertown, where he had assisted in deciding on and administering the crucial first steps of Massachusetts's most populous town.[1] He had been granted six parcels of upland, meadow, and plowland in Watertown, totalling 117 acres, one of the larger proportions of the first grants, indicating a prosperous life before he arrived in New England. Since he had lived in London, he had more than likely been trained as a businessman, and he was known later as a land speculator, military leader, and politician.[2] Undoubtedly he was alert for natural resources, and perhaps more than tolerant of a settler who might prove to be a shrewd investor.

Noyes, Rice, and Walter Haines, although they did not have years of actual administrative experience in English governing institutions, all knew the open-field system well and had seen a variety of local governing bodies operate for more than thirty years. All were in the prime of life, and since their townsmen repeatedly re-elected all of them to every major town post, their judgment must have been respected in the early critical years.

Certainly their task was a formidable one. The General Court had shown practical wisdom in refusing to define their administrative powers with any precision, for these four men had to achieve a synthesis of a wide variety of English experience. Their settlers came from at least twelve different counties, stretching from the midlands to both the south and the east coasts of England, and such boroughs as London, Sudbury, Berkhamsted, Cambridge, and Trowbridge.[3] (See map, Figure 8.)

One of their very first problems was to determine the method by which these fifty-odd families could survive. The fact that at least 50 per cent of the farmers had grown crops in villages like Weyhill meant that they came with a marked shortage of agricultural equipment. Twenty years later, as wills began to be filed at the county court, only one third of the Sudbury men had plowshares and pairs of oxen as plow teams, and one farmer, Henry Prentis, owned only one hoe.[4] Noyes and Haines were well accustomed to this, for wills in their open-field villages indicate that open-field farmers expected to share equipment, labor, and administration, as they always had done.[5]

The absence of specific bylaws in the Sudbury Town Book, 1638–1639, indicates group harmony and co-operation in developing an open-field land system in the Musketaquid valley. The first recorded order, of April 1639, decreed that fences should be made around the two "general fields" and that four men, Rice, Darvell, Thomas Goodnow, and Andrew Belcher should patrol these fences.[6] This order was just as spare, and just as meaningful, as very similar bylaws passed by the jury of the Weyhill court-baron. There was only one major difference. The commissioners gave the four fence surveyors the power to fine "any who default," but the fine was twice that which Noyes and others had known at home.

Peter Noyes, standing on Reeve's Hill, could have seen North Field, South Field, and a cluster of thatched cottages circled around a common "for working cattel," the pasture for oxen which made their settlement possible. The size and place of the individual house lots was either not recorded in the Town Book, or possibly has been lost, but subsequent local historians and antiquarians have made it possible to draw a reasonably accurate early map of the village center (Figure 9).*

The government that emerged in Sudbury's first year was a mutual agreement among four parties: General Court, commissioners, inhabitants, and the Indians. Above all, it was orderly in the best English sense. Each group instinctively knew some of the rights and powers of the others, at least for a while. The General Court was the source of power and had told the commis-

---

* The house lots were made four acres each, in accordance with the English law of that time. (See order to constables, reproduced farther on.) For the map, I have assigned each grantee an arbitrary number and given all land grants the appropriate number, where possible. Examples: Peter Noyes #46, Edmund Rice #5, John Parmenter #22, Edmund Brown #51. The complete numerical system in Sudbury Records, I, pp. 5–7.

sioners that if any serious "difference" should break the harmony, the government's "Council," acting like the Privy Council in England, "should order it."[7]

The commissioners, assuming the role of justices of the peace, sanctioned the written orders for the town. In due course they drew up an English land deed and paid the Indian chief £5 for "all rights and appurtenances" in an area five miles square.[8] Apparently they respected their heathen neighbors enough to give the name of Jethro to one chief and Cato to another.[9] It is not known whether Jethro repeated the Old Testament ritual and gave advice to "Moses" Noyes, but other early settlers in other towns relied greatly on Indian agricultural experience and suggestions.

Both the commissioners and the central government respected the desires of all the inhabitants. After finding that they could grow crops successfully in the valley, these inhabitants petitioned the General Court, in the summer of 1639, for a larger committee of seven Sudbury men, "to lay out lands to the present inhabitants, according to their estates and persons."[10] The Court acknowledged this in exactly the same manner as the court of general sessions, sitting in Woodbridge, Suffolk, responded to two petitions of the inhabitants of Framlingham in 1639 regarding taxes and the burden of caring for the poor.[11]

In an orderly English fashion the General Court in 1639 also appointed Peter Noyes as surveyor of arms and Brian Pendleton as captain of the Sudbury military company. The Court was willing to make the large grant of land, partly because it expected Sudbury to be a defensive outpost, just in case the Massachusetts tribes started acting like the Narragansetts or the Pequods. But Sudbury was still to be an English town, not a disorderly frontier settlement, and the Court appointed Edmund Goodnow as first constable.[12] It was assumed that he knew the standard charges to a constable. They consisted of a list of reports which the constable had to make to his local justice of the peace:

1. What felonies have been committed – of what, against whom, and what pursuit has been taken? What are the results?
2. Are there any idle, vagrant or suspicious persons?
3. Have there been any riotous, outrageous, or unlawful assemblies tending to break the peace?
4. Have there been any recusants who came not to church?
5. Have there been any extortion or apprehension by any officer?
6. Have there been any engrossers, forestallers or regrators of the market?
7. What alehouses do you have? Are they licensed or unlicensed? Do they observe orderly behavior?

8. Have there been any masters who retain servants and give better wages than those set down by law?
9. Have there been any common drunkards or common haunters of taverns?
10. Have any new cottages been built?
11. Have there been any new cottages erected without four acres of land adjoining?
12. Have any of the inhabitants tried to sell goods twice?[13]

But since neither the General Court records nor those of the Middlesex County Court show an indication of any dispute in Sudbury for the first decade, Goodnow's job may have been an easy one, compared with any similar service he may have had in Donhead St. Andrew, Wilts.[14] The most difficult job was in the hands of the new commissioners: Noyes, Pendleton, Rice, Walter Haines, John Parmenter, and George Munnings. They had the responsibility of assigning social and economic status to every one of Sudbury's adult male inhabitants.

Despite all that has been written by historians damning early Massachusetts leaders for attempting to establish a "rule by Saints," not enough attention has been paid to the essential fact that both the Bay government and the town government were accomplishing a virtual social revolution in the systems of social and economic status of each community. For the first time in their lives, the inhabitants of an English town were assuming that each adult male would be granted some land, free and clear. Noyes, for example, was shifting from a village in which about half the adult males were landless laborers, and the other half tenants paying yearly rents and feudal fees, to a Massachusetts town in which he had the power to grant lands to all inhabitants, according to "estates and persons." Under the radical new social philosophy he was free to grant land either according to the number of persons in a family, or according to an assessment of the wealth and property each family had brought with them, or in relation to some combination of both these sets of data.[15]

Both Munnings and Pendleton had seen this system established in Watertown, and Pendleton had assisted in its administration. There was no indication that a person's religious faith had anything to do with the Watertown grants of 1636 and 1637. Of course, if it seemed that a family might be a public charge, the Watertown committee had been reluctant to give it social and economic status in their town.

The new Sudbury committee of 1639, using the phraseology of a justice of the peace, made a sweeping proposal: "We have ordered that the meadows . . .

shall be given to the present inhabitants . . . according to the following rule: to every Mr. of a family: 6 acres; to every wife: 6½ acres; to every child: 1½ acres; For every mare, cow, or other cattle amounting to £20: 30 acres."[16]

To open-field folk, this order must have seemed remarkable. For men like John Bent and John Rutter, it meant that every family with but one child was going to gain possession of more meadow than the amount of land which two thirds of the men in Weyhill rented at that time. In addition, the plow-land and upland were still to be divided up.

Perhaps this decision was too radical for the community, too egalitarian, or too favorable for the wives. It was never acted upon. Instead, the town adopted a division of meadow based on a clear distinction between the vary-ing amounts of property which each male inhabitant possessed. The division was made for two purposes — to grant property and to constitute the basis for a town tax which would pay the Indians for the town grant. In one "river meadow" list drawn up during the winter of 1639–1640, the committee as-signed economic status to each one of the male inhabitants of Sudbury, mak-ing each at once a landlord and a taxpaying citizen.

Having briefly examined approximately fifty candidates for citizenship, each one of whom had come from a very distinct English background, the committee ranked all of these men in an economic hierarchy that was to be fixed and final. The minister, Edmund Brown, was first man; Brian Pendleton second; Thomas Cakebread, a miller who had been lured from Watertown, third; William Pelham, brother of an important investor and government official, fourth; Peter Noyes, fifth; Edmund Goodnow, sixth; John Knight, a wealthy Watertown man, seventh; Edmund Rice, eighth; George Munnings, ninth; William Ward, tenth; Walter Haines, eleventh — and so on down the list.[17] (See Appendix VI.)

The committee did not distribute all of the available river meadow but kept the major part in reserve, as a type of town bank account, on which they later drew to "gratulate" town officials for time and service rendered. Out of an estimated 3000 acres, the committee allotted only 848, but this was ten times the amount of meadow in Rice's old village of Berkhamsted and un-doubtedly more river meadow than most of the settlers had been accustomed to using.

The committee made meadow grants slowly. After staking out the first strips on the east bank of the river, they determined the placement of the sec-ond division "by lot." This old open-field system meant that the meadow strips were numbered. The numbers were placed on pieces of paper with a description of the plot, and the slips put into a container. The farmers each drew out a slip and thus learned, by chance, whether they would have to walk one mile for their hay or possibly five.*

Extremely careful distinctions were made in the size of the meadow grants — they ranged from seventy-five acres (the minister) to one acre (John Loker) and even reached quarter-acre precision.† The type of holding was very vaguely expressed, although perhaps clearly understood by the committee. Above all, every farmer had to be a responsible citizen. Watertown had decreed that if any person neglected to make his share of the fence around the common plowland, his land would "return to the Town."[18] This philosophy was implicit in the Sudbury grants of both meadow and other land, with unhappy consequences later on.

At any rate, each landowner in both Sudbury and Watertown was expected to come to a member of the land-grant committee, later the town clerk, and have a description of his lands recorded in the Town Book.[19] Probably the settlers regarded the Town Book as a type of manorial court roll, giving a man legal title to his possessions, with right to bequeath, sell, or rent them.

But the very fact that each settlement was starting to record orders in a Town Book was indicative of a strong desire to institute a political entity known as a town. The Sudbury committee, in making the meadow grants, stated clearly that they were giving status to "all the inhabitants of this Town."[20] Three months later, the commissioners, instead of speaking in terms of a grant of power by the central government, called themselves "the commissioners of the town" and appointed two highway surveyors, Peter Noyes and John Parmenter, to see to it that "every inhabitant of this town shall come forth to the mending of the hyways."[21]

The order of April 1, 1640, reads as if the selectmen were recording it in the minutes of the old borough of Sudbury: "It is ordered and agreed that all such hogs and pigs as shall be kept in the town of Sudbury . . . shall not go about the town without yokes and rings in their noses."[22] Furthermore, this order instituted a town treasury, decreeing that every man who found an unyoked pig should collect ten shillings fine, half for himself for leading it to the pound, and "the other half for the town." (See Town Pound, Figure 10.) At this rate, only twenty offenses would fill the treasury with as much money as

---

* This was the method I used in assigning numbers to the Sudbury map, Figure 9. I employed a regular, north-south placement on the east side of the river, an irregular placement on the west side of the river.

† For example: G. Witherell: 6 acres; J. Blandford: 5¾ acres; H. Prentice: 5½ acres.

the mayor of the Suffolk borough spent in an entire year. The settlement's fine for unruly hogs was thirty times the fine levied in Brown's old borough in 1622. Inflation had seeped into New England, but the extraordinary size of this ten-shilling fine also implied a determination to institute an orderly life.

By May, 1640, the desire to form a distinct town had taken deep roots in Sudbury. Thirty-four per cent of the landholders were ready to sign an agreement, not only to pledge their incomes in behalf of their town, but also to tax themselves to fight a legal battle should the occasion arise. They were worried that the treasurer of the colony might distrain someone's goods, because Sudbury had obviously not yet paid its "country rate," for that year. A very large colony tax, at least £1200, had been passed. Watertown had been assessed at £90, and Concord, to the north, £50.[23] Seventeen citizens of Sudbury, led by Pelham and Noyes, passed a very significant law, stating that "the town will bear all the charges that may in any way arise by standing suit with the Treasurer, the charges to be paid by a town rate."[24]

Every type of citizen added signatures to this critical town order. Leading landowners, such as Walter Haines and Edmund Goodnow, signed, but so did John Maynard (2½ acres), John Blandford, an indentured servant, and two men, William Kerley and John Moore, who had not yet been allotted river meadow grants. Even more significant, at least ten of the seventeen men were not colony freemen.

Whether they consulted with Reverend Edmund Brown or not is not evident from the records. It is certain he did not sign this order, although he did sign two orders in the first years. But the absence of his signature and the wording of the order, together with the variety of inhabitants pledging loyalty to "the town" all seem to imply one important decision: that in May, 1640, one third of the male settlers were officially instituting a political entity which was distinctly different from any English political institution they had known.

This order went beyond English law and custom. It could not be considered analogous to a vestry bylaw, because the minister always conducted vestry meetings, signed such orders, and usually confined the meetings to the oligarchy of the parish. The Sudbury order obviously was not an agricultural bylaw. It was somewhat similar to the decrees passed by an English borough council. It certainly implied that "the town" could be a party in a suit at law and that the town could pass its own taxes. But, on the other hand, the orders emanating from the council of the borough of Sudbury were the product of an oligarchy appointed to political position for life, and were issued under the seal of a borough whose rights and powers had been granted by charters from the King of England.

It is impossible to call this the product of a town theocracy. In the famous Massachusetts *Body of Liberties,* then being debated by towns in the Bay Colony, Liberty 12 allowed "every man, whether inhabitant or foreigner, free or not free," to come to any town meeting and present any orderly motion. Nonetheless, the *Body of Liberties* had a strict definition of a town government. Liberty 66 stated that "the freemen of every township shall have power to make such by-laws and constitutions as may concern the welfare of their town . . . not repugnant to the public laws of the country."[25] By "freeman" this early Massachusetts constitution meant an official church member who had taken an oath to uphold the colony.

But 60 per cent of the Sudbury men who passed this 1640 order were not on the books as colony freemen, although they may well have intended to become staunch members of their church and, eventually, freemen. Their move indicated that they wanted a political entity, with full legal power and with a broad base of responsible citizens.

The central government sanctioned their status. When "the inhabitants of Sudbury" petitioned the General Court in the spring of 1640 for an additional 3200 acres on their southern border, the Court quickly granted six extra miles of territory.[26]

Having received support for their local plans for a town which owned over 19,000 acres of upland and meadow, the inhabitants met in June to choose a committee of two leading citizens, Brian Pendleton and Edmund Goodnow, who would distribute the "third division of upland."* This "order of the inhabitants of the town" gave Pendleton and Goodnow power to make grants that would "stand for ever, without contradiction," in what can be termed a type of Sudbury freehold.[27]

The committee felt that it was acting in behalf of a legally constituted town. They prefaced their list of land grants with the statement, "Being chosen by the Town of Sudbury, and put into commission to assign upland to the inhabitants." They staked out a total of 751 acres of farmland to 43 grantees, ranging from 76 acres (Pendleton) to 4 acres (John Wood), most of them lying together in "great fields," but some of them laid out as separate plots and

---

* The first two divisions were probably strips in North and South Fields. No records of these grants were entered into the Town Book or have been found in local manuscript collections.

widely scattered on both sides of the river.* They did not explain, however, the basis for their distribution of different amounts of land.

Goodnow and Pendleton closely followed the hierarchy of the first meadow-tax list, but dropped the minister down to seventh place in size of grant, replacing him by the miller, Cakebread. Peter Noyes, Walter Haines, and Edmund Goodnow kept their leading positions, but William Pelham dropped from the list, without explanation. Everyone must have begun to understand the source of Sudbury's power — the will of all the landowners, expressed at a town meeting.†

This will of the town dictated Sudbury's decisions on land grants and, therefore, the social status of its citizens. The fate of Munnings and John Knight are clear proof. Sudbury, at first, welcomed George Munnings of Watertown. He had been admitted to Watertown's church, ran an inn there, and had been granted a house lot of 14 acres, 8 acres of meadow, 4½ acres of upland, and a farm of 73 acres.[28] The inhabitants of Sudbury gave him a grant of 28 acres of meadow in 1639–1640 and elected him to the committee to decide on all meadow grants in the town. In terms of meadow and taxes, Munnings ranked ninth in Sudbury, just below Edmund Rice. By November 1640, however, something had happened to his reputation, or possibly he had indicated a lack of interest in the new town. At any rate, the town committee dropped him to twenty-fifth place in a list of forty-three men, giving him only 10 acres of upland. In a few years he left the town and returned to his inn at Watertown.[29]

John Knight had a somewhat similar fate, although the extent of his land grants in Watertown labels him, from the start, as a land speculator. Watertown had granted him an 8-acre house lot, 9 acres of meadow, 10 acres of plowland, 19 acres of "planting ground," 78 acres of upland, and a farm of 270 acres, a total of 394 acres of land. He was given, in Sudbury, 38½ acres of meadow, ranking him seventh in the list of grants. In the division of upland, Pendleton and Goodnow moved him up in rank to fourth place, with 61 acres.

Knight's progress illustrated why each town was insistent that a man de-

* The lots placed on the 1650 Sudbury map, Figure 9, particularly those on the west side of the river, have been located according to the reasonable estimates of antiquarians, the descendants of original grantees now living in Sudbury and Wayland, the former Town Clerk, Mr. Forrest Bradshaw, and the author.

† Another principle of division was clearly written out after a town meeting of 1664: "The town of Sudbury for future time will grant no lands whatsoever within the town bounds of Sudbury except the major part of those who have power to grant lands in the Town of Sudbury do affirmatively act in the granting and giving of the said lands." (Order of 1664.)

clare his loyalty to one town by "settling" there. If each town allowed men like Knight to move to another new settlement, and still retain the grants they had been given elsewhere as part of their overall "estate," it is not hard to see how such speculators could pyramid holdings almost indefinitely, as they moved from new town to new town. Sudbury must have made Knight decide between his two towns, for he was one of the very few leading Sudbury land-holders not elected selectman, and he returned to Watertown after a few years. Sudbury did not favor absentee landowners, however, and dropped Knight from all successive land-grant lists.

There is no record of a complaint against this policy by such men as Mun-nings and Knight, either in the town records or in the records of the General Court. But a complaint would not have been likely. After all, by showing loy-alty to one town alone, a man stood the chance of greatly increasing his status over that which he had known in his English community. By a single majority vote, a town like Sudbury could enhance a man's position with a rapidity im-possible to achieve in England.

The men from Weyhill and Berkhamsted can serve as examples. Although Peter Noyes did not gain in relative economic status, being fourth in Weyhill (61 acres) and fourth in Sudbury (121 acres), he gained in acreage and, most important, in leadership. His uncles had dominated the community in Wey-hill, and Peter assumed a similar role in his new town. Two men whom he had brought over, Robert Davis and John Rutter, moved from the status of landless laborers to that of householders and citizens in less than a decade. Edmund Rice made one of the most significant advances. From a position as an outsider trying to gain land in Berkhamsted and finally achieving 15 acres, he shifted to a position as one of Sudbury's outstanding leaders, was granted 87 acres, and was soon elected as Sudbury's deputy to the General Court in Boston.

The rise in status, however, was far from automatic. At least two men ap-pear to have lost in the transition, although, of course, we do not have any ex-pression of their actual feelings. While John Bent was in Weyhill, he stood fifth in land (45 acres) and was inheriting his father's role as an active commu-nity leader. In the town on the banks of the Musketaquid, however, he slipped to eighteenth place in economic status (40 acres) and was elected only twice as selectman in the first fifteen years. Robert Darvell, a lifetime chief burgess of Berkhamsted, increased his acreage from 22 acres to 47 acres, but stayed in the same economic position (fourteenth) and was elected to the governing council of his new town only once. Thomas, the son of Darvell's old mayor, William

Axtell, gained even less recognition. While he might have inherited his father's position had he stayed at home in Berkhamsted, Thomas chose to emigrate to a town which did not even grant him land or meadow. He had to buy
five acres of upland from Edmund Rice, and it is not surprising that his son,
Henry, moved to another new town to try his luck.[30]

Sudbury was perfectly willing to entertain the requests of its citizens. As
the townsmen agreed in 1643, "if any man shall lack any such quantity of
meadow or upland, as by proportion he ought to have, if he appeals to the
town, he shall have satisfaction in some land or other."[31] The townsmen
meant to imply a moral sanction, because they clearly wished to refuse status
to men and women who did not meet their standards, particularly proprietors
who refused to live in the town itself.

The Pelhams, for example, presented a real problem. Both William Pelham, a Cambridge University graduate, and his brother Herbert, had come
over in the Winthrop fleet and were granted extensive farms in Sudbury by
the General Court to compensate for their investment. The grants were not
laid out at first and were never entered in the Town Book. While the townsmen granted William Pelham a large plot of meadow, 50 acres, they dropped
him from the land list in other divisions, stalling until 1646 before granting
him any more meadow or upland. Since he did not establish a home, they
were probably glad to see him go when he decided to return to England to
take part in the Civil War.[32]

Sudbury was particularly resentful of the attitude of William's brother
Herbert, a resident of Cambridge and a member of the upper house of the
legislature. When Pelham appealed to the General Court about his land in
Sudbury, the townsmen reminded him that "he had promised to build a
house there, settle a family there and be there as much as he could in the summer time."[33] They refused to record his farm in their Town Book for years and
disputed his "right" to share in the town grants. Pelham put pressure on the
town through President Dunster of Harvard, whose wife, the former Mrs.
Glover, had six hundred acres of land to the south of Sudbury.[34] The town appointed a committee to see about "his demand," and grudgingly admitted his
right to some land; but they staunchly refused to admit his right to vote in town
meetings by absentee ballots, on the principle that he was not a resident.[35]

Within two years after the initial grant of land, then, fifty settlers in the
valley of the Musketaquid developed a distinct type of social, political, and
economic unit known as the town of Sudbury. Of dubious legality, in terms of
English common law, and of questionable validity under the terms of the

Massachusetts *Body of Liberties,* Sudbury developed its own version of orderly reform.

Although right next to Watertown and formed by some of its important landowners, Sudbury copied neither its neighbor's farming system nor its political hierarchy. Where Watertown's East Anglians had laid out enclosed farms in large rectangular lots and began to abandon the temporary general fields, Sudbury laid down a type of expanding open-field system.

Where Watertown's first records cited "the Freemen" as a source of local political authority, Sudbury's governing body hardly used the term at all. Now and then Noyes, Pendleton, Haines, and Goodnow signed as "freemen" in the first five years, but the overwhelming majority of the early laws stated boldly, "ordered and agreed by the inhabitants of this Town of Sudbury."

CHAPTER VII

"All Liberties As Other Towns Have"

WHEN Peter Noyes and his fellow petitioners were granted "all liberties as other towns have," by the General Court in 1638, the Bay government was referring to the seventeen other Massachusetts towns which had already been established.[1] But neither Noyes nor his leading citizens had lived in any New England town except Watertown, and they had never been elected or appointed to a governing council.

They brought with them years of experience in English communities, and it is only natural that they relied on this training, in addition to whatever reports they heard about Boston, Salem, Charlestown, Cambridge, and other early Bay settlements. To Noyes the phrase, "liberties of a town," undoubtedly stimulated memories of the power and government of the borough of Andover, Hants, where his relatives served as members of the borough council.[2] Since Andover is adjacent to Weyhill and was the market town, Noyes knew it well.

Edmund Goodnow and his brothers, cited in the Wiltshire church courts for going to hear sermons in the borough of Shaftesbury, must have known the liberties of "Shaston," particularly since Thomas Goodnow lived in the city. Edmund Rice and Robert Darvell certainly knew the powers granted their borough of Berkhamsted. Hugh Griffin, elected town clerk of Sudbury, Massachusetts, had previously lived in London, as Brian Pendleton had also. The knowledge of the functions of borough administration, which these men brought to Sudbury, could not have been easily forgotten.

FIGURE 13
Edmund Rice's House and Barn, Sudbury

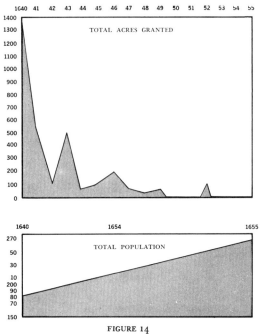

FIGURE 14

Sudbury Land Grants and Population Growth, 1640–1655

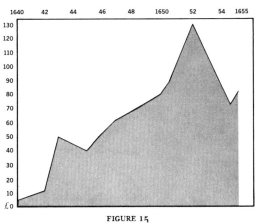

FIGURE 15

Sudbury Taxes, 1640–1655

FIGURE 16

Sudbury Bridge, 1643

FIGURE 17
First Sudbury Meetinghouse, 1643

Noyes, Rice, and Goodnow were trying to weld together an independent synthesis of local laws, responsibilities, and rights, an amalgam of English institutional influences, as well as new solutions to new problems. Noyes, Haines, and Goodnow insisted on open-field agricultural co-operation and the tradition of passing agricultural bylaws by the farmers concerned. Perhaps Rice contributed the tax system of Berkhamsted, with changes, a system which Noyes, at least, had not used in his village. Perhaps Griffin gave sanction to the increasing number of town officers, paid from the town's treasury. To all of their English experience, fresh ideas were added each year. Quite possibly Rice, Haines, and Noyes, traveling to Boston to speak for Sudbury in the General Court sessions, took heart in the realization that other towns were being allowed to experiment, much in the same way.[3]

The leading men of Sudbury, however, did not act like an English borough council, nor assume the exclusive powers of freemen as decreed by the *Body of Liberties*. Every major issue was discussed in open town meetings, and over 132 meetings were held in the first fifteen years. More than 650 orders, "agreed by the town," were passed in this period, a staggering number contrasted with the legislative activities of the Suffolk borough. Two charts well illustrate the amount of time and thought which the citizens of Sudbury were contributing to their new political entity. (Figure 11.)

In terms of numbers of orders devoted to particular topics, the citizens of early Sudbury called meetings and passed laws on the following items: land (45 per cent of the total number of orders, 1639–1656), town government (35 per cent), economic regulations and taxes (9 per cent), church affairs (6 per cent), personal quarrels in the town (2 per cent), relations with neighboring towns (1 per cent), relations with the Indians (1 per cent), and relations with the colony government (1 per cent).

Land Problems

Once the committee had drawn up the basic "proportion" of all male citizens in 1639–1640, and individual grants of meadow and upland had been made on this basic ranking system, the rest of the 19,200 acres was declared to be "the commons," a sort of town bank account in land. It was considered good soil but very difficult to farm. Edward Johnson, in his brief survey of New England made in the 1650's said of Sudbury, "It is very well watered, and hath a score of plowlands, but by reason of the oaken roots, they have little [land] broken up, considering the many acres the place affords; but this kind of land requires great strength to break up, yet brings very good crops, and lasts long without mending."[4] The farmers probably used the wooded areas for pasture of cattle. This extensive area of woodlands was free from underbrush owing to the ancient Indian practice of burning all the undergrowth once or twice each year, making the Sudbury forest seem similar to an English park.[5] In a number of years, the townsmen were taking in cattle from other towns, but the inventories of the period show few sheep owned by Sudbury men. The farmers were shifting from wool-growing to cattle-raising.

This general "commons," an estimated 89 per cent of the total town plot, stretched out from the town center east, west, and northwest. About 2750 acres lay on the east side of the river, and its boundary was staked out in 1643, with the optimistic decree that it was "to lie forever." In 1647, a corresponding grazing area of about 5000 acres was laid out on the west side of the river, stretching northwest to Pantry Brook, south to Lanham Brook, and west to the far town line, "to remain in perpetuity."[6]

Every meadow-holder in Sudbury was assured of a "town right" in the commons. This meant, as it had in every open-field village, and in the old borough of Sudbury as well, that "the inhabitants of the town are to be limited or sized in the putting in of cattle upon the said commons according to the quantity of meadow they [obtain] by the division of the meadow or [which they] purchase, providing that they buy with the meadow the liberty of commonage allotted to such a quantity of acres purchased."[7]

The town decided in 1643, however, that the commons were so extensive, and the town herd so small, that "it is permitted to the said inhabitants to put on their cattle without size [limits] until the herd or herds shall decrease the feed, at which time they shall come to size." In other words, the townsmen warned everyone that each person would be limited as to the number of cattle which he could put on the town commons as soon as the Sudbury herds seemed to be getting too large for the amount of pasture available. The great difference between this bylaw and a traditional "sizing of the commons" in England lay in the fact that this order of 1643 was a legislative decree, subject to the vote of the citizens, not a custom which had existed "time out of mind." This limitation of the commons was to become a controversial issue in little more than a decade.

Nonetheless, in 1643, the townsmen asserted their complete authority over all undivided land and even over individual enclosures on the commons. They warned that "all upland meadow not yet granted to any person . . . shall be left open to be fed by the common herd until May 1, provided that if any person possess such meadow, he must withstand ingresse and egresse of the herd or herds or shall forfeit for every acre confined five pounds." This was a staggering fine to impose, equal to the price of a cow in England, or one fourth the price of a cow in the inflated New England prices at that time.

The townsmen, then, were militantly opposed to any farmer who cared more about his own selfish aims than he did about the common good. At the time, the men were continuing their open-field farming customs in Sudbury, sharing the labor, and the making of bylaws to administer the general fields.

John Goodnow, for example, a Wiltshire man, had grants of roughly 100 acres of plowland, upland and meadow, scattered all over the town plot. (See map, Figure 12.) When he collected the hay from all his meadow strips, he had to travel a minimum of eleven miles. But he still preferred to work in co-operative agricultural groups, just as the farmers in his old village of Donhead St. Andrew were doing at the time, and always had done.

With the possible exception of meat and milk sold, Goodnow, in the first years, probably used an economic philosophy which calculated in terms of the production of food for his family and for his animals, not cash for crops sold. He and his fellow farmers, nevertheless, slowly expanded their production of crops as well as the size of their town herd. In good open-field fashion, a whole set of complicated town orders was passed, year by year, involving pasturage of the common herd, designation of the fields which were to be planted and which were to be left fallow, the dates by which the fences had to be made following the plowing and harrowing, and appointment of the various town officers to supervise all these operations.

There were two general fields in 1643, two more were added that year, six open fields were added in 1644, eight open fields in 1654, and twelve open fields in 1655, demanding the services of three general surveyors and twenty-five regular fence viewers, two to a field.[8] Some Sudbury men, like Edmund Rice, were buying large farms, and building houses on them, perhaps influenced by the farms being developed in Watertown. (See Rice's house and barn, Figure 13.[9])

But the Sudbury townsmen, as a group, were expanding their open-field system and not following Rice in a shift toward individually managed farms. The younger sons, however, were undoubtedly influenced by the fact that the Watertown farmers, by 1655, had almost completely changed to individual farm management, appointing only two fence viewers for the town commons in the town center.[10]

The Sudbury land committee did not entertain requests for sales of town land to those who wished to farm on their own, although it sanctioned the sales of land by one citizen to another.[11] Over the common and undivided land the townsmen exercised a type of landlordism in which some land automatically returned to the town's control. In 1646, for instance, the committee, acting "by joint consent of the town," told William Brown that "he shall quietly enjoy the land which he hath now fenced in, which is the second division of upland formerly granted to Thomas Brown."[12] Apparently Thomas Brown had left the settlement, but the Town Book records no deed or order by which either he, or the town, clearly altered his original grant from the town.

Both John Goodnow and his brother Edmund opposed a policy which made the Sudbury commons freely available to new citizens, once the "due proportions" of the original settlers had been drawn up. Both men were appointed, in 1644, by the town to a committee given power "to dispose of so much land to any [person], as they shall see each occasion, provided they decree not to any above six acres."[13] They admitted that men could "appeal to the town," but they guarded the town resources carefully. For a few years they granted plots to town officers in lieu of wages, or, as they said, "to gratulate them for services rendered."[14] They also rented certain swamps to men for the hay in them, but they much preferred that their citizens buy additional land from each other.

The resources of the commons could not be used indiscriminately either. The townsmen, as early as 1640, authorized Edmund Goodnow and John Bent to "assign all timber to be befallen to any man's necessity," with power to fine anyone who either failed to get permission before felling a tree or who disobeyed his town's timber keepers.[15] From 1640 onward, all the town's land resources were thus jealously guarded by "joint consent."

This policy of absolute control of the town over its land, despite specific grants to individuals, seemed to work without friction as long as each landowner was a citizen who fully understood the intent of his fellow townsmen. But when a man left Sudbury or disagreed with his neighbors, grave misunderstandings about land titles flared into angry disputes.

The land committee sharply decreased the amount of town land granted as the years progressed. And as the younger sons matured and began to take part in town meetings, the elder generation was shocked into the realization that their sons could use political power to demand far more than their fathers were prepared to give. Whether the land committee realized it or not, the contrast between the rise in population and the decrease in land granted (see Figure 14) was to threaten the entire order of Sudbury.*

Town Government

The political order of the town was imposed year by year through the concerted efforts of devoted townsmen. It is not known how many men attended the meetings in the first five years, but it is obvious that in a time of crisis, demanding town loyalty and clarity of purpose, a third of the citizens were ready and willing to sign an order pledging their crops and their estates to support the legal actions of the town of Sudbury.

Following the significant order of 1640, pledging money to go to law against the colony in behalf of the town, the townsmen were content to have their land committee divide up and stake out the land and to obey their Court-appointed constable, Edmund Goodnow, in his effort to maintain peace and order. By 1643, once the land was plowed and sown, and houses built, the townsmen were ready to assume political power and to delegate this authority to an ever-increasing number of town officials.

At a town meeting in February, the town appointed three officers, a marshal, a man to write town orders, and a ferry-keeper. The Sudbury citizens seem to have been making a careful choice of titles for their officers. For ten years they called their police officer "marshal" and not "constable," and during Hugh Griffin's lifetime of service they never officially called him a town clerk but elected him to "write the town orders."[16] The town levied a tax to pay Hugh Griffin a salary of ten shillings and empowered the marshal, John How, with authority to levy the stiff fine of £1/00/12 for every distraint he was forced to make.[17]

The curious aspect of this Sudbury marshal is that no records of his actions have been found. Whether he exercised merely moral restraint and simply warned the town inhabitants is not known. Whether he reported disorders and distraints to the Middlesex County Court or to his town meeting can be only a guess. Perhaps he informed his selectmen, since the General Court had granted power to selectman Walter Haines to "grant summons and attachments in all civil actions," and since the constable of Watertown reported misdemeanors to the selectmen there.[18] Whereas the English court records of this period are filled with warrants served by constables, indictments levied, and

* The population graph is an estimate, based on fragmentary statements in the Town Book and in the Stearns MSS.

fines imposed, no records of these penalties appear in the Sudbury Town Book.

The contrast between the entries in the Borough Book of Sudbury, Suffolk, and the Town Book of Sudbury, Massachusetts, is startling. While the constables and justices of old Sudbury could count on an income of at least £2 to £8 from numerous fines imposed, the Town Book of Sudbury does not record a single fine levied or received in the first fifteen years of town government. This surpasses the record of Noyes's Weyhill, where, despite a spirit of co-operative farming, a few fines were imposed by the juries each year. Consequently, if the Sudbury marshal and governing officers controlled their citizens with only moral pressure, a remarkable social harmony prevailed in the Musketaquid valley for a decade and a half.[19]

In 1644, the town clarified the function of its officers slightly and added a governing council. The marshal was instructed to "compose the rate," with the clerk, or to make tax assessments, giving the inhabitants notice of the amount of their tax and designating a time and a place of payment. The marshal could add to his own fee, if he was forced to "go afterward to gather" the tax payment.[20]

The town re-elected How as marshal and Griffin as writer of orders and gave John Bent and John Blandford "power to call out men to the highway for the year." Since these men were not given any authority to levy fines, the town assumed apparently a strong spirit of mutual co-operation among its citizens.

By this year the farmers had opened up six general fields, and eleven men were appointed to see that all the planters built fences in each field in proportion. This work was to be completed by May 16. The appointed men had the power to levy a 12d. fine for "every rod of defective fence." The fifteen appointments mentioned above indicated how representative the town government was becoming. Not only did William Brown and John Ruddock join Peter Noyes and the former leaders in signing this order, but almost a third of the taxpayers were delegated authority to administer town affairs, including nine men hitherto listed as mere citizens.[21]

In the summer of 1644, power was "granted by the town" to Peter Noyes, Walter Haines, Edmund Rice, Brian Pendleton, William Ward, and John and Edmund Goodnow "to dispose of town affairs for one year." This was the seven-man council to which the town also gave authority to grant plots of upland.[22] The government of Sudbury was now in the hands of the townsmen.

The government was still flexible and experimental, nonetheless. Almost once a month the drum would beat, calling the inhabitants to a town meeting. At all times this town meeting was assumed to be the source of local power and authority, granting limited amounts of authority to individuals, or to committees, for a limited time, at most a year. Elections had not yet been made specific, as the citizens held four separate elections in 1645 to name men as highway supervisors, meadow supervisors, fence viewers, and selectmen.

For the next ten years, the town continued to indulge in several separate elections of men to various posts, and no official list of town officers was entered in the Town Book. The selectmen eventually were appointed each spring, but other men were named at different times. When specific jobs had to be done, the townsmen looked around the meetinghouse to see who was there and who would assume the responsibilities. Probably after some sort of agreement had been reached, the names of the new officers were entered in the Town Book.

The following are the various offices to which men were elected during the period 1639–1656. "Major Posts" are those repeated each year; "Minor Posts" those offices created for special occasions:

Major Posts	Minor Posts
"To Order Town Affairs" [Selectmen]	Tax Gatherer
"Writer of Town Orders" [Clerk]	Commissioner
Marshal [Constable]	Swine Keeper
Highway Surveyor	Pound Keeper
Fence Viewer	Tithingman
Field Surveyor	Drum Beater
Invoice Taker	Man to "Divide the shot"

It was impossible for the citizens to predict how many officers would be needed in any given year. The government was flexible. Whereas three men sufficed in 1643, the town required the services of about thirty-eight men in 1655, twenty-five of whom were fence viewers for general fields. Inevitably, most of the male inhabitants served in one post or another, although they shifted from one type of job to another quite readily.

The term which the inhabitants of Sudbury used to distinguish their citizens was "free townsman." This status, which implied both rights and responsibilities, was clearly granted by the town to men whom they wished to have a share in the town's common property. If there was any controversy about a man's status, the governing officers asked only one question — was the man granted common land?

There was some disagreement, apparently, about William Kerley, Jr., and

Thomas Cakebread, in 1647. The town clerk used the same phraseology to define the status of these men: "Wm. Kerley, Jr. is acknowledged to be a free townsman by virtue of the first grant in his commonage to the town . . . it is also acknowledged that Thomas Cakebread was a free townsman by virtue of his first grant of land as his commonage to the town."[23]

The phrase "free townsman" was very similar, of course, to the same phrase used in the old borough of Sudbury. But the new Sudbury had a very different philosophy. All male adult citizens, once sanctioned by a town-meeting vote and given a grant of common land, were considered free townsmen. For this privilege, they were expected to live in Sudbury, pay all taxes, and be called on to serve in any town post which the town meeting decided was necessary for that particular year.

Furthermore, the citizens expected that their large landowners would give almost unlimited time and service to affairs of the town. This demand of social responsibility seems to have been considerably stronger than had been true in most rural villages which the settlers had known. In Noyes's parish of Weyhill, for instance, Peter Gale, Sr., who stood number two in terms of land farmed, served only twice on the Ramridge jury and only one year as highway surveyor. On the other hand, Noyes's uncles had served in many parish posts, as had John Bent's father, Robert.[24] Sir Philip Cary, holder of 114 acres in Berkhamsted, was absolved from parish or borough posts, although one does not know whether he served the national government. But it was possible, in an English rural community, to be a wealthy landholder and to avoid any concomitant responsibility in manorial or vestry posts. The Sudbury, Massachusetts, citizens did not wish this to be possible, although they did make an exception for Cakebread, probably accepting his services as town miller and ensign as sufficient.

The Massachusetts town had at least two effective means, other than group pressure, to enforce their demands for social responsibility. They could refuse to grant men any new divisions when these lands were opened up, as they did to sixteen men in Sudbury in 1655, or they could hurt a man's pride by refusing to re-elect him to a town office that carried dignity and honor.

For the first eighteen years, however, harmony seems to have prevailed as the town government evolved. Men such as Peter Noyes, Walter Haines, Edmund Rice, and Edmund Goodnow served again and again in almost all the governmental posts in the town. But they did not constitute an exclusive borough council. At least thirty-nine different men, 52 per cent of the male land grantees, served as selectmen during the period 1639–1655. And these selectmen could count on their townsmen to assist them. All but two of the men who were granted new lots in 1655 had served in some Sudbury town posts.[25] The new political entity enjoyed, then, almost complete self-government in its first decade.

Economic Regulations — Taxes

The citizens of Sudbury showed a definite willingness to tax themselves for the good of the town and to make economic regulations in the name of orderly government. As has been explained, the necessity for paying the Indians for the deed to the town plot, and the possibility of being distrained for refusal to pay the colony tax caused the townsmen to think deeply about the very nature of their government by 1640.

The next economic crisis which affected the town occurred in 1641 and was widespread throughout the Bay Colony. As Winthrop expressed it, news arrived in December of "the Scots entering into England, and the calling of a parliament, and the hope of a thorough reformation . . . some among us began to think of returning back to England." Others, despairing of receiving any more supplies from England, considered emigrating to "the south parts, supposing they could find better means of subsistence there," and sold their property at a loss. This, "together with the scarcity of money," caused a sharp drop in the prices of all commodities, making it very difficult for men to pay their debts. At the same time, laborers and workmen, owing to the scarcity of labor, began to demand high wages, throwing the "principal men" into something of a panic.[26]

Consequently, the General Court passed wage regulations, with the unhappy result that the laborers "would either remove to other places where they might have more, or else, being able to live by planting and other employments of their own, they would not be hired at all." In this dilemma the General Court authorized "the several towns to set down rates among themselves," that is, to set wage ceilings.[27]

Accordingly, Noyes, Pendleton, Haines, Goodnow, Parmenter, Bent, and Ruddock ordered the following wage and price restrictions in Sudbury:[28]

Every cart, with four oxen, and a man, for a day's work	5s.
All carpenters, bricklayers, thatchers	21d./day
All common laborers	18d./day
All sawyers, for sawing up boards	3s./4d. per 100

All sawyers, for slit work	4s./8d. per 100
Yearly covenant servant	£5/year
Maid servant	£2/10 per year
Charge for carting corn from Water- town to Sudbury	5d./bushel
Charge for carting any other goods from Watertown to Sudbury	20s./ton

Although given explicit authority to act by the General Court, these seven men were exercising a power reserved in England for the justices of the peace and imposing wage rates then current in many parts of England.[29]

The records do not indicate whether this governing committee actually imposed these wage ceilings, but the townsmen of Sudbury expected, from the earliest years onward, to limit their incomes to cover town expenditures. Adopting the borough practice of paying a yearly salary to the town clerk, the men of Sudbury soon voted this fee to Hugh Griffin and instructed Griffin and the marshal to make a tax assessment and to collect the tax.[30]

In this same year the town voted both the clerk and the marshal a yearly salary and then started their minister off with £30 a year, a sum which was considerably lower than the average pastor's salary in the Bay towns at that time.[31] Such wages demanded a yearly tax and a definite tax system.

The townsmen adopted a property tax, levied almost always on land, although in 1643 they did assess some animals.[32] They continued much the same system which Rice and Darvell had known in Berkhamsted but substituted a more reasonable assessment in place of the arbitrary "ability" tax used in England. Each year the Sudbury invoice takers, recognizing the growing wealth of the inhabitants, evaluated each man's estate, making up the tax assessment.[33]

Unfortunately, the Sudbury invoice takers, unlike the clerk of Watertown, did not write down the tax lists, with amounts assessed, in the Town Book. But they did record the values of land in Sudbury, which indicates that the men emigrating from the West Country did not think highly of the quality of their new property. In 1647, the clerk recorded that land was "prized" in Sudbury as follows:[34]

Upland "broke up" [plowed]	20s./acre
Meadow	5s./acre
Land fenced but "not broke up"	2s./acre

One can only be sure of the value of Noyes's former property in Weyhill, but this value will serve as a representative example. Tilled land in one of Noyes's open fields was worth £6/10 an acre, while land of a similar nature in

Sudbury was worth one sixth this amount. Acre by acre, the value of meadow in Sudbury was low, even compared with that in neighboring towns. Watertown, in 1642, valued its meadow at £1/acre, four times as valuable as that in Sudbury.[35]

Of course Noyes gained in amount of land. In both Penton and Andover he had a total of 116 acres, which can be estimated as worth £696, according to the recorded value of open-field land in Weyhill, and for which he paid an annual rent of £31/09/04, plus feudal fees. In Sudbury, in 1647, he owned 48 acres of meadow, 73 acres of upland, and perhaps 80 acres in the general fields. It is not possible to estimate what his grant of 111 acres in Watertown was worth, but the value of his Sudbury land was about £104.[36] It can be readily understood, therefore, why Peter Noyes held on to his land outside Andover, Hants, and bequeathed it to his three sons, Thomas, Peter, and Joseph. It was his most valuable property.

It would appear, then, that in shifting from land in England to land in Sudbury, Massachusetts, a substantial English landholder, while he might gain in acreage, did not gain in value of property. Furthermore, it is also apparent that he paid a higher tax rate in his new town, despite the fact that he owned his land and had no feudal fees.

The Sudbury clerk recorded the amounts of each tax voted by the town. In 1647, this tax amounted to £70 and was probably assessed on both upland and meadow. At that time 1440 acres of meadow had been granted in Sudbury to its citizens, 1500 acres of upland, and about 570 acres in the general fields. Without attempting to differentiate between a tax on these three types of land, one can estimate that the tax rate was 10½ pence per acre. This was substantially larger than the parish rates which either Darvell or Rice had been paying in Berkhamsted, Herts.

Darvell had paid from 2d./acre to 4d./acre on his arable, and from 6d./acre to 12d./acre on his meadow. Only in the drought year of 1630 had he been assessed at 5s./acre, probably the highest rate any one of the parishioners paid during his lifetime in Berkhamsted. His normal tax, then, had been about 4s./9d., total, on his 22 acres, and his largest tax in 1630, £4/15.[37]

In Sudbury, however, using the 1647 estimated rate, he was assessed at twice his average rate in Berkhamsted, paying an estimated 41s. on his meadow and upland, alone, and perhaps 17s. more on his share of strips in the general fields, or about 58s. He had received a grant of land three times the size of his English holdings, but he was paying a town tax which was about ten times higher than his previous parish rate.[38]

Sudbury's tax for the first decades was paid partly in commodities, "in wheat, peas, butter, cheese, pork, beef, hemp or flax."[39] An estimate of how much of his crop of wheat Darvell had to pay in 1647 can be made. His 20 acres of arable in the general fields, sown with wheat, would have yielded at that time at an average of 15 bushels/acre, a total of 300 bushels of wheat. The current "country price" in Sudbury was 5s./bushel for wheat, 4s./bushel for rye, and 3s./bushel for Indian corn.[40] At these figures, Darvell's town tax was 11.6 bushels, or 1/26 of an estimated yearly yield. It could be argued, on the basis of this computation, that Darvell did not have to continue to pay both a tithe and a parish rate on his land and crops and, therefore, that his total yearly local taxes were less in Sudbury than in Berkhamsted.

Another and more comprehensive comparison can be made for Nicholas Danforth, who gained farm land just below Sudbury's southern border and whose English property and expenses are known. In Framlingham his total land taxes and rents would have been a summation of rent, tithe, parish rate, and, starting in 1635, King Charles's ship-money tax. His tithe and rent in 1632 was £1/15. The largest rate his parish levied came during the drought year of 1630. On the basis of Edward Alpe's payment, which was forced by court decrees and may have included court fines, Danforth's tax on his 70 acres of arable and pasture could have been no larger than £21. His ship-money tax was probably 7s., the tax levied on the man who bought his Framlingham property.[41] The totals of all yearly rents, tithes, and taxes, then, could have been no larger than £23/10/00.

Had Danforth received land within Sudbury's borders in the same proportionate increase that Darvell had enjoyed, he would have owned 250 acres of meadow, upland, and plowland, which would have meant, in 1647, a tax of £11. His town tax in Sudbury would have been substantially less than the highest possible payments in Framlingham, but, of course, he would have had to pay a Sudbury tax each year, with progressively increasing assessments.

The Sudbury 1647 tax was but an average one in the period 1640–1656. Taking the combined tax rates, as voted to cover the various town expenses year by year, one can construct a graph of Sudbury's taxes, showing a steady climb from 1640 to 1652, at which date the second meetinghouse was built. (See Figure 15.)

The townsmen used their tax income for the same variety of purposes that parish churchwardens in England did, although Sudbury's problems were unique. The townsmen had to build a community and had little patience with those inhabitants who would not contribute or who were poor.

The one consistent expense which the town was forced to meet was the construction and maintenance of the bridge over the Sudbury River. The seasonal flood of the "great river," combined with the treks of the town herds to western pasture, continually "decayed" even the stout oaken timbers of the first bridge. The town in the first two decades spent far more on bridge repair than on building meetinghouses. Perhaps because Sudbury farmers took in cattle from other towns to put out to pasture, the selectmen asked the Middlesex County Court for financial assistance for their bridge repairs.[42]

Within the first year after the original bridge had been constructed, Sudbury ordered Hugh Griffin to "get sleepers and lay them" and to pin on planks with wooden pins. Within five years the town paid Griffin for more repairs, more pine timbers, and more planks. Two years later, the bridge was defective again. Rails, planks, "buttingends" — all were needed.[43] But the town decided that Griffin was a better clerk than a carpenter. In half a year, they contracted with John Rutter and William Kerley and drew up such a detailed contract for repairs that it has been possible to reconstruct a picture of the whole bridge[44] (Figure 16).

Highway construction and military expenses were much heavier in Sudbury than in former English parishes. Surveyors were repeatedly ordered to call out men to work on the roads, which were to be from thirty-three feet to ninety-three feet wide, and a large tax of £17/10 was voted in 1655 for road work.[45] As a frontier defense post, Sudbury bought powder, bullets, a drum, a halberd, and a "flight of colors" for its trained band of militia.[46]

The townsmen ignored the provisions of the English Poor Law until 1655 and did not even appoint overseers of the poor to be sure that the sick and lame were relieved.[47] Education suffered as well, despite the insistence of the General Court that every town have some schooling. There were no master and free scholars in early Sudbury, as in old Berkhamsted and Sudbury, Suffolk. Instead, Parmenter and three other men in 1655 were appointed to "see into the several families in town to see whose children and servants are employed in work and whether in the ways of God and in the grounds of religion," according to the order of the General Court.[48] The town had to wait until 1692 before they had the money, or the concern, to appoint a "Writing school master, to teach the children to write and to cast accounts."[49]

The clerk recorded neither tax assessments, nor income, nor expenditures in the Town Book, but he kept a record somewhere, which has not been preserved.[50] In 1648, he noted in the Town Book, "Hugh Griffin gave his account, and the town was in debt 4s./4d."[51] The book is surprisingly free of indications of quarrels over taxes in the town, although in 1652 the town "appointed H. Griffin to sue J. Smith and R. Smith for that they are behind in the rate for payment of highways." Griffin by that time could take the case up to the Middlesex County Court, where he had served as clerk of the writs in 1651.[52]

By the 1650's the citizens of Sudbury had been accustomed to strong town pressure, forcing payment of yearly taxes. The selectmen did not feel that they had to obtain a warrant of power from the General Court or the county court. They had the power themselves. In 1654 the town gave it to them, legally or illegally. "It is ordered by the town that the selectmen shall give warrants to the constable to distrain any that are behind in paying any rates already levied by the town."[53] And apparently the colony supported them in their show of independent authority over their own economic and financial problems.

Church Affairs

Contemporary commentators wrote that "a majority of the Sudbury settlers" took the usual Puritan covenant, formed their church, and elected deacons and elders to assist the Reverend Edmund Brown.[54] Nonetheless, the townsmen ran almost every function that Brown, with his sexton and curate, had been accustomed to administering in his English parish within the borough of Sudbury.

No longer did Brown call vestry meetings and sign vestry orders. The town ran its own meetings, granted Brown land and meadow, and elected its own officers independently. No longer did Brown visit each farmer to collect his tithes. He probably made many family visits, but he was paid a salary from the town treasury, just as the town clerk and the constable were; and the town invoice takers gathered the tax for these salaries. Brown's new church did not even have glebe land; the only perambulation was the one around the town plot.[55] No sexton rang the bell or recorded births and deaths. A town drummer drummed for a meeting, and the town clerk was ordered to record all births, deaths, and marriages.[56]

The minister did not even sign the order describing the dimensions of his first "church" and contracting John Rutter, Noyes's man, to build it. The town agreed with Rutter on the details, the town consented to draw timber and to help "raise the house," and "two men of the town" were ordered to be sure that the cost of £6 would be paid.[57] Perhaps Brown was startled when he faced the building which he was to share with the selectmen, the men on military watch, and the town clerk. He was now going to function in a meetinghouse, practically indistinguishable from any other cottage on Mill Road, except that it lacked a chimney.

The town had decided on a framed building, thirty feet by twenty, and it knew just what it wanted. Noyes, Haines, Pendleton, Ward, How, and White were the architects. Rutter was the carpenter, instructed to "fell, saw, hew and frame a house." The town provided the labor.[58]

Noyes wanted his new church to emphasize lectures and sermons, rather than embody ritual and symbolism, to serve as a hall for meetings, not a sanctified place for popish mysteries. The interior had little or no architectural decoration which might have caught the glances of the inattentive. The windows were called "clearstory windows." They were high enough to prevent the congregation from looking outside. Nothing was to prevent the town from meeting Peter Noyes or Edmund Brown face to face. (See sketch, Figure 17.)

It is not hard to understand why, after a few years, the minister began to resent the power of the town. He had few church functions left. Even the seating arrangement in the church was taken away from him and given to the town clerk, who was authorized to sell seats, but who had to sanction all sales of seats from person to person, particularly when a family left the town.[59] The minister might consult colleagues in neighboring churches, but he could appeal to no church courts and could expect no visitations, for these had been abandoned in the Bay Colony.

According to Puritan doctrine, a magistrate or an elder appointed by the General Court performed marriages, not the minister.[60] Peter Noyes was granted his power in 1648 in addition to his many other functions.[61] As the years went on, it became obvious that Peter Noyes and his selectmen, not Edmund Brown, administered the church affairs of Sudbury.

Quarrels in the Community

The absence of records of quarrels, refusals to pay taxes, or misdemeanors in the Sudbury Town Book, when compared with the town and borough records of England or to the Watertown records during the same period, is one of the most intriguing aspects of the book. Of course, one of the foremost ideals of the New England Nonconformist movement was to produce "select societies" with a harmony radiating from a deep religious faith and from a spirit of Christian charity. We know, however, that New England towns and church meetings at times could be anything but harmonious. Militant beliefs also produced strong feelings and actions when differences suddenly appeared.

The explanation for the apparent social harmony in the early years of Sudbury is that the townsmen were doing everything possible to force group agreement by discussion. The Sudbury men had clearly abandoned their customary legal institutions for the enforcement of social order and law. The courts-baron and courts-leet were left in England, along with the out-hundred courts. No one even dared mention the hated church visitations, or the archidiaconal and bishops' courts. Moreover, neither Sudbury's constable nor any of its selectmen rode off to the quarter sessions every three months, recording their expenses or their dinners with judges. Apparently a case in the Middlesex County Court was a rare event for a Sudbury citizen, for from 1638 to 1656 only three have been found dealing with Sudbury men and their "civil differences."

The General Court had high hopes for harmony in each town and church and great faith in the wisdom of leading townsmen. For Sudbury's first decade, the Court appointed outstanding selectmen to a new type of civil court and gave them the title, "judges of small causes." Three men were appointed, almost yearly, to judge all local civil actions under £2, but they were left with wide discretion as to procedure and precedent. They had no assurance that they could continue to function as judges, which seems a radical break from the English precedent of appointing justices of the peace for lifelong terms of good behavior.

The oath for a Massachusetts judge of small causes required that he judge cases under forty shillings according to the "laws of this jurisdiction" and that he give "true judgment" without any favors or affection according to his "best light."[62] Prominent selectmen such as Peter Noyes, Edmund Goodnow, Edmund Rice, Walter Haines, and William Ward held the court from 1641 to 1648, and after 1648 Sudbury was given the power to elect its own civil judges. William Brown, Edmund Goodnow, and Edmund Rice were elected in that year; and Peter Noyes, Walter Haines, and Edmund Rice in 1654.[63]

The oath mentioned laws and asked each judge to use his "best light." But what laws? English common law? Old Testament law? Some sort of synthesis of the two, as in the *Body of Liberties?* Reports from the town deputies on the General Court debates and decisions? Certainly no judge could have referred to any volume containing the Court's "law" — none was printed until 1648. Until then, Noyes, Goodnow, Rice, and Haines had to turn to their own sources of "light."

Peter Noyes had in his library two works which he probably consulted during difficult quarrels. One was a compilation of Old Testament law by Henry

FIGURE 18

Second Sudbury Meetinghouse, 1653

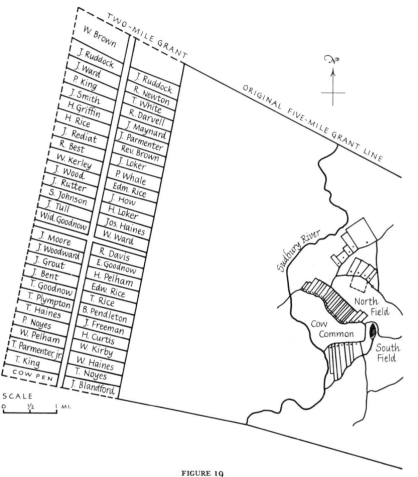

FIGURE 19

Sudbury's Two-mile Grant Lots, 1658

Ainsworth, *Annotations upon the First Book of Moses,* the title page of which read, "Moses commanded us the law, the inheritance of the Church of Jacob. Remember the law, with the statutes and judgments."[64] The second book was "Mr. Perkins's works," the many "fixed principles," gathered and explained by Cambridge University's famous William Perkins, a favorite writer among Nonconformists.[65]

Nonconformists had often been advised to use "God's law" in this formative period. Samuel Ward, for instance, had preached to justices sitting at the assizes in Bury St. Edmunds, Suffolk, that magistrates should "heed the 'Holy Writ' for the venerable antiquity of it . . . in which respect it must needs be of sovereign use for discovering and reforming of whatsoever error time has soiled governments withall."[66]

If Noyes, meditating on a case in Sudbury, had dipped into Ainsworth, he could have found many scholarly comments on Leviticus and on Deuteronomy. But Perkins would have been more immediately useful. Volume One outlined all the basic principles of Christian religion, gathered into "a Golden Chain." Volume Two presented "the whole treatise on cases of conscience" in easy question and answer form. "Justice" was clearly defined — there were two sorts, public and private. Public justice was that "given and administered by a public person in a public place, such as the judgment of a Magistrate."

Perkins had explicit rules for magistrate Noyes. He had to examine the men before him and judge three things: "Men's facts, men's doctrines, and men's persons." He was to attempt to answer three questions in judging a case: "Do we know any good thing of that man? Do we know any evil thing of that man? Are we truly informed?" And above all, "Love and charity must direct your speech and judgment."[67] Noyes may well have tried to follow such principles in settling differences between his townsmen. But the vital question remains: did all the townsmen know and accept such principles of law? In other words, did the "law" as interpreted by Sudbury's judges of small causes coincide with "the law" as understood by the inhabitants, with their wide variety of English background?

The Sudbury judges have left only one case. In this the following actions seem to have occurred: Thomas White, a Sudbury farmer, had failed to make up part of the fence around the general field in which he, John Ruddock, and others had planted crops; Ruddock's hogs had gotten through the "defective" part of the fence and rooted up certain crops of another farmer, John Rediat; Ruddock, as the elected fence viewer, and acting according to the custom of open-field farming, had attempted to make White pay for the damages caused by his negligence, and White had refused. Accordingly, Ruddock had presented his charges against White.

Judges Haines and Ward ordered the following written in the Town Book: "It is agreed between W. Haines and W. Ward, by way of arbitration between Thomas White and John Ruddock that: whereas Thomas White had been defective in the field wherein John Ruddock dwelled, and is appointed surveyor, the inhabitants shall pay the damage which John Ruddock's hogs did in the corn of John Rediat, be it four bushels of corn, more or less, and pay one bushel of corn to the said John Ruddock for his trouble, and damage, and the said John Ruddock shall get part of the forfeit."[68]

The case raises several interesting points. It was not Rediat, whose crops had been damaged, but Ruddock, the fence viewer, who pressed charges against White. Ruddock, whose hogs had committed the trespass in the first place, was bringing suit, as a town officer, against the farmer who had failed to live up to his duties. It is not apparent whether this was a civil or a criminal case, or whether the judges of small causes made such a distinction. It is also not clear what White objected to. Perhaps he felt that Ruddock should have been responsible for his own hogs. Or perhaps he questioned Ruddock's police powers.

White had come from Wiltshire, as had Ruddock, and therefore must have experienced manorial justice in regard to open-field farming practices. Perhaps this is why the farmers of the general field concerned shared a type of group obligation toward local justice and together contributed, or were ordered to contribute, grain to pay Rediat "for the damage." They were to pay in kind, just as Rediat had been damaged, in kind. But how curious that they were ordered to pay Ruddock one bushel "for his own trouble and damage," when it had been Ruddock's hogs which had rooted up the crops. Perhaps the judges were supporting Ruddock's authority to be a local police officer and making the inhabitants recognize this. Without much question, the Sudbury townsmen were experimenting in government and in law, imposing a type of local justice by mutual agreement of all concerned.

Noyes, Haines, Ward, and the other judges of small causes were apparently able to force, by group pressures, agreements on petty "differences" in Sudbury for a decade. But, as will be seen, when a major problem arose involving the fundamental policies of the new town, both the wisdom and the new institutions of Sudbury's citizens were hopelessly inadequate to handle the frustration and the hostility engendered.

Relations with Neighboring Towns

The relations between Sudbury and its three neighboring towns, Water-town, Concord, and Nashua were co-operative for the most part during the period 1638–1656. When quarrels did arise, Sudbury tried to settle them as it resolved differences within the town, through arbitration and discussion.

The first controversy occurred in 1647 when Pendleton, who had returned to Watertown, sent down a "warrant of complaint," and threatened to sue the town. William Pelham and Edmund Goodnow were instructed to answer in behalf of Sudbury, but to attempt to avoid a legal suit by "pressing a re-form" on Pendleton. Since the Middlesex County Court shows no record of this case, the three men must have come to an amicable agreement.[69]

But the townsmen of Sudbury were periodically alarmed by the growth of Watertown and occasionally by that of Concord. After boundary lines had been staked out on the north and east, Sudbury improved the road to Water-town but appointed representatives "to prevent Watertown's coming so near."[70] A special tax was levied, "for the stopping of Watertown's proceed-ings in coming too near our bounds," and men were appointed to consider the possibility of getting more town land, should the encroachments of the more populous town be impossible to prevent.[71] When a townsman of Concord seemed to be trespassing on Sudbury's woods by "burning up our pine for making tar," William Ward and John Maynard were instructed to sue the trespasser "in behalf of the town" only if they could come to no agreement.[72]

If there seemed to be major quarrels, the selectmen of Sudbury were ready to proceed to the courts in a manner quite similar to that employed by parish churchwardens of two disputing towns in England, who always referred such troubles to a nearby justice of the peace. The court to which the Sudbury men turned, that of Middlesex County, either was inactive during Sudbury's first ten years, or its papers have been lost for this period. Although by English law and by growing New England custom, each town was expected to elect one man yearly to serve on the jury of the county court, the Sudbury Town Book never mentions its choices.

As far as one can tell, Sudbury did not receive an actual warrant from the court to send men to serve on the grand jury and on the trial jury until March, 1652. The Sudbury constable was ordered to "call the Freemen to choose one fit and able man" to serve on each jury for the April court, and Edmund Goodnow and Henry Rice were chosen.[73] This is the only record that the Sud-bury freemen elected anyone during these years. The town preferred the status of "free townsman" and after the first years dropped the term "free-man" from the Town Book entirely.

Goodnow and Rice appeared before the court to find that their town had been "presented for having a defective bridge between Sudbury and Concord," but there is no record of action taken or fines levied. Not many Sudbury men appeared in the county court, although Robert Darvell was called as a witness in a case involving infant baptism, in which one Thomas Arnall had reportedly said, "The churches in Watertown are no churches, and no fit matter for churches."[74]

There was one long civil case to answer the complaint of Richard Barnes for a debt of £20, which involved Peter Noyes, John Bent, and others, but except for these instances, Sudbury seems to have had a very infrequent relationship with its county court. The townsmen were deciding most of their own problems, with little help or interference from the magistrates of the Middlesex court.

Relations with the Indians and with the Colony

During the entire period of Sudbury's settlement and growth, the General Court in Boston provided the guiding hand and was looked to as the official source of authority and power. The Sudbury townsmen assumed that their liberties came from a chartered government, in which their own deputy represented their wishes and in which he debated laws for the other Massachusetts towns at large.

At no time in the first forty years did the Sudbury townsmen, selectmen, or clerk ever mention in the Town Book the King, the Privy Council, the English church, Parliament, or English justices of the peace. The book reads as if these institutions simply did not exist. One can hardly believe that Peter Noyes, churchwarden at Weyhill, or Robert Darvell, chief burgess of the borough of Berkhamsted, are the same Peter Noyes and Robert Darvell who governed an English town.

The customary English political, religious, and legal vocabulary was profoundly altered in the Sudbury Town Book. Constables and churchwardens did not report to justices of the peace to obtain orders. Free burgesses did not consult justices and members of the Privy Council. Members of Parliament and knights of the shire were not elected. Sidemen did not make presentments before archdeacons and bishops. No sheriff brought royal writs or decrees. These officers had all vanished.

Instead, Sudbury marshals reported to "men granted power to order civil affairs," or, by the 1650's, selectmen. The selectmen listened to and were directed by "orders of the General Court," transmitted by the town deputy. Townsmen built a meetinghouse, hired a pastor, passed agricultural bylaws, taxed themselves, and administered their independent political activity.

Watching this profound transformation of political and religious institutions and slowly expanding "liberties" of Sudbury was the General Court in Boston. Having granted "Mr. Brown, Mr. Noyes and their petitioners" an extensive plot of land, the central government appointed a three-man committee to allot the land.[75]

The Court recognized that the group, almost from the first day of settlement, would constitute a political entity, and it allowed it to choose its own seven-man land committee, merely authorizing the choice.[76] To be sure that division of land did not absorb all their energies, the Court appointed Noyes as surveyor of arms, Pendleton as captain of the military company, and Goodnow as constable.[77]

Within the year, a deed had been drawn up with the neighboring Indians, a petition for more land had been entertained, and Sudbury's first deputy, Edmund Rice, arrived in Boston to take his oath as freeman and to sit as a member of the General Court.

From this point on, the Court, probably calling on Rice from time to time to give reports, gave less and less direction to Sudbury and began transferring powers to the citizens and to their own officers. The town, in turn, started paying its yearly colony tax and never failed to send its deputy to participate in the general government of all the towns. Edmund Rice and Walter Haines represented Sudbury most consistently, serving five years apiece, but Edmund Goodnow and Peter Noyes also came up to the yearly sessions of the legislature numerous times.

Each year the Court permitted Sudbury to take over powers of town government itself. The Court allowed the town to elect its surveyor of arms in 1641, its captain and ensign after 1645.[78] The elections of marshal, clerk, and men to "order the affairs of the town," were tacitly approved in 1643. The Court first appointed Walter Haines to be clerk of the writs, in 1641, then Hugh Griffin in 1645, then apparently approved the transfer of this power to the Sudbury selectmen.[79] The Court appointed judges of small causes from 1641 until 1648 and then allowed the town itself to elect its own judges.[80] The colony tax was finally established at a set rate in 1646, and Sudbury appointed an assessor to gather it each year.[81]

Although the Court directed few specific laws at Sudbury, the town appointed a man, in 1655, to "keep all the General Court orders relating to the Town."[82] The town, thus empowered with many responsibilities, still relied on the Court to give guidance in one of the most unnerving problems the citizens had to meet — that of relations with the Indians. They had a problem of discerning the attitudes and movements of members of an entirely different culture, a challenge few townsmen of New England had ever faced before.

While technically at peace with their Indian neighbors, the towns had to be constantly on the alert against sporadic attacks of a nature almost inconceivable to English farmers. These rural folk were accustomed to wars being fought by professional men, by gangs of unfortunates pressed in the market towns, or, as in Framlingham and Sudbury, Suffolk, by a "trained band" hired for the purpose. Even these English trained bands were accustomed to a type of war that was fought by certain rules, in which no soldier fought at night, or in the rain, and in which the commanders tried to avoid fighting during the winter or during the harvest seasons.[83]

In New England the townsmen were shocked to hear that there were no rules of warfare that they understood at first. The "tawney serpents" attacked "in a monstrous manner" at night, in the rain, during harvests, over the snow, recognizing no standards of warfare as understood by Europeans, no accepted civilities; and they seemed as ready to slit the stomach of a pregnant woman as they were to scalp any man who crossed their warpath.[84] The men of Sudbury had to steel themselves for such barbaric tactics. Their town was considered an outpost on the frontier, the front line of attack, and their selectmen turned to Boston for advice on how to proceed.

The central government was establishing rules year by year for times of crisis. There were to be military companies in each town, and all members of each company were given the unusual privilege of electing, from the colony freemen, a captain and the officers. The surveyor of arms was to see that not only each man in the company but also each man in the town had a musket and ammunition. Although the constable had authority to set and to administer the town's watch and ward, or the nightly patrol around each town, the militia captain could assume full military authority in any town in any emergency or in the event of an Indian attack. For the sake of preparedness, each town was to appoint a number of training days for its militia at various intervals, at least eight days every year, or approximately one day each month. The company was to drill during these days and to prepare itself for immediate action.[85]

Rumors of dangers from the Narragansett and Pequod country had convinced the General Court that the whole colony was imperiled and that the respective towns had to bear the major share of responsibility. Declaring that the colony was at war, the Court, in 1642, gave the military officers of each town considerable authority. They could fine men for not obeying orders; they were to instruct men how to sound a general alarm; they were to see that each town had a safe place for its powder, one barrel of which Sudbury was required to buy, and that it had a place of retreat for wives and children. Furthermore, each town was to see that each family took steps to "help raise salt peeter," for the making of explosives.[86] Sudbury, as one of the frontier towns, had grave obligations toward the whole Colony.

By 1645 Sudbury assumed direction of its own troops, and as an outpost agreed to send scouts out into the woods daily and to have thirty soldiers ready within a half hour after notice. The town elected William Pelham as captain and Edmund Goodnow as ensign, and in the next four years levied special taxes to cover the purchases of powder and ammunition.[87] Having assigned John Goodnow to beat the drum, and having purchased a halberd and a flight of colors to provide the necessary military symbols, Sudbury organized and drilled a band of soldiers and scouts, nominally under the head of the United Colonial Army, but ready to meet the enemy at the first warwhoop.

The four colonies of Massachusetts Bay, Plymouth, Connecticut, and New Haven, with the continuous threat of an Indian uprising or conflict with the Dutch hanging over them like a black cloud, in 1643 had formed the United Colonies of New England. The General Court accordingly had appointed a War Council for Massachusetts, with a hierarchy of officers under a Sergeant Major General.[88]

For better governmental and military administration, four shires had been created in Massachusetts, and the town militias had been organized into shire companies, with an elected shire military officer over them. Extensive military regulations were laid down, but the burden of responsibility lay squarely on a citizen army, armed and maintained by each town, and principally commanded by the various town officers.

Sudbury was ready, therefore, by the 1650's to fight for the liberties which it had been granted, and for the institutions which its townsmen had evolved. But the crisis which the town had to face was not a military one. It lay deep within its own heart.

CHAPTER VIII

"We Shall Be Judged by Men of Our Own Choosing"

EDMUND BROWN had made many sacrifices to come to the Musketaquid valley as pastor of Sudbury's first church. A scholar, a gentleman, a man of wealth, he was also a man of deep religious faith. Perhaps he did not expect to accomplish a great deal with his first small congregation in the wilderness. But he did demand respect. There were attitudes and actions which he was not willing to suffer.

Perhaps his age was his downfall. He arrived in Sudbury aged thirty-two, thirteen years younger than Peter Noyes and some years younger than Edmund Rice. And yet he had had considerable experience, for he had trained at Cambridge and had served in a church in the old borough of Sudbury for fourteen years.[1] Furthermore, the towns in New England were full of men he had known at the University — Shepard and Mellowes and Allen in nearby Cambridge and Charlestown, Perkins in Roxbury, Miller in Rowley, Denison and Knight down in Ipswich, Hobart in Hingham. There were Cambridge men in almost every New England town to give him advice and comfort as he formed his new church.[2]

During his years in New England, Brown had enlarged both his property and his church relationships. He had been granted 140 acres of upland and meadow in Watertown, worth £20. His house in Sudbury had not only a kitchen and a parlor on the first floor, but a study as well, stocked with over one hundred books, folios of music, and his bass viol. His barn had grain and hay in the loft, and below oxen, cows and calves, sheep, pigs, two mares, and a colt. One servant, one maid, and a wife completed the minister's household.

When he wished to let pride get the better of him, he could throw his "plush saddle" on the mare and ride off to consult with his colleagues of the cloth.[3] There was much to discuss. In 1646, a synod had been called to face the threat of Samuel Gorton, who challenged the whole jurisdiction and authority of the Massachusetts government and who was determined to take the case to Parliament.[4]

The rise of Presbyterianism in England had been the cause of the second synod, the famous one of 1648 at Cambridge, where many ministers had suddenly realized that perhaps they were the only refuge of a Congregational polity. In meeting after meeting, discussion after discussion, Edmund Brown helped form a whole statement of church discipline, a confession of faith, and a unified polity for all New England churches. The "Cambridge Platform" was then sent to the General Court, to be adopted by the civil government.[5]

But Edmund Brown's work was opposed in his own town. Sudbury's deputy to the General Court, Walter Haines, voted staunchly against sanction of any church discipline that might threaten the independence of his own church body.[6] Trouble was brewing in Sudbury. Perhaps Brown did not really know his townsmen.

Brown's sermons for this period have been lost. But there is a letter from Peter Bulkley, the pastor in Concord in 1650. Bulkley was also suffering indignities: "Shall I tell you what I think to be the ground of all this insolency, which discovers itself in the speech of men? Truly, I cannot ascribe it so much to any outward thing, as to the putting of too much liberty and power into the hands of the multitude, which they are too weak to manage, many growing conceited, proud, self-sufficient, as wanting nothing. And I am persuaded except there be some means used to change the course of things in this point, our churches will grow more corrupt day by day, and tumult will arise, hardly to be stilled."[7]

There was arrogance in Brown's own town, and there was tumult in his own heart. The selectmen were gaining too much power. He was not the only man in Sudbury annoyed with the selectmen. There was another, a man who had become a leader of the youth of the town, where Brown had failed. This was John Ruddock, a man with a fierce pride and a sharp tongue. He was prepared to battle for his point of view, whether against selectmen or against the pastor. He had learned the politics of a New England town. He knew how to speak boldly to a town meeting, and he knew the power of the vote. Moreover, he was determined to have his way, despite Noyes, despite Brown, and despite tradition. He knew that he had the hot-blooded youth of Sudbury behind him.

Peter Bulkley might well have been thinking of the town just to the south when he had written of "the putting of too much liberty and power into the hands of the multitude." The power was land. The liberty was "Liberty 12," the right of every man to come to a town meeting and to "move any seasonable question or to present any necessary motion or complaint."

Both Ruddock and Brown became angered at Sudbury's policy toward the land. Both took advantage of Liberty 12. In short, they turned into rival politicians, to the amazement and the despair of their friends in both church and town.

"Joint consent" of the town had slowly become joint discontent. As in so many towns at the time, it was the product of two important factors, growth of population and the availability of land not being used. In 1649, the inhabitants of Sudbury, casting envious glances at land to the west, had petitioned the General Court for an additional strip of land on their western boundary, two miles in width, containing 6400 acres.

The deputy to the General Court, Edmund Goodnow, wheedled the grant from the government and presented the gift to the selectmen of Sudbury in the summer of 1649.[8] The selectmen, Peter Noyes, Edmund Rice, Walter Haines, Edmund Goodnow, Thomas Noyes, John Moore, and John Grout, aware of the growth of their families, well realized that there were at least twenty-six sons who had grown to manhood and yet had been granted no meadow strips and, with the exception of four of them, no land whatsoever. They knew that there were, in addition, at least eighteen men who were not on the original meadow-grant list, some of whom had bought land in the town and all of whom could attend town meetings. On the other hand, they well knew that Sudbury had then at least six open fields, demanding the strength and co-operation of all the young men of the town.[9]

Undoubtedly, they wanted to continue to use open-field farming and feared lest the young, vigorous men go off to farms of their own. But they postponed the apportionment of land in the new grant. Edmund Rice knew that they had avoided an issue. He had five sons who had been granted no meadow, and he had been buying plots of land every year to provide for them. Ruddock knew. And Edmund Brown realized the situation. Brown had 74 acres of Sudbury meadow, 12 acres more than Peter Noyes. In fact, he was the largest meadow-holder in the town.[10]

Brown had more meadow than he could use. He granted twenty-five acres of it to Thomas Walgrave, Esq.; and the town approved.[11] Perhaps he did not realize how dangerous this grant was to become. In making a meadow grant to Mr. Walgrave, father-in-law of Herbert Pelham, and an original investor in the Bay Company, he was giving rights to a nonresident.[12] Neither he, nor the town, realized that the title to this land was so vague as to permit grave misunderstanding. No one had made explicit the vital question: could the landholders vote in a Sudbury town meeting, or merely the men who held meadow rights?

The whole land policy of the town was thrown open to discussion. At a town meeting called in October, 1651, someone proposed a radical change: "When the two miles shall be laid out, that every man shall enjoy a like quantity of land."[13] When the men voted, the selectmen were amazed by the show of hands. Whether Ruddock maneuvered this meeting, and this vote, no one can be sure. But it is obvious that he was determined to gain land for the young men of Sudbury. Some of the selectmen were equally determined that the elders should have their way.

The phrase "every man" was too egalitarian. For what had the fathers given up their good English property and risked everything to begin a new settlement? To become one of a mob of men with mere "carnal desires" for land? Certainly not. Age and rank had to command respect. The status of a Sudbury townsman had already been clearly defined. A man was a free townsman if he had been granted a strip of meadow, or bought these rights in buying such meadow. Otherwise, he had no rights to future land grants.

The townsmen were beginning to divide on two issues. The clerk could no longer write "by joint consent," indicating a uniform agreement among all the citizens. Town meetings were becoming exciting and well-attended, so much so that the new citizens demanded a meetinghouse in which all of them could discuss town issues, in which the church members could "come to the Lord's supper," in which they could hear their leaders speak. For three years they debated whether they should enlarge the old meetinghouse by building "ten foot on the south side, all the length of the meeting house," or not. Many in the town wanted the meetinghouse to be a dignified structure. They wanted it "mended and made handsome." They wanted "two gable ends in the front." But they knew it would be costly.[14]

The pastor was consulted. He agreed to contribute twenty shillings toward the work, little enough, considering his wealth. A large group wanted no "enlargements," no mere mending of an outmoded structure. They wanted an

entirely new building. Consequently, they called a town meeting in the fall
of 1651, packed the meeting, and demanded a count of hands. The clerk dutifully obeyed: "25 voted for the building, 14 on the contrary wise."[15]

These figures are a clear indication that at least half the townsmen went
to important town meetings and stood up to be counted. Thirty-nine votes
represented 83 per cent of the original number of meadow grantees, and
about 45 per cent of the total adult males in Sudbury at the time. The anti-
building faction went out to look for these.

Two months later this faction called another town meeting and obtained
their majority. With glee, they told the clerk to write, "The town in a public
town meeting did repeal the orders formerly made for the enlargement of the
old meeting house, and for a new meeting house, to be of no good." They had
another solution, much less expensive. They ordered Edmund Rice and John
Ruddock to go to find the pastor and to obtain his permission to "build gal-
leries in the old meeting house."[16]

For a while the conservatives were triumphant. They would shove the
youngsters up under the thatch and avoid unnecessary expense. Furthermore,
they would somehow make the meetinghouse "for a watch house," just in case
the Indians did emerge unexpectedly from the woods.[17]

The expansionists, however, became politicians. They presented arguments and new designs. Just open up the new land to the west, start farming
in the East Anglian competitive way, and each citizen would have money to
pay for a really dignified building. These liberals did their work well. By December, 1652, they had convinced a majority of their fellow townsmen. They
had an architectural design, and they knew where to get the money. They
filled the town meeting, presented the description of the building, and led
their citizens to vote a tax of £85, the largest single tax that had ever been
voted in Sudbury.[18]

If Edmund Brown read the contract, his blood must have boiled. Not only
were the townsmen going to build another meetinghouse, but he was going to
be forced to contribute. The town had voted that the contracting workmen
"could have the meadow and upland for a minister, to gather hay thereupon
this year."[19] For Brown, this was outrageous. Had he been granted this
meadow and upland free and clear by the town, or had he not? This led to a
more fundamental question: what was the town's land policy? No one seemed
to know. But tempers were rising. To make matters worse, workmen were constructing the new meetinghouse and using the pastor's land at the express

command of the town. The building (Figure 18) was raised in 1653, and at least two political factions were ready and waiting to crowd into it.[20]

In January, 1654, the selectmen of Sudbury called to order a noisy group of townsmen, "to take some course for dividing of the land, that was last granted by the Court to the town." The meeting was a heated one. In the clerk's terse words, there was "much agitation." And why not? The entire social, political, and economic philosophy of Sudbury was at stake.

The conservatives had drawn up a careful proposal, designed to satisfy everyone, but one which maintained the basic concept of rank and proportion. The original meadow-list ranking was to be abandoned. The men who had prospered in the town were to be rewarded. The men who had produced large families were to get their share. But there was to be no monstrous "democratical" contempt for an aristocracy of the productive leaders of the town. The conservative proposal embraced five clear definitions of policy: (1) The land granted to the town by the General Court was to be divided to the inhabitants; (2) The division was to be based on an assessment of estates and families; (3) A family was to be defined as husband, wife, children, and such servants as had been "either bought or brought up"; (4) The value of a man was to be considered £40, that of every wife, child, and servant, £10 each; (5) The town was to give their consent by "lifting up their hands."

After the proposals were thoroughly discussed, the selectmen called for a vote, and the clerk counted the raised hands. The proposal was soundly defeated. But this was not all. Two young men and one emigrant from the borough of old Sudbury itself demanded to be heard and to be recorded: "Walter King, Obadiah Ward and John Smith did dissent."[21]

It is not known what these three men objected to, or what they proposed as an alternative. Yet they demanded their right to dissent, and this was accorded them. Their independent thought was respected and put into the Town Book. The eldest was not penalized, although the younger two had to wait their turn for land. In time, Smith was given a lot in the Sudbury land granted by the General Court.[22]

The liberals forced another town meeting on the following day. They packed it well. The conservatives, probably sick at heart, must have stayed away. Twenty men stood up and demanded a clear, simple proposal for dividing the new land: "to every man an equal portion in quantity." Three men voted for the conservative proposal, as outlined the previous day.

But there were still dissenters. Six men demanded to be counted and their scheme recorded. John Parmenter, Sr., John Parmenter, Jr., John Bent, John Haines, Robert Darvell, and Herbert Pelham's "agent" made proposals "which were neither of the former ways." The clerk, however, neglected to give details.[23]

Although the issue was decided once and for all, the selectmen refused to follow the town vote and actually stake out the lots. They had their own scheme for maintaining some sense of dignity and rank, and for keeping the traditional open-field system. They would interpret the phrase "every man" in their own conservative way. They would show the ordinary townsman that they would not bow to the crude desires of the multitude.

The selectmen controlled the town land within the old plot, and they intended to maintain control. Edmund Goodnow wanted to use the hay on the plot of river meadow near his house, "formerly reserved for the minister." The selectmen agreed to his request and in June, 1655, rented it to him for five shillings.[24]

They did not intend, necessarily, to slight their pastor. But they would take care of him in their own way. Perhaps as compensation for the meadow and upland which they had snatched away from him, they raised his salary to £60 per year at the same meeting at which they voted the deputy to the General Court, then Edmund Rice, six pounds in wheat for his "services done at the Court."[25]

Only in the following January did Edmund Brown realize the full meaning of the selectmen's power. Undoubtedly angered that their conservative proposal had been beaten in an open town meeting, the selectmen met by themselves to establish their authoritative control over the undivided town commons. If the ordinary townsmen were going to move out to the "new grants" and raise crops there, let them. But the selectmen were determined to impose respect for the efforts of the first settlers. There was still the original meadow-grant list, a clear indication of the social and economic status of each original founder of the town.

The selectmen well understood the gravity of moving against the will of the majority. But Peter Noyes, his eldest son Thomas, Edmund Goodnow, and Walter Haines were proud and resourceful men. They called a special "solemn selectmen's meeting," in January, 1655–1656, to debate a new question — was the town herd of cattle too large for the Sudbury commons?

Noyes reminded his council of their previous order, made in 1643, which all but two of them had signed, stating that "all the common lands" would eventually be "sized," or limited as to the number of cattle which could be placed upon them.[26] He felt that the commons should be "sized speedily" and asked for a vote of confidence that this was a "righteous act." Five selectmen voted with Noyes. But John Ruddock and William Ward "voted the contrary," demanding the privilege of reversing their decision of November, 1643.

The majority group of selectmen then proceeded to draw up a motion to present to the town meeting. It contained five principles: (1) The act of the selectmen, to "size all the common lands," was a righteous act; (2) All inhabitants of the town would be limited in the number of animals which they could place on the town commons according to the number of acres of river meadow granted in the first, second, or third divisions of meadow, or granted "for some services done by them"; (3) The proportion would be: for every 2 acres of meadow — one beast; (4) A cow, a bull, a steer, or heifer above a year old, a horse or a mare above a year old — each was to be considered 1½ beasts; (5) Every five sheep were to be considered "one beast," but all cattle under a year old were to be allowed on the commons, "without sizing until further reason doth appear for sizing them." After hearing the proposed act, Edmund Rice abstained, and "John Ruddock, being then present did, by his vote for himself and William Ward, dissent from the act."[27]

Ruddock and Ward had a definite reason for their dissent. They knew that at least thirty-two young men had been given no meadow grants whatsoever, had little chance of receiving them, and thus would be prevented from putting any animals on most of the pasture within the Sudbury town plot. They were not convinced that the large area of common pasture, amounting to approximately 8000 acres could support no more than 775 "beasts," the maximum number according to the meadow acreage already granted.

They went out of the selectmen's meeting determined to fight. They were going to pack the town meeting with younger sons and vote down their own selectmen's proposal. But another townsman was equally aroused, equally prepared to play politics. Edmund Brown had had enough.

Brown had a dual problem. With part of his meadow snatched back by the selectmen, the passage of the sizing act would severely limit the number of animals he could pasture on the commons. And yet, if Ruddock had his way, the youth of the town would follow a rival leader, show contempt for age and position, and split the town in half.

The pastor acted swiftly. According to a charge made by Ruddock later on, Brown, in an open town meeting, "took up" the twenty-five acres of meadow which the town had demanded be returned to the town. Not only this, he called a private gathering in the house of one of the townsmen and outlined a plan of attack. He is supposed to have "told some there that the way to bring it about was to send men from house to house to see what they could get to be on their side." The battle was on.[28]

The entire citizenry of Sudbury was deeply involved and deeply upset. As they admitted, "the peace and comfort of our meetings both in Church and town was despoiled." But they looked to the town meeting in their distress. Somehow, they felt, the split could be healed by group discussion and a majority vote. A week after the selectmen's order, a town meeting was "warned purposely to take notice of the act of the selectmen for sizing the commons." A considerable number packed the building and voted to have the pastor "seek the Lord for his blessings in the actings of the day," and then, "the act of the selectmen was publicly read and debated."[29]

Immediately John Ruddock charged Peter Noyes with pushing through the sizing order at the selectmen's meeting and refusing to allow any substantial debate, a charge which Noyes hotly contested. After debate, John How spoke for those who had little meadow. Owning only eleven acres of meadow himself, which by the order would have allowed him to place only five and one half beasts on the commons, How said bluntly, " 'That it was oppression,' and added, 'If you oppress the poore, they will cry out; and if you persecute us in one city, wee must fly to another.' " These were solemn words. How was not only charging the elder selectmen, as well as the town, with neglect of a fair land policy, but he was threatening to lead a group out of the civil organization which, as first Sudbury marshal, he had done so much to establish.

At last the town decided to vote on the issue. To make sure that the town clerk made no error in recording the decision of the inhabitants, it was decided that "You that judge the act of the Selectmen for sizing the commons to be a righteous act discover it by drawinge yourselves together in the one end of the meeting house . . . and those who were of a contrary mind . . . draw themselves together in the other end of the meeting house."[30]

With Edmund Rice, Robert Davis, and Thomas Plympton abstaining, the first vote stood at 27 to 27. The clerk recorded the voters, name by name. The Parmenters, Noyeses, Haineses, Goodnows, together with Edmund Brown and Hugh Griffin, stood solidly for the sizing order, against the Rices, Bents, Newtons, Lokers, selectmen Ward and Ruddock, and some of the younger sons. Almost as soon as the vote had been recorded, the town realized another damaging fact: the basis for the right to vote had not been made clear, and several significant objections were immediately raised. John Parmenter, Sr.

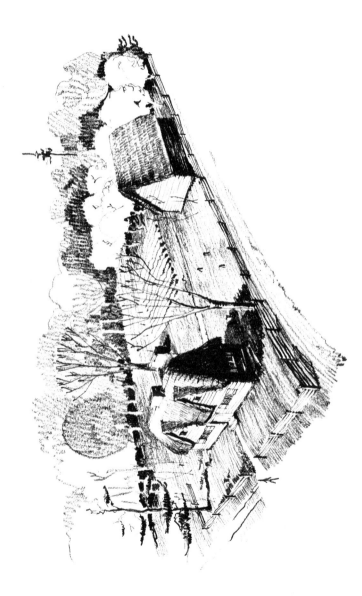

FIGURE 20

John Ruddock's House and Barn, 1661

FIGURE 21

Third Sudbury Meetinghouse, 1688

had cast votes as agent for three nonresidents, Herbert Pelham, Esq., Mr. Thomas Walgrave, and Capt. William Pelham, but his status as the legal agent for Herbert Pelham was challenged. More important, a dispute arose over the right of Pelham, a nonresident, to vote, even though he had been granted meadow.

John Ruddock was particularly angry at Edmund Brown for putting in three votes for "our Brother Whale, which was denied by our Brother Whale that he gave any order so to do." The sizing group, on the other hand, challenged the voting right of ten of the opposition, probably on the basis that none of them had been granted any meadow by the town. And yet two of the sizing party had voted without having title to meadow grants themselves.

The shaken town was too split to come to any decision about the basis for a vote in the town meeting, although the problem was crying to be solved. There were at least thirty-seven men who did not show up at the meeting, twenty of whom had been given no meadow grants, and the rest of them with an average of twelve acres apiece. Had all the men who still lacked meadow grants from the town come to oppose the order which denied them access to the town commons, the elder statesmen and their sizing party would have been completely overwhelmed.

Some of the men, probably including Ruddock, went to the pastor, "to desire him not to meddle about the sizing of the commons." Somehow, they had assumed that because he was a professed man of God, he did not have a stake in this political and economic crisis. Brown, however, well understood his position. Suspecting that the basic loyalty of the townsmen was really to their secular, civil affairs, he had decided to enter the political struggle like any other good citizen, using what influence he could to gain votes. His visitors, the opposition party, gave these reasons why they did not want him to "meddle": "1st: that it would be a dishonor to God; 2nd, a prejudice to his ministry; 3rd, a scandall to his name; 4th, also a hindrance of the conversion and building up of souls."

Brown realized that he was at the mercy of town opinion, and he made it quite clear that he was dissatisfied with the position which the town had forced him into: "Our pastor's answer was that if it did blunt his ministry, he should then see his call clear to England, for he had waited for it for a great while."

Although the visitors were startled by Brown's frankness, they were still not willing to countenance his position as a town political leader. They left his house with more of a threat than with a complete understanding. "Our brethren answered him that the saving of one soul to Christ was worth more than all the commons in the world; but further our brethren pressed our Pastor not to meddle with sizing the commons."

It did not take the younger generation, now the opposition party, many months to realize their political strength, despite the split vote and the dispute over the basis for voting. In March, 1655/6, Peter Noyes, Walter Haines, and Edmund Goodnow were all swept out of public office. Parmenter was the only conservative elected as a selectman, and the anti-sizing party elected six out of the seven selectmen, including John Ruddock and William Ward. Even faithful Hugh Griffin, town clerk consistently since 1643, was replaced by John Stone.

Edmund Brown recognized the challenge and rose to meet it. He moved carefully but firmly. First, he asked the selectmen to call some meetings, "to see to the constraining of youth from the profanation of the Lord's day in time of public service."[31] Having then attained his role of moral guide to the youth, he turned the meetings to other purposes. In fact, "the thing was neglected, and the stinting of commons set on foot and strongly presented, and prosecuted with violence."

Furthermore, he turned to outside assistance. A petition to the General Court was drawn up to help "settle the differences among them," for the townsmen were still arguing not only the sizing issue, but also the question of how to divide the two-mile grant of land on the west. Although the General Court appointed a committee of three neighboring citizens to look into the matter, many Sudbury inhabitants greatly resented what they considered unwarranted interference.[32]

After about ten months in office, the new selectmen felt that they had enough of the townsmen behind them to take some drastic steps. Five of the selectmen, excluding John Parmenter, Sr., who had originally voted for the limitation of the commons, deliberately crossed out the order of January, 1655/6, calling for "sizing the commons" and then moved to allot the two-mile grants in equal lots.

Although these selectmen were not yet ready to decide on the actual list of grantees, they were willing for the town to vote on the structure of the new allotments. The inhabitants, after having continued the traditional system of open-field agricultural management for fifteen years, contemplated a radical shift of land management and community structure.

They decided that the two-mile strip was to be divided into four rectangular but somewhat equal "squadrons," looking very much like a modern suburban lot division, with two extremely wide roads, thirty rods in width, running north and south, east and west, through the center of the grant. (See map, Figure 19.) Each of the lots "shall be layd out meddow and upland together all in one lump," indicating that despite the unsuitability of the actual land in the grant, the townsmen were thinking in terms of individual farm management. Whether they were planning to build houses in their new suburb cannot be determined from the records. As a matter of fact, not many families did want to move away from their own town center, and few houses were constructed in the new area. But, in theory at any rate, the inhabitants were abandoning their original closely knit land policy for one of individual competition, and, except for the insistence on equal lots, were repeating a type of four-squadron layout, which Watertown had first used in the northwestern area of its town section in its early years.

The possibility of using the new lots for individual farms and therefore individual animal pasturage, as well as for selective breeding, did not make the sizing party of Sudbury any less furious than that their specific order had been crossed through with a large, inked "X" in the Town Book. The Reverend Edmund Brown was said to have threatened to "sue the Select men," and took every occasion he could to speak publicly to force the issue to a final decision.

He waged his battle both as a citizen and as a member of the group of Puritan ministers. When some of the Sudbury brethren persisted in asking him to keep silent, "he promised that he would never appear in a towne meeting agayne about it; yet notwithstanding he did afterward appear and prosecuted it with great violence. For upon a time in a town meeting, he stood up and sayd, 'Put it to Vote, before I would be nosed by them; if we do not carry it, let them laugh at us when we have done.' "

Brown's determined political leadership not only angered John Ruddock and Walter Haines, but also had great effect on church attendance, to say nothing of the spirit of loyalty and reverence toward the religious institution of the town. Ruddock was blunt in his feelings toward Brown and spoke up in a town meeting to say, "Setting aside your office, I regard you no more than another man."

Others in the town began feeling the same way and carried their hostility to the point of refusing to come to the Sabbath lectures and services. Their defense of this defection was piquantly accurate, "Whereas we are charged with Sin in not coming to Meetings, our answer is, we came not, for fear of being ensnared by *them*." Mr. Brown recognized that he was in the midst of a serious crisis and decided that it was necessary to obtain help from neighboring ministers: "Our Pastor upon a Lord's day, made proposition to the church to put our differences to a Counsel of Elders; we answered that of our selves, we could not do it, because the town, as it was a civil difference, were engaged in it, and they would not consent to it. Our Pastor answered that if the church would consent to it, he did not care for the town; which thing was taken very offensive."

The implication is clear. The economic spirit of self-interest, which both Peter Bulkley in Concord and John Cotton in Boston, among others, had feared most, was rapidly spreading in Sudbury. Management and control of land, with consequent administration of town affairs, had become the interests and activities which commanded the most intense loyalty among the majority of the Sudbury inhabitants, and the minister had been bitten by the same desires. When some of the town actually challenged his position on the political issue of stinting the commons, pointing that to order a limit on the number of cattle "would breake the peace of the town," Brown answered, "You keep my goods, and then you say you will be at peace, if I will let you alone."

Naturally, certain townsmen, recognizing Brown's secular interests, were upset that he was not only becoming a dominant town politician but that he was also trying to use the church politically to protect his property. It is not surprising that when some of his more devoted and loyal followers came to him and "told him he was the Pastor, and sheppard of our soules and had the charge of them, he answered that he knew not whether he were our sheppard or not."

The metaphor, whether Brown knew it or not, was double-edged. Brown felt that he no longer had the complete loyalty of the townsmen; men like Ruddock pointed out, however, that by caring more about his goods than about people's souls, he had abandoned his traditional role of shepherd. In fact, it was very evident that many of the townsmen had far outgrown the position of dependent sheep and had become mature, perceptive individuals. They were angry that their pastor "did not care for the towne," and they were raising a fundamental and most necessary question when they asked him on what grounds he recommended calling a committee of "Reverend Elders" to investigate the dispute. Many of them felt that since it was an issue of contention having wholly to do with the inhabitants of Sudbury, their vote in the town meeting was adequate to resolve the disharmony. But they could not prevent a visit by an investigating committee.

The committee appointed by the General Court held a number of meetings in Parmenter's tavern, calling in witnesses and trying to determine the facts of the case. They were convinced, somehow, that a majority of the town favored the limitation of the commons, and on the basis of this, recommended that "every allowed inhabitant" should have the right to pasture animals according to the acres of meadow he owned, or his estate, at his pleasure. They added, however, that no one should be able to vote on this issue who was either a noninhabitant or who did not own some meadow acreage.

Furthermore, they recommended that anyone who objected to the equal division of the two-mile grant should have "their interests according to their estates and persons." As a last part of their report, the committee declared that they saw no just ground for the "objection . . . and clamorous reports" against the title to lands held by Reverend Edmund Brown, or against similar title held by Hugh Griffin. This recommendation had to be presented to, and approved by, the General Court.

Meanwhile, an investigating committee of neighboring clergy, led by Cambridge's Jonathan Mitchell, wrote to the church of Sudbury. The "Reverend Elders" claimed that they were called on to make an inquiry by the Colony Council, "to procure peace and unity amongst" the members of the church of Sudbury. As friendly and interested neighboring churches, they had written "in an amicable way to advise and council them forthwith to call into their help such counsel as the rule prescribes." The church of Sudbury, however, only resented the letter and refused such help.

The elders nonetheless, "judging it to be their duty to take an effectual course for the healing of their breaches," ordered the churches in Cambridge, Watertown, and Concord to send "two messengers" each to meet at Sudbury "to endeavor to compose and settle the distractions at Sudbury . . . and it is expected and desired that the church of Sudbury and all persons concerned therein give this Council . . . the opportunity of meeting with them . . . to declare what shall concern themselves or the Council . . . [to determine] where the fault hath bin." The purpose of this was to determine "such further course . . . as may most conduce to the Glory of God and the Unity of their hearts to Unity in truth and praier, according to the rule of the Gospel."

The men of Sudbury, on the other hand, continued to maintain that this was a perfectly normal civil dispute, having nothing to do with the church. They rejected the first letter of "friendly advice" by the neighboring churches; they rejected the council's sterner admonition; they refused to set aside a day on which the Cambridge-Watertown-Concord committee should meet; in short, they tried to be as unco-operative as they possibly could be, without being actually rebellious.

As before, selectman John Ruddock was the town spokesman. In regard to the calling of the committee, he objected both to the activities of Jonathan Mitchell, minister of Cambridge, and to the recommendations of the elders. Of the latter, he said, "It was easy for them to advise, so when they were informed or told what to advise." When he was told that he would be "heard in his place," he said that "they should not, nor ever have an opportunity to speak." The most articulate statement of his whole position followed his initial objections. He said bluntly, "We shall be, or should be, judged by men of our own choosing."

Furthermore, he made good his words. Together with many of the Sudbury men, he refused to come to the meetings of the elders in Sudbury, although he had the boldness to appear briefly to tell both Brown and the elders that Sudbury would not comply with the council's advice, and that they would not testify about a quarrel which was strictly a local matter concerning the town.

Jonathan Mitchell and his committee were reduced to writing a long report on their efforts, in which they attempted to define the grounds of their authority as well as the basis for their judgment. Their authority stemmed from the fact that the council had advised them to meet, simply because both of them felt that "the rule of the Gospel," and hence the rule for Sudbury, was "unity of their hearts." They made ten specific charges, with many additional derogatory comments on the lack of co-operation they had received in Sudbury. Their charges, summarized, were primarily directed against John Ruddock, although, by their own admission, they had gained their "evidence" by hearsay and not by direct examination of the Sudbury leader:

1. Brother Ruddock's charging speech, in a town meeting, that the selectmen "would not suffer any agitation" over the sizing question.
   A BREACH OF THE 9th COMMANDMENT — "beside the evil effect it had."
2. Brother Ruddock's speech, when a Committee was recommended, "It was easy for them to advise, so when they were informed or told what to advise."
   A BREACH OF THE 9th IF NOT THE 5th COMMANDMENT
3. Ruddock's charge against Reverend Mr. Brown: that he seized the 25 acres of meadow which he was supposed to have given back to the town.
   A BREACH OF THE 9th AND 5th COMMANDMENTS
4. Brother Ruddock's words in reference to the Council, "We shall, or should be, judged by men of our own choosing."
   A BREACH OF THE 9th COMMANDMENT
5. Ruddock's words: when he was told that he would be heard in his place, "That they should not, nor ever have an opportunity to speak."
   A BREACH OF THE 9th AND 5th COMMANDMENTS

6. Ruddock's irreverent carriage toward Reverend Mr. Brown; "Setting aside your office, I regard you no more than another man."
   A BREACH OF THE 5th COMMANDMENT

7. Ruddock's words: Casting aspersion on "our military Commissioned Officers . . . irreverent speeches."
   A BREACH OF THE 9th AND 5th COMMANDMENTS

8. Ruddock's words: That it was only Mitchell's act that procured the order to investigate Sudbury.
   A BREACH OF THE 9th COMMANDMENT

9. Sudbury's refusal to join in calling in a Council of Elders.
   A SAD BREACH OF ORDER, AGAINST THE 5th COMMANDMENT

10. The crossing and defacing the stinting order in the Town Book:
    JUDGED A GREAT SIN[33]

John Ruddock took these stern rebukes without flinching — at least in public. He answered the ministers and elders with actions, not with words. He was still the leading selectman of Sudbury, and he insisted that Sudbury alone had the right to define and to solve its own civil disputes.

But the fundamental conflict had become an extremely deep one, a split in the body politic which caused hostility, not understanding; aggression, not resignation to the will of the majority. Former selectman Edmund Goodnow, out of office for the first time in his political life in Sudbury, had become so angry that he stated publicly, "Be it right or wrong, we will have [the sizing] . . . if we can have it no other way, we will have it by club law."[34]

No one traded blows, however. No one fired a shot. John Ruddock knew how to turn his dissent and that of his young men into constructive political action. With Edmund Rice as Sudbury deputy to the General Court, the plan was relatively easy. The two leaders, together with eleven other men, petitioned the government for another grant of land. They would form still another town, another religious and political institution with a different spirit.

Their claims were skillfully worded. "God hath been pleased to increase our children, which are grown to man's estates," and the fathers "should be glad to see them settled before the Lord take us away from hence." The implication, of course, was that it was impossible to settle them in Sudbury. Furthermore, "God having given us some considerable cattle so that we are so straightened that we cannot so comfortably subsist as could be desired."[35]

The voice of Moses was heard once again: "Some of us having taken some pains to view the country, we have found a place which lyeth westward" — ever the sight of New Canaan.

The General Court was sympathetic. Edmund Rice helped them to understand the new vision. As a result, Ruddock, severely censured by the ministers who could not examine him face to face, was rewarded for his defiance by the members of the legislature. Together with his petitioners, he received a large town grant "westward." Once again, the children of Israel were on the march.

But not Peter Noyes. Crushed by seeing his settlement split asunder, its spirit of love turned to hate, its dignity flouted and threatened, the old man lost all his strength. While the sound of axes rang in the forest, Peter Noyes confessed his failure and journeyed to ask God the reason thereof. When his townsmen voted him down in 1655, his spirit was too broken to rise again. Bequeathing a slight token of affection to his pastor, with perhaps an implied plea for forgiveness, Peter Noyes left his town by the river for the eternal city in his heart.[36]

CHAPTER IX

"Interest in This Town of Marlborough"

JOHN RUDDOCK was given even more liberty in forming his town than Peter Noyes had been granted. The General Court required that there be "twenty or thirty families," together with a minister, and that these families had to settle in the new grant within three years.[1] Except for the fact that a committee was appointed to stake out the new town, the rest was left to Ruddock, Rice, and their young citizens. They knew how to proceed. They had learned the necessity of order.

In September, 1656, Ruddock and Rice called a meeting of thirteen petitioners at the site of their proposed settlement to discuss citizenship and entrance requirements for the new town. After due discussion, they voted that each male petitioner who agreed to be a resident of the town within two years, and who agreed to pay town taxes based on the value of his property, would be granted a house lot and farm, all in one piece.[2]

John Ruddock, as leader of the rebel group, proposed a social system similar to the one created in Sudbury. No man would be granted property who would not be an active citizen. Each settler had to live in the town, serve in the town government, and pay taxes in proportion to the size of his grant of land.

But in the case of Ruddock's settlement, the government preceded the land distribution. At a meeting of "proprietors" in the spring of 1657, five men were elected selectmen for a year: Ruddock, Edmund Rice, William

Ward, Thomas King, and John How, Sr. Their powers were as loosely defined as ever, "to put the affairs of the said plantation in an orderly way."

Just as Noyes and Pelham had obtained a broad support in their settlement, so Ruddock, Rice, and How received a pledge of loyalty should they get into legal difficulties with outside authority. In July, 1657, they got twenty of their most substantial settlers to sign an agreement "to secure E. Rice, J. Ruddock, and J. How from any danger of damage that may come on their persons or estates. . . ."[3] This band of former Sudbury men called their new settlement "Whip Suffrage," but no one now seems to know what they implied by this name.

As in Sudbury, the settlers waited a few years before dividing the land. The title was not entirely clear, for the General Court had allowed them to place their town grant almost on top of the Indian settlement of Ockocangansett, to the northwest of Sudbury, and a detailed compromise had to be worked out with the Indians.

During their wait, Ruddock and his followers discovered the full meaning of the elder selectmen's decision to limit the Sudbury commons to holders of meadow grants. Given political power again by the General Court, the selectmen refused to destroy the social hierarchy they had so carefully constructed and preserved. Without comment, without tumultuous town meetings, they drew up a list of men who deserved additional land, "according to previous town acts." Although they were willing to bow to popular demand that the plots be equal in size, they limited the grants to 130 acres each and wrote down forty-seven names.

This new list represented an aristocracy who had shown real devotion to Sudbury and who, for the most part, had decided to live there. Men who had returned to Watertown, as Knight and Munnings had, or had left for other settlements, as Thomas Brown and Andrew Belcher had, were excluded. Other settlers, even though they had received original grants, were dropped from consideration; they had not met the tests.

On the other hand, nineteen new names were added. Some had served as town officers; some had not. But they were considered worthy. The list of forty-seven names was submitted to a public town meeting. Perhaps for political reasons, Ruddock was to be granted two farms. Respected older Sudbury men, such as Edmund Rice, William Ward, and Thomas Goodnow were not forgotten, even though they had joined Ruddock in the new venture. The selectmen had learned to be charitable — or, one could say, to face the inevitable. Fourteen men who had expressed a "straightness" in Sudbury were on the

list. On the other hand, the selectmen did not favor the few sons who had decided to desert Sudbury for Ruddock's new settlement. They had already
made their choice.[4]

The Sudbury town meeting accepted the new aristocracy and agreed to
draw lots to decide on the placement of farms. The lots were drawn, and the
clerk recorded both the names and the numbers. Sudbury had an East Anglian
suburb. (See map, Figure 19.)

Ruddock could not be turned away from his move to the west. He continued to go out, axe in hand, to chop trees and to prepare for his new citizenry.
He knew that crops and houses came before town meetings. But he could not
postpone the critical decisions for long. His younger men demanded to know
how much land they were going to receive, and on what basis.

At last, in the fall of 1660, at a full town meeting of "inhabitants and proprietors," the first land distribution was made. Ruddock and Rice had been
granted a town plot much larger than that of Sudbury, six miles square, containing 24,000 acres, and they had a complicated task of distribution. Their
inhabitants were thirty-eight in number, and at least half of them were the
sons of ten leading Sudbury families: Rice, Ward, King, Goodnow, Bent,
Newton, Maynard, How, Kerley, and Johnson.

Almost all of them who had possessed the power had voted against the limitation of the Sudbury commons. This is probably explained by the fact that
only 30 per cent of the rebel group had been granted meadow lots in Sudbury.
Without meadow lots, they would have been prevented from putting any
"beasts" on the huge commons, had the sizing order been passed and enforced.
But thirteen of the thirty-eight men had upland in Sudbury, ranging from
Rice's 164 acres to Rutter's 9, not counting the recently granted 130-acre
farms in West Sudbury, which fourteen of them had received.

The new group, then, consisted of the older landed men and the younger
landless settlers. On what basis could the Marlborough land be distributed?
Hardly on the basis of "estate" or wealth. Two-thirds of the men had little but
youthful vigor.

At least Ruddock and his followers had grown beyond the complicated
general-field stage of farming. Each man was ready to handle his own property, which would contain pasture ground and plow ground. And the leaders
wished to set out the fresh-water meadow in four "squadrons," each squadron
divided into rectangular lots.

Ruddock had no intention of granting all the 24,000 acres, or even a large
part of it, at first. Nor did he intend to grant the land on the basis of assessed

wealth. Perhaps he felt that the range of grants would have been too large, for Rice and Ward clearly dominated the others in landed wealth, while young men, like John How, Jr., had none.

When the new settlement was officially named, the settlers switched from Whip Suffrage to Marlborough, in honor of the thriving borough in Ruddock's old English county of Wiltshire. To assure community loyalty, the leaders of the Massachusetts town established a new social scheme, defining it as an "Interest in this Town of Marlborough." They decreed that any persons who "lay claim to any Interest" in this new plantation had to perfect their house lots by a certain date. Further, all who claimed any interest had to pay "all public charges"; the penalty for refusal in both cases was to "lose all Interest in this town."[5]

Apparently, then, Ruddock and Rice drew up a list of their first settlers and granted them land in a public meeting on the basis of "Interest." The proportion of grants is significant. No one was allowed to be too rich or too poor. No one was allowed to be a "top man" or a "low man." Three men received 50 acres apiece; nine men received 30 acres each; and, at the low end of the scale, six men were granted 16 acres apiece. Out of 24,000 acres, only 992 acres were given out in the first division.[6]

As in Sudbury, this first list determined each man's share of the town tax, and a substantial tax of 13d./acre was levied at the time.[7] This proportion also determined every subsequent division of land or meadow. When four squadrons of fresh-water meadow, totaling 427 acres, were granted a month later, "every man's proportion for his first division meadow is to be half the number of acres granted in his previous lot."[8]

Again, as in Sudbury, this new wealth dictated social responsibility. Ruddock became town clerk and was made selectman each year, and he also found time to survey the roads and supervise the chopping of trees. Rice and Ward were selectmen each year for six years, and Thomas King served as selectman, constable, timber keeper, and highway supervisor.

Some of the attitudes generated by the Sudbury dispute were incorporated into the Marlborough social system. The minister was granted only 30 acres of land. He was eighth in the scale of landed wealth, a position held by the blacksmith and seven other men, all former Sudbury inhabitants. Marlborough had made specific Ruddock's acid comment to the Reverend Mr. Brown, "Setting aside your office, I regard you no more than another man." Perhaps this explains the reluctance of any minister to serve in Marlborough during its first decade. A new generation had almost grown up before Reverend William Brimsmead consented to join the recalcitrant group.[9]

With or without a minister, Marlborough intended to be a closed society, observing its constituents with care and constantly assessing any inhabitant on the basis of "his Interest." No man was allowed to join the community unless he passed their inspection: "It is ordered that Obadiah Ward shall have power in behalf this Town . . . to prosecute any man and all persons whatsoever that shall come into this Towne to dwell and abide without or contrary to this Towne's consent."[10] When new land was divided up, the basis was made clear: "Allotted out to every proprietor, a due proportion according to his Interest in this Town, to be enjoyed by him, his heirs and assignes."[11]

Such orders meant that these Englishmen, within thirty years or less, had helped to create another of that powerful and significant new entity, the New England town. This entity absorbed their energies, gave a hearing to their ideas and to their plans, and commanded some of their deepest loyalties.

For two of the leaders in Marlborough, Rice and Ruddock, this formation of a new town must have represented a great personal triumph. Edmund Rice had moved four times within forty years. Stage by stage, he had risen from an English parish and manufacturing center, in which he had stood near the bottom of the social scale, with few or no significant social functions, to a position of landed wealth and community leadership, in which he served in every important civic post available to him.

John Ruddock had probably enjoyed a similar rise in power and prestige, but one cannot be certain until more English documents from his area become available. Certainly, however, he had been able to express, and to fight for, his own concepts of political and economic organization. Ruddock, indeed, in 1663, was in a position to choose those who might judge him, as well as to demand that principles of justice dominate the spirit of the new town. Since he and the other Marlborough leaders were still giving away divisions of land, the phrase "Interest in this town" could have had as much an idealistic tone as one of speculative financial investment.

Ruddock had led a group of landless young sons away from a town which had too quickly forgotten some of its original principles of land distribution, and which had been unable to adjust to the change inherent in the reform of English institutions. Ruddock and his young men, after public debate, were once again formulating principles of their society and expecting certain obligations of those who asked to join it. Having suffered through the profound experience of building one community out of various elements and institutions of English society, Ruddock and his townsmen were starting afresh.

They had the power to raise a man's social and economic status dramatically, but they demanded that he become an active, responsible citizen of a community which was acting in moderation as it grew. And they required that any new citizen respect a significant spirit, which was becoming a deep faith — a respect for the orderly processes of law, an alertness to social justice, and a desire to improve society by forming, ever and again, self-governing entities called New England towns.

CHAPTER X

The Origin and Stability of a
New England Town

THE historical debate on "the origin" of a type of social and political structure called "the New England town" is probably not over, but the question itself may be superficial today. We can now realize that there were multiple origins and many distinct early towns, and that all of these towns and their relationships need careful examination.

How far back to search for origins was an unsolved dilemma for a previous generation of historians. Charles Andrews was undoubtedly correct when he insisted that there were only superficial likenesses between the German *tun*, the Anglo-Saxon village, and the New England town, despite Herbert B. Adams's insistence to the contrary.[1] There are three major difficulties in this whole investigation — the difficulty of finding and transcribing much of the documentary material; the complex interaction between village, regional, and more extensive social, political, and economic structures; and finally, the validity of the search for "the origin." A geneticist can watch the growth of biological structures in controlled experiments and can observe the intricate linkages through hundreds of generations. But the purpose of his experiments is to discover means to eradicate deleterious genes and to improve human genotypes. The purpose of those historians who insisted on the origin of the town has no such clarity.

If the question of the origin seems superficial, the investigation of the change, transition, and stability of English local institutions across the Atlantic ocean in the seventeenth century is not. The members of these groups came from quite diverse social and political locales in England, with definite sets of attitudes and drives, usually expressed in religious terms — but not always. England itself contained a large variety of local institutions. As a skilled archivist and local historian has said, "No place is 'representative' of English local government in seventeenth-century England. The evidence one finds tells us what local government was like in one distinct village, or parish, or town or borough, no more, no less."[2]

Apparently those men and women who emigrated to New England and formed new groups were inventive, as were some who settled in southern areas.[3] Certainly they had the unique challenge of a "town grant," which could be defined more or less as the inhabitants wished.

They made a staggering number of changes. How many men today, founding a "godly plantation" on the moon or on any habitable planet, would make as many significant alterations in religion, in social organization, in local government, and in attitude and values generally? Consider what might be called the constructive dissent in the first generation of Sudbury men. What were the selectmen there actually doing? They were constructing a community of free townsmen. This seems to have been their principal ideal, and their loyalty to the town even transcended their professions of religious faith. They had been trained in a variety of local institutions in England. They knew how to function as jurymen, vestrymen, borough councilors, or parish officers. But they must have wanted more, for they constructed an entirely new type of town.

Even the minister succumbed to the charged atmosphere. When his leadership over the youth was threatened by John Ruddock, when his sermons did not prevent "prophanation of the Lord's Day," he appeared in town meetings and prosecuted his cause "with violence."[4] "Put it to vote!" shouted Edmund Brown. He could not believe that the new political entity would abandon him. But it did — at least for a while. John Ruddock and his group, facing severe restrictions, wanted to construct a new town.

Examine the solemn meetings in Sudbury in January, 1655. Note how completely absent the traditional legal sanctions are. The selectmen did not bolster themselves with citations of Elizabethan laws, English customs, or warrants from local justices of the peace. As far as one can tell from reading the Sudbury orders, the selectmen assumed that once the General Court had made the initial town grant, they were the principal source of power in their area, subject only to the approval of the townsmen. It was very significant that when the General Court sent out an investigating committee in 1656, not only was there resentment in Sudbury, but also there is no indication that the townsmen followed the recommendations on the sizing of the commons.[5]

There seems to have been deep meaning to the phrase in the Sudbury Town Book, *free townsman*. Since it is never fully defined, it may have implied a status more like that of borough freeman than that of freeman written in the orders of the General Court. In Sudbury at any rate, such a man knew he could dissent and that he would be heard.[6]

To quote the town clerk, "John Ruddock, being then present, did, by his vote, dissent from the act." At that point Ruddock was the leader of a minority group. But did he, full of frustration and ill-will, call his youth to arms and resort to violence? He did not. Finding his ambitions blocked in the Musketaquid valley, he proceeded to construct another community. Once again, he rebuilt human institutions in the face of necessity.

Ruddock developed his constructive faith in relation to the area about him and with the full permission and support of the Massachusetts government. When he dissented in 1655, Ruddock hoped that another land area would be available to him and to his petitioners. He could have swallowed his pride and remained in Sudbury. He could have moved across the river and settled on the plots which the selectmen offered him. But he did neither. Whether tacitly or explicitly, he made a series of daring assumptions, involving predictions about his own leadership, his group, the General Court, the Indians, and the opposition party in Sudbury. With his confidence fortified by the grant of town land from the General Court, he then proceeded to express his ideals and his will.

Each step demanded both logic and leadership. Ruddock had to "view" the area to assure his group that it would be productive and satisfying to them. He then recognized the rights of the Indians, although there is no evidence that he tried to communicate with them to see whether they understood his purpose. Had he tried to do this sincerely, he might have made the unhappy discovery that the English concept of the individual, exploitative ownership of soil was causing apprehensions among the original natives.

Next, Ruddock needed to display confidence in his woodsmen and farmers, and to develop this into a reciprocal relationship. Not only did he have to prove that crops could be raised, but he had to show that a market for them could be found and a road built for their transportation. In addition, he had to hope that even though he might be considered immoral, some minister would forgive him and join his new group. This took many years, as the new town later learned.

Above all, Ruddock had to display a type of idealism that could transcend his previous failures. He probably had to achieve a remarkable synthesis of the new awareness of the ideals of his young followers and his own ability to assist his men in fulfilling them. In short, to be able to establish a community that would function "forever" in the same spot where the leaders planted it, Ruddock must have had a complex mind and a profound faith which he could communicate to others.

Later generations use the term "New England town," and thereby assume the established set of relationships and attitudes which New Englanders have known for decades. Today we think we know what a "town" is. But to the first settlers, the term "town" must have meant a life of uncertainty, balanced by a faith in social order and stability.

To emigrate from accustomed social institutions and relationships to a set of unfamiliar communities in the way in which Noyes and Ruddock shifted from England to Sudbury, and the latter from Sudbury to Marlborough, meant a startling transformation. The townsmen had to change or abandon almost every formal institution which they had taken for granted.

The Sudbury Town Book, read in the context of close examination of English local records of the period, actually describes this set of reforms. The first clerk, Hugh Griffin, began using a new vocabulary as he recorded the orders made by his selectmen and his free townsmen.

Gone were the courts-baron, courts-leet, vestries, out-hundred courts, courts of election, courts of record, courts of the borough, courts of orders and decrees, courts of investigation, courts of ordination, and views of frankpledge. In their place came meetings of men to order town affairs, or later, selectmen's meetings and town meetings, with a few references to the General Court and the county court.

Gone were the seneschal, bailiff, jurymen, virgate, yardland, reversion, messuage, tenement, toft, croft, heriot, close, fealty to the lord, admission, hayward, annual rent, copyholders, coliarholders, and freeholders. In their stead came selectmen, grants of land, freemen, and free townsmen.

The medieval church calendar was completely abandoned in the first generation. Whereas the Hampshire farmers had started the year in England with Lady Day (March 25) and ended it with Plow Monday, which was the first Monday after Epiphany (January 6), the entire calendar in early Sudbury was reduced to a numerical sequence of months, monotonous in their prosaic designations, starting with "the first month" or March. The second generation in both Sudbury and Marlborough returned to the old calendar. The men of Marlborough had a town meeting on December 25, 1663. They were using the day not for the ancient ceremony they had celebrated since childhood, but for a new kind of ritual — the formation of a godly community.

Gone also were the rector, curate, sexton, ringers, glebe land, terrier, tithe, parish perambulation, churchwardens, sidemen, questmen, overseers of the poor, and all the many familiar objects of church "furniture," from the cross to the goblet. The town clerk of Sudbury spoke of pastor, deacon, meeting-house, town perambulation, and a town "rate" to pay the pastor and to repair or rebuild the meetinghouse.

Into the dark mists had disappeared articles of visitation, Book of Common Prayer, presentments, commissary, archdeacon, church courts, purgation, certificate of penance, and holy days. Hugh Griffin had no substitution for these. As far as local historians can tell, the first Sudbury "church" did not even keep a separate book. Only the visit of the "Reverend Elders" tried to impose an external church discipline on Sudbury, and Griffin did not even record their presence in the Town Book.

Abolished too were the quarter sessions, justices of the peace, knights of the shire, king's sheriff, house of correction, Marshalsea payments, king's bench, assizes, Privy Council, and Parliament. The King and Queen were never mentioned. In their places were governor, magistrates, General Court, and town deputy.

Sudbury was no longer an ancient borough and had no mayor, bailiff, collector of rents of the assizes, chamberlain, chief constable, sergeants at mace, coroner, burgess, aldermen, market overseers, ale tasters, or master of the grammar school. No one met in the Town House or aspired to build paneled rooms for the "select fraternity" who governed the town. There were only selectmen, marshal, clerk, and various townsmen doing various specific jobs, as assigned by the town meeting.

Hugh Griffin did not have to note any maimed soldiers, travelers from Ireland, Dunkirkers, or soldiers from Bohemia. Someone had tried to dignify the resident Indian chiefs by giving them the names Jethro and Cato, but it seems there were few visitors during the first generation, and few people "warned out."

Life in Sudbury was indeed a "new" England. No wonder men like Samuel Gordon and Thomas Morton were amazed and alarmed as they inspected other towns. What held these communities together and gave them stability? What welded relationships and created loyalties and mutual respect?

Bold leaders, the tacit and sometimes actual approval by the General Court, concern for every inhabitant, and a deep faith were sufficient for the first generation of Sudbury townsmen. One can argue that three institutions gave a structure and a harmony to the community: the open-field system of farming, the town meeting, and the town church. Sudbury continued "general and particular" fields until 1694, and Professor Ault has clearly shown how this joint administration of agriculture led to a kind of local democratic government.[7] The Sudbury town meeting considered a wide variety of social problems, from the granting, renting, taxation, and sale of land to bastardy and the mental health of its citizens. When one reads the Town Book closely, one is impressed that the selectmen were aware of the precise "condition" of every inhabitant and quick to note any "dangerous" or "suspicious" person amongst the group. Any unusual occurrence which caused a problem seems to have been brought before the town, and the townsmen voted on the policy of warning out "maimed, defective, or suspicious persons," the problem of finding a smith and keeping the mill running, the correct height of field fences, an inventory of "all mens' estates," and the sickness of any citizen. They also considered the menace of hungry crows and marauding wolves, the correct placement of roads between communities, and any infringement of town meadow or town land, which seems to have been managed as a kind of corporate bank account, to be granted, rented, or called back at the will of the inhabitants and selectmen.[8]

The Sudbury church seems to have been virtually indistinguishable from the town throughout the seventeenth century, but it must have given a sense of order and security until 1655, after which the church was "in a most deplorable state, from which it was long in recovering."[9] Town meetings discussed the problem of finding a substitute when the Reverend Edmund Brown fell ill in 1678, hired his successor, the Reverend James Sherman, and set the conditions of his contract, drew up the design and levied taxes for the third meetinghouse 1686–1688, appealed to those citizens who were negligent in paying their share of Mr. Sherman's salary, and decided who could or could not build pews in the church in place of the normal "seats left open at both ends."[10]

The first generation found that it could not abandon the traditional calendar, and from 1648 onward the pagan names of February, March, and the rest were introduced into the Town Book and have been used ever since.[11] The second generation, however, returned to several deep-seated English institutions and customs. The farmers grew "English pasture" and sedge fences, the military company purchased a "flight of colors," men were elected tithingmen to collect the church tax, and town accounts began to appear in the Town Book, making some pages read like any English borough book, citing income and expenses.[12]

The most significant institution which was reintroduced was the English common law. When Widow Loker refused to resign to the town the housing, ground, trees, and privileges which she had sold to the town, the selectmen turned to the county court at Cambridge and started a suit at law.[13] Another entry indicates the relationship of Sudbury to the courts and to ultimate authority. "This day Sarjt. Barnard made report to the Town what success hee mett withall att the Quarter Sessions; and then did chuse a commity to meet with and treat the Jury that shall be appointed to state his Majesties hy way betweene our Town and Marlbrough and Indevor to the uttmost of thear power that it may bee layd out so as it may bee least prejudijuall to our Town."[14]

Ten years before Barnard's report, Sudbury acknowledged that it was now part of the British empire, for the town, desiring to be rid of one D. Hedley, warned him out in "his Majesty's name."[15] The King's tax started to be collected by the town constable by April, 1693, and once again these town officers relied on the ultimate authority of the King. It is particularly interesting to read that the town voted a special tax of "eight pounds in money . . . for the sending and transporting of Thomas Blake to Old England."[16] The absence of any references in the Sudbury Town Book to "his Majesty" during the famous governorship of Sir Edmund Andros, 1686–1690, clearly illustrates the spirit of insubordination of which the governor constantly complained while he was in Boston.[17] Apparently Sudbury was willing to acknowledge the authority of the King, but on its own terms and at specific times.

Sudbury, like the other early New England towns, was a remarkable experiment in the formation and growth of a social community. Now that this town presents an explicit case study, further examination in group behavior can be made of the whole problem of the growth and stability of such communities, provided that accurate categories of investigation are formed. William Caudill suggests the concepts of the "stress" on various groups and the formation of "linked open systems" and feels that students should consider the Atlantic only as a highway between related communities. He advises that we try to define and discover "cultural pairs" of communities on both sides of the ocean and then ask why some citizens left, why some stayed, why some shuttled back and forth in the whole Atlantic system.[18] Bernard Bailyn has clearly shown that the Boston merchants returned to the British trade system by the end of the seventeenth century,[19] and certainly both the inhabitants and the free townsmen of Sudbury felt the compelling need of the authority of the King and common law by the second generation.

If, as it seems, we today are in a period of radical social upheaval and violent transformation of communities and entire national and international populations, much perspective can be gained from close examination of a somewhat analogous period in the seventeenth century. Above all, we should not lose the faith in our ability to create "godly, orderly communities," or our desire to rely on law and common consent, rather than on violence and the authority of a powerful central government. If we abandon our New England heritage, we do so at our peril. The Sudbury townsmen might not have been able to order their community "forever" as they hoped, but they set a remarkable example for all the generations which have followed them.

Notes

1. Herbert B. Adams, *The Germanic Origin of New England Towns* (Baltimore, 1882). The debate is summarized in A. S. Eisenstadt, *Charles MacLean Andrews, A Study in American Historical Writing* (New York, 1956), pp. 13 ff. Adams's thesis is contested in *Proceedings of the Massachusetts Historical Society, 1892* (Boston, 1892) and in Charles F. Adams, *The Genesis of the Massachusetts Town* (Cambridge, 1892). John Sly, *Town Government in Massachusetts, (1620–1930)* (Cambridge, 1930), pp. 20–21.

2. W. E. Tate, *The Parish Chest* (Cambridge, 1946); Wallace Notestein, *The English People on the Eve of Colonization, 1602–1630* (New York, 1955).

3. John Winthrop, "Declaration In Defense of an Order of Court, 1637." Later incorporated into a General Court order applicable to each town. Printed in Mark Howe, *Readings in American Legal History* (Cambridge, 1949), p. 161.

4. Howe, *op. cit.*, p. 204.

1. Col. Henry E. Noyes, ed., *Genealogical Record of Some of the Noyes Descendants of James, Nicholas and Peter Noyes* (Boston, 1904), I, 43–44. Both men finally settled in Newbury, Mass. Both became freemen, while Nicholas served as deacon of the First Church and deputy to the General Court. A deposition of 1652, a copy of which is in the Weyhill Rectory MSS, attests to the fact that both Nicholas Noyes and other inhabitants of Newbury, Mass. knew various families in Weyhill, Hants, and knew of the details of their trips to New England.

2. Weyhill Rectory MSS. Indenture of P. Noyes, 1652: Middlesex County Court, Registry of Deeds, III, 292–293; Middlesex County Probate Records, VIII, 425.

3. Compiled from the Town Book of Sudbury, Vol. I. (Town of Sudbury MSS.) Details in Chapter VII.

4. All land grant statistics in Sudbury, Mass. taken from the Town Book of Sudbury, Vol. I (MSS).

5. For full description see C. S. and S. Orwin, *The Open Fields* (Oxford U.P., 1938), p. 3.

6. Reconstructed by the Reverend Cyril Williams and the author on the basis of maps and documents at the Weyhill Rectory, Hants Record Office, and Muniment Room, Queen's College, Oxford University.

7. Weyhill Rectory MSS: See Mildred Campbell, *The English Yeoman* (New Haven, 1942), 68–73. Howard L. Gray, *English Field Systems* (Harvard History Studies, Vol. 22) (Cambridge, 1915), pp. 72, 109, 152.

8. Enclosure Act of 1812: Weyhill Rectory MSS. I am indebted to the Reverend Cyril B. Williams for extensive information on all aspects of Weyhill.

9. Tables compiled from court rolls of the Manor of Ramridge, 1600–1640 (MSS in Muniment Room, Queen's College, Oxford), Weyhill Churchwardens' Accounts (Weyhill Rectory MSS); *The Victoria History of the County of Hampshire* (London, 1911), IV, 394, gives the following survey for Weyhill: 1214 acres arable; 434 acres of grassland; 124 acres of woodland. Total: 1772 acres.

10. These names were compiled from the Weyhill Churchwardens' Accounts, 1600–1640. Each man served as some type of parish officer. The rector, in 1672, reported that there were about 28 "landless laborers" in the parish. (Weyhill Rectory MSS.)

11. Campbell, *op. cit.*, p. 217. Campbell feels that a yeoman, at that time, considered £50 to be a good yearly income.

12. Data from the Ramridge Court-baron rolls: Piece 1 — 1 cottage, "land" and 1 acre meadow; Piece 2 — cottage and 15 acres arable; Piece 3 — 30 acres of arable; Piece 4 — cottage and 15 acres arable.

13. The concept is historically traced in George Homans, *The English Villagers of the*

Thirteenth Century (Cambridge, 1941). The hostile reaction of the Weyhill men to the demands of T. Drake for enclosures of two fields in 1648 are amply documented in the Weyhill Rectory MSS.

14. The description of the vicar's copyhold land has been preserved: (1) one acre in Ridge Field, shooting E & W; Mr. Manning on the South and Peter Noyes on the North; (2) One acre in Nudle Field, between the two harrow ways, shooting N & S; (3) One acre in Nudle Field, shooting N & S; (4) One acre in Nudle Field, shooting E & W; the little harrow way on the South; land of T. Grace on the North; (5) One acre in Gore Ridge Field, shooting N & S; (6) One acre more in Gore Ridge Field, shooting N & S; Longmeadow on one side, Blissimore Hall on the West; (7) One acre in Great Field, shooting N & S; on the North long croft, belonging to Blissimore Hall; (8) One acre more in Great Field, shooting E & W; (9) One acre more in Great Field, at West Lynches, shooting E & W; the land of J. Noyes on the South; (10) Half an acre more in the Great Field in Rowberry, shooting E & W; (11) Half an acre in Far Penton Field, shooting E & W; (12) Three quarters of a acre of enclosed ground, called croft; (13) Three quarters of an acre of enclosed ground. Total: 11½ acres; Rent £00/00/07 per year. (Additional MSS, Weyhill. Queen's College Muniments. Agreement of 1651.)

15. Weyhill Rectory MSS; Copy of 1651 Deed in Muniment Room, Queen's College, Oxford.

16. F. J. C. Hearnshaw, *Leet Jurisdiction in England* (Southampton, 1908), p. 81.

17. It must be admitted that these court rolls are not complete. Only court sessions for 1608, 1613, 1616, 1624, 1629, 1631, 1632, 1635, 1637 and 1638 remain. Court-baron rolls of the Manor of Ramridge (Muniment Room, Queen's College, Oxford).

18. Views of frankpledge, 1604–1624: Andover out-hundred (Borough of Andover, Hants, MSS Records). See data on service of Weyhill men, Appendix II.

19. Sidney and Beatrice Webb, *English Local Government* (London, 1906) II; Wallace Notestein, *The English People on the Eve of Colonization, 1602–1630* (New York, 1954), Chap. 18; William B. Willcox, *Gloucestershire, a Study in Local Government, 1590–1640* (New Haven, 1940).

20. Further details in Chapter VII.

21. Andover Corporation Records; "Titeredge's Report On Andover Records" (Borough of Andover, Hants, MSS Records).

22. The tithes, at best, gained the vicar £11/year. (Additional MSS, Weyhill. Muniments of Queen's College, Oxford.)

23. Churchwardens' Accounts of Weyhill, 1601–1640. (Weyhill Rectory MSS.) See data in Appendix II.

24. W. E. Tate, *The Parish Chest* (Cambridge, 1946), Part II, Chs. III, IV.

25. Hants Diocesan MSS (Diocesan Registry, Winchester). Visitation Books, Deposition Books, 1600–1640.

26. See comments of Hon. Mellen Chamberlain on Toulmin Smith's *The Parish* in C. F. Adams, *The Genesis of the Massachusetts Town* (Cambridge, 1892); see also comments of Sly, *op. cit.*, pp. 63–68. Both seriously question "the parish" as a prototype. See variety of parish activity in W. E. Tate, *The Parish Chest*, Part I, Chap. III; Part II.

27. Hants Quarter Sessions Books, 1607–1640 (Hants Record Office MSS, Winchester).

28. W. O. Ault, "Village By-Laws By Common Consent" in *Speculum*, XXIX:2, Part 2 (April, 1954), 378; *The Self-Directing Activities of Village Communities in Mediaeval England* (Boston University, 1952).

29. See G. Homans, *English Villagers*, Chap. II; Norman S. B. Gras, *The Economic and Social History of an English Village (Crawley, Hants)* (Cambridge, 1930); H. L. Gray, *English Field Systems*; Crawley Manorial Rolls, printed in N. S. B. Gras, *op. cit.*, pp.

587–589; Gilbert Slater, *English Peasantry and The Enclosure of Common Fields* (London, 1907), pp. 22–23.

30. Thomas Hardy describes the Weyhill Fair vividly in Chapter I of *The Mayor of Casterbridge.* "Weydon Priors" is Weyhill of the nineteenth century.

31. Letter printed in Alexander Young, ed., *Chronicles of Massachusetts Bay* (Cambridge, 1846), p. 264.

32. Middlesex County Probate Records (MSS), I, 112–114.

33. Willcox, *op. cit.,* pp. 18–72.

34. R. M. Heanley, *The History of Weyhill and Its Ancient Fair* (Winchester, 1922), p. 57 ff. Additional MSS, Weyhill, Muniments of Queen's College, Oxford.

35. Weyhill Rectory MSS.

36. Weyhill Rectory MSS; Middlesex County Court Files; the "invoice of the carryers" printed in *New England Historic and Genealogical Register,* XXXII, 410. Most of the emigrants were close relatives or friends. Anis Bent was a widow, mother of John Bent, who had gone in 1638, and mother of Agnis Blanchet. This Agnis Blanchet had been previously married to John Barnes of Clanville, and the boy Richard Barnes was her son by the first marriage. She married Thomas Blanchard in Penton Mewsey, and he accompanied her on the trip. She died, however, on the way. Her niece was Elizabeth Plympton, whose brother was Mr. Noyes's servant. Thomas Blanchard stayed in Charlestown, Massachusetts, but his son Samuel helped to found Andover, Massachusetts.

1. Genealogical data to document these movements: Appendix I: The Sudbury Settlers.

2. It is not certain that Robert Darvell came over with E. Rice. Thomas Axtell came later in 1642. But all three men had lived together in Berkhamsted, as had a man named Philemon Whale, who might have been the same P. Whale listed in the Sudbury (Mass.) land grants and records, although genealogists think that Whale came from Bures St. Mary, Essex. (Appendix I.)

3. All statistics taken from Berkhamsted Churchwardens' Accounts, 1600–1645. (British Museum MSS.)

4. W. Page, ed., *Victoria County History of Herts* (London, 1908), II, 167.

5. *Calendar of State Papers, Domestic Series* (London, 1857), IX, 126. J. E. T. Rogers, *History of Agriculture and Prices in England* (Oxford, 1887), VI, 426 ff.

6. J. Cobb, *Two Lectures on the History and Antiquities of Berkhamsted* (London, 1883) p. 113.

7. The 1905 survey described the parish as: 1484 acres arable, 1265 acres grass, 312 acres woods; total: 3061 acres: *Vict. Cty. Hist. Herts,* II, 162 ff. See totals in Appendix III.

8. *Vict. Cty. Hist. of Herts,* p. 167 ff. See the extracts of the manorial court rolls in Cobb, *op. cit.,* which support this conclusion.

9. *Vict. Cty. Hist. of Herts,* II, 173.

10. All information on charter and government of the borough itself from Cobb, *op. cit.* The charter is reproduced in Cobb's Appendix.

11. Entry of 1602, Churchwardens' Accounts. Tolls were fees levied on "strangers" who paid for the privilege of selling their grain at the central market in the borough.

12. Cobb, *op. cit.,* p. 96 ff. The receipt of "market tolls" in the Churchwardens' Accounts support his statements.

13. This is *not* the total amount of the church rates — only that part spent on church repair. All statistics from Churchwardens' Accounts, 1600–1645.

14. See Appendix IV: Table of government posts held: W. Pitkin had 204 acres in 1637; O. Haines had 52, and S. Besouth had 26. Each served in at least 6 church posts.

15. Berkhamsted Churchwardens' Accounts, 1602–1618 (MSS). See also Tate, *op. cit.*, pp. 26–27.

16. Tate, *op. cit.*, pp. 95–96. Note his excellent bibliography of studies of various church and village institutions in England.

17. *Articles to Be Inquired Into . . . by the Bishop of Winchester* (London, 1619–1639): Bodleian Library Collection.

18. Tate, *op. cit.*, Chap. 5; also p. 149.

19. *Ibid.*, p. 241.

20. *Calendar of State Papers, Domestic Series (1629–1631)* (London, 1860), p. 8, 406 ff., 500.

21. This entire order made: Feb. 10, 1630/1. Berkhamsted Churchwardens' Accounts.

22. W. Le Handy, comp., *Calendar to Herts Sessions Books, 1619–1657* (Hertford, 1905–), Vol. V.

23. Churchwardens' Accounts, 1630–1631. Wethered's tax of £25 would be roughly $1250 in terms of 1960 prices. See Tate, *op. cit.*, for canonical court procedure in tax cases, p. 143. The vestry did not always lose such a case. Contrast this case of Wethered *vs.* Berkhamsted with that of E. Alpe given in Chapter IV.

24. *Calendar to Herts Sessions Books, 1619–1657*, V, 75, 139, 149.

25. *Ibid.*, p. 263, 262.

26. Tate, *op. cit.*, p. 9 ff. Contrast the parish of Berkhamsted with the two and one-half parishes within the borough of Sudbury, Chapter III.

CHAPTER III

1. C. F. D. Sperling, *A Short History of the Borough of Sudbury*, (Sudbury, 1898), p. 148. Also Norman C. Tyack, "Emigration from East Anglia to New England, 1600–1660" (MSS Thesis, University of London, 1951). Tyack counts fifty-four persons leaving Sudbury for New England before 1660. At least four capital burgesses left Sudbury for Massachusetts, and their departure is noted in the Borough Book of Records, 1630.

2. The parish officers of the two largest parishes, St. Gregory's and St. Peter's, claimed in 1636 that there were 1200 communicants in their two parishes. (Sperling, *op. cit.*, p. 116.) The communicants of the other parish, All Saints, comprised about 25 per cent of the total taxable borough population. The 1 per cent–2 per cent figure is reached by a statistical analysis of the total number of borough court cases, 1618–1638. The title "yeoman" occurs only four times in all these indictments. This does not mean, of course, that the townsmen did not have their small gardens in the "backsides" of their row houses. (See map.)

3. W. Notestein, *English People on the Eve of Colonization*, p. 110.

4. Bernard Bailyn, *The New England Merchants in the Seventeenth Century* (Cambridge, 1955), Chapter I.

5. Parish of St. Gregory's: 812 acres on N. and E. of the borough; St. Peter's: 29 acres around the central market place; All Saints: 64 acres in Sudbury and 850 acres in Essex. (Sperling, *op. cit.*, p. 36). The seventeenth-century parish records have not survived, but the borough's population was 3283 in 1801.

6. Liber Quintus: MSS Borough Book of Records, 1618–1640 (Borough of Sudbury Records. Translated by the author). Gen. Sess. Peace: 4 Oct., 19 Jas. I.

7. Gen. Sess. Peace: 13 May, 17 Jas. I, Liber Quintus.

8. The fee was 30s. at the Court of Elections, 2 Sept., 20 Jas. I, Liber Quintus.

9. Notestein, *op. cit.*, Chap. 10, "The Businessman," Chap. 18, "The Justices of the Peace."

10. *Ibid.*, Chapter 19; Tate, *op. cit.*, pp. 175–186, especially the rare set of Constable's Accounts from Doveridge, Derbys.

11. Oaths of Office (Borough MSS Records).
12. Oath of the Weaving Surveyor (Borough MSS Records).
13. Sperling, *op. cit.*, p. 77.
14. General Court, 7 Sept., 5 Chas I. (1629), Liber Quintus.
15. Order of 21 March, 7 Eliz. (Borough MSS Records).
16. *Calendar of State Papers, Domestic, 1628–1629* (London, 1859), p. 6. describes how a Member of Parliament was elected: "The Knights of the Shire for Essex were chosen in the following manner: the freeholders were called upon by the constables to give their voices for the side supported by most of the Justices of the Peace; and there was also a very irregular creation of freeholders, in order to secure the return of Sir Francis Barrington and Sir Harbottle Grimston. Sir Edward Coke and Sir Nathaniel Bernardston have been returned for Suffolk, but they would not have been chosen if there had been any other gentlemen of note, for neither Ipswich had any great affection for them, nor most of the country. But there were not ten gentlemen at this election." Such elections, held within the borough, prompted Dickens, two centuries later, to write the famous satire of the Reds and the Blues in *Pickwick Papers*. His "Eatonswill" was Sudbury.
17. W. Page, ed., *The Victoria History of the Counties of England: Suffolk* (London, 1907), II, 265.
18. *Ibid.*, pp. 263–264.
19. *Calendar of State Papers, Domestic (1603–1610)* (London, 1857), p. 550.
20. *Calendar of State Papers, Domestic (1629–1631)* (London, 1860), p. 120.
21. *Ibid.*, p. 415.
22. St. Gregory's Church has account books from 1662–1829; St. Peter's Church has similar records from 1675 on. A church rate for the 1670's lists 53 men and a tax of £19, about 7s. each. Perhaps this indicates that the parish rates were heavier than the borough taxes.
23. *Calendar of State Papers, Domestic (1631–1633)* (London, 1867), p. 22. *Vict. Cty. Hist. Sflk.*, II, 269. Suffolk wheat prices at that time had climbed from 6s. to 8s./bushel.
24. First published in London in 1626 as *A Song, or Story, For the Lasting Remembrance of Diverse Famous Works, Which God Hath Done in Our Time,* reprinted in Perry Miller, T. H. Johnson, eds., *The Puritans* (New York, 1939), p. 553.
25. Court of Pie Poudre, 9 May, 19 Jas. I (1621), Liber Quintus. The first actual town order of Sudbury, Mass. concerned the ringing of hogs and pigs: April 1, 1640. Town Book of Sudbury (Town of Sudbury, MSS Records).
26. Court of Orders and Decrees, 13 May, 20 Jas. I, Liber Quintus. The 5s. fine was a heavy one.
27. Gen. Sess. Peace, 8 March, 21 Jas. I, Liber Quintus. "Sea coal" was hard coal which was imported, by sea, at a nearby port, such as Ipswich.
28. Gen. Sess. Peace, 20 August, 4 Chas. I, Liber Quintus.
29. Gen. Sess. Peace, 6 July, 22 Jas. I, Liber Quintus. The salary of the master of the house of correction was set at £12/year.
30. Court of Elections and Orders, 7 Sept., 5 Charles I, Liber Quintus.
31. Orders of 6 June, 7 Charles I; 6 July, 10 Charles I, Liber Quintus.
32. General Court, 7 Sept., 5 Charles I, Liber Quintus.

CHAPTER IV

1. Norman C. Tyack, "Emigration From East Anglia to New England, 1600–1660" (MSS), Appendix A. From Essex: 634; from Suffolk: 644.
2. See Appendices I, VI, VII for statistics.
3. Court-baron of Thomas Barrington, Kt: 22 Sept. 1637; 27 March 1633. (MSS at Essex

Record Office). Barrington held the three adjoining manors of Hatfield Broad Oak, Matching Barnes and Burnt Hall. The Matching map was made by John Walker and is deposited in the Essex Record Office.

4. Court-baron at Barrington Hall: 30 May 1637. (MSS at E.R.O.)

5. Calendar of County Records, Quarter Sessions Records, Vol. 18 (MSS at E.R.O.): 26 March 1610. By 10 Jan. 1611 "case" discharged because "insufficient in law."

6. N. C. Tyack, *op. cit.*, Suffolk map of emigrants, Appendix A. John Booth, *Nicholas Danforth and His Neighbors* (Framingham, Mass. Historical Society, 1935), p. 5.

7. R. Hawes and R. Loder, *The History of Framlingham* (Woodbridge, 1798), pp. 330–331, 201. List of taxpayers in J. Booth, *op. cit.*, pp. 47–57.

8. Map of Danforth property reconstructed by J. Booth, on basis of original Danforth deed discovered by the author. See J. Booth, *The Home of Nicholas Danforth in Framlingham, Suffolk, in 1635* (Framingham, Mass., 1954), pp. 7–15.

9. R. Green, *The History of Framlingham* (London, 1884), pp. 176–177: Danforth served on the upland leet jury in 1628.

10. Framlingham Churchwardens' Accounts, 1629–1639 (MSS at Ipswich and East Suffolk Record Office).

11. All details taken from Churchwardens' Accounts, 1629–1639.

12. All citations from Suffolk Quarter Sessions Records, 1639. (MSS at Ipswich and East Suffolk Record Office.)

13. Hawes-Loder, *op. cit.*, pp. 333–387: Alpe held twenty-nine parcels of land, at a rent of £3/year.

14. Account Book of the Reverend Richard Golty (privately owned MSS); partly transcribed in J. Booth, *Nicholas Danforth and His Neighbors*, pp. 18–23 ff. Some of Golty's expressions have been modernized.

15. The only evidence we have of the value of such crops is one deposition in the Archdeaconry of Suffolk MSS for 1632: in Baraham, Suffolk, barley was said to be worth 26s./8d. per acre; oats at 3s./4d. per acre. (East Suffolk R.O. MSS.)

16. Deed in E. Sflk R.O. Reprinted in J. Booth, *The Home of N. Danforth*, pp. 22–24.

17. J. Booth, *N. Danforth and his Neighbors*, p. 18. Danforth left for New England in 1634.

18. Cotton Mather, *Magnalia Christi Americana* (Hartford, 1826), II, 59.

19. All depositions from Archdeaconry of Suffolk: Book of Depositions and Allegations, 1632 (East Suffolk Record Office MSS). The depositions were apparently heard in many parishes: Ipswich, Brandeston, Wattisham, Woodbridge, Ottlea, Orford, Stradbrook, and Framlingham — and this is not a complete list.

20. Bishop of Salisbury: Act Book, 1634–1635 (Wilts Diocesan Registry MSS).

21. Thomas Shepard, *A Defense of the Answer Made Unto Nine Questions Sent From New England Against the Reply Thereto By Mr. John Ball* (London, 1648), p. 3.

22. See the latest counterblast against the economic interpretation in Alan French, *Charles I and the Puritan Upheaval* (Boston, 1955). He uses only State Papers, though.

23. N. Tyack, *op. cit.*, emigration maps. John Stone was probably born in Great Bromley — see Appendix I, Sudbury Settlers.

24. Compiled from Great Bromley Churchwardens' Accounts (E.R.O. MSS) and Archdeaconry of Colchester Act Books (E.R.O. MSS).

25. Case of May–June 1625: the penalties were excommunication for the woman, public penance for the father of the bastard, and for the couple. The "adulterer" denied the charge and had to appear with compurgators to prove his innocence.

26. See genealogical notes in Appendix I.

27. Book of Depositions, 1634–1635. Archdeacon of Sarum (Salisbury) (Wilts Diocesan Registry, MSS Book 19), Walter Haines prominent selectman of Sudbury, Mass., came from Sutton Mandeville. We have a sketch of Haines's old barn: Figure 8.

28. All depositions from Archdeacon of Wiltshire Act Book, 1636–1639 (Wilts Diocesan Registry MSS).·

29. See Figure 7, St. Peter's Church, Shaftesbury. This was well known, at the time, for the fiery sermons of the Nonconformist, Reverend Thomas Hallett.

30. See Appendix I for genealogical details. The Goodnows of the small villages of Donhead and Semley were joined by their relative, Thomas, of Shaftesbury.

CHAPTER V

1. *Watertown Records* (Watertown, 1894), I, 8–10; checked with H. Bond, *Genealogy of . . . The Early Settlers of Watertown, Mass.* (Boston, 1860), C. E. Banks, *Topographical Dictionary of 2885 English Emigrants to New England, 1620–1650* (Philadelphia, 1937) and C. H. Pope, *The Pioneers of Massachusetts* (Boston, 1900). Banks's statements should always be checked against later genealogical work.

2. Compiled from *Wat. Rcds,* I, Bond, and Tyack. Appendix I.

3. *Wat. Rcds,* I, Land Section, pp. 3–5. The boundaries of the "dividends" in map, Figure 5, are approximations.

4. The listings of holdings of homesteads, upland, meadow, and plowland in *Wat. Rcds,* I, Land Section, pp. 17 ff. are very similar to Reverend Richard Golty's listing of holdings of farmers in Framlingham, Suffolk. The men were making enclosed fields for themselves, and the orders pertaining to the Watertown common fields disappeared within the first decade.

5. *Wat. Rcds,* I, 2–3.

6. *Wat. Rcds,* I, Land, p. 46.

7. *Wat. Rcds,* I, 2.

8. Samuel E. Morison, *Builders of the Bay Colony* (Boston, 1930), pp. 87–88.

9. *Wat. Rcds,* I, 2.

10. *Ibid.,* p. 3.

11. In the first five elections to the 11-man governing committee, 1634–1638 28 different men were chosen. (Compiled from *Wat. Rcds,* I.)

12. Bond, *op. cit.,* p. 1002.

13. *Ibid.,* p. 993.

14. Estimate of Edward Johnson, cited in Bond, *op. cit.,* p. 982.

15. The first petition had been submitted to the General Court in 1637. Brown arrived in 1638 but seems to have been influential in obtaining the grant.

16. Collection of Early MSS in relation to Sudbury, Mass., of Dr. Alfred Stearns, Goodnow Library, Sudbury. (Referred to hereafter as Stearns MSS).

17. Harrold Ayres, *The Great Trail of New England* (Boston, 1940).

18. James K. Hosmer, ed., *Winthrop's Journal* (N.Y., 1908), I, 62.

19. Alfred S. Hudson, *The History of Sudbury, Mass.* (Sudbury, 1889), p. 2. Also: Stearns MSS.

20. Hudson, *op. cit.,* p. 4.

21. *Winthrop's Journal,* I, 178.

22. See recent soil analysis in "Sudbury Landscape Survey," Dept. of Landscape Architecture, Harvard University, 1952.

23. Pond Letter, with modernized phrases. Original letter, dated 1631, printed in *Winthrop Papers* (Mass. Historical Society, 1943), II, 18–19.

24. Quoted in *Mass. Historical Society Collections, 3rd Series,* III, 37.

25. P. Bidwell, J. Falconer, *The History of Agriculture in the Northern U.S. 1620–1860* (Washington, 1925), pp. 19–23.

26. N. B. Shurtleff, ed., *Records of the Governor and Company of the Massachusetts Bay in New England, (1628–1686)* (Boston, 1853–1854), I, 238. Referred to hereafter as *Mass. Col. Rcds.*

156 PURITAN VILLAGE

CHAPTER VI

1. Town officer in 1634, 1635, 1636: *Wat. Rcds,* I, 1–2.
2. Bond, *op. cit.,* p. 402. Bailyn, *N. E. Merchants,* p. 82, 125.
3. See Appendix 1 for details.
4. Middlesex County, Probate Records, Vol. I (1655–1667). Total of 15 Sudbury wills listed in this period.
5. The inventory of W. Batchelor, yeoman, of Weyhill (d. 1675) shows very few agricultural implements. He farmed 75 acres, but had only 2 carts, 2 harrows, and 3 rakes, plus a few scythes. Other men who farmed less had even fewer implements at their deaths. (Weyhill Wills, Muniment Room, Queen's College, Oxford.)
6. Sudbury Town Book, transcribed by the author. (Town of Sudbury MSS.)
7. Stearns MSS.
8. Deed confirmed and signed in 1648; printed in A. S. Hudson, *History of Sudbury,* pp. 64–65.
9. Sud. Rcds: Order of 1640: "Jethro's Field"; Hudson, *op. cit.,* p. 64.
10. *Mass. Col. Rcds,* I, 271.
11. Quarter Sessions of Suffolk (E. Sflk R.O. MSS): orders of July, October, 1639, Sud. Rcds.
12. *Mass. Col. Rcds,* I, 291–292.
13. Charges of 1616 at Stowmarket, Suffolk, printed in W. E. Tate, *The Parish Chest,* p. 177. Quarter Sessions Courts had been ordered by the Massachusetts General Court in 1635, and in 1643 Sudbury became part of Middlesex County: *Mass. Col. Rcds,* I, 169; II, 38.
14. The Middlesex County records do not begin before 1649, and no citation of Sudbury was made before 1655: Papers in Cases Before County Court of Mdsx. (MSS).
15. There is just such a list found in the old Roxbury records, with four categories: name, "persons," evaluation of estate, and the amount of acres proportionately granted: C. M. Ellis, *History of Roxbury Town* (Boston, 1847), p. 17. No such list remains for Sudbury, unfortunately.
16. Order of Fall, 1639, Sudbury Town Book. In these years of inflation, a cow in New England was worth £20, where at home it had been worth £5.
17. *Wat. Rcds,* I, 2, 8. Sudbury Order: February, 1638–1639. Sudbury Town Book. Note in Appendix VI that J. Parmenter, despite his place on the land committee, was given 28th place on the meadow-list.
18. *Wat. Rcds,* I, 2, 6. Stated in 1634 and again in 1640.
19. *Wat. Rcds,* I, 1, 3 (1638). Order of 1642, Sudbury Town Book.
20. Order, Fall of 1639, Sudbury Town Book.
21. Order, February 1639/40, Sudbury Town Book.
22. Order, February 1639/40, Sudbury Town Book. Compare order of Borough of Sudbury, May 1622, Ch. III.
23. Table printed in Bond, *op. cit.,* p. 983.
24. Order of May, 1640, Sudbury Town Book.
25. "Early Laws of Massachusetts," *Mass. Historical Society Collections, 3rd Series,* VIII: Body of Liberties, 216–237.
26. Gen. Ct. order of May 13, 1640. Entered into Sudbury Town Book.
27. Order of June 18, 1640, Sudbury Town Book. No definition of title was ever made, and occasionally the townsmen took back property granted to inhabitants, particularly when they left the town. Such grants "reverted to the town's use."
28. *Wat. Rcds,* I, Land, p. 28.
29. All statistics from tables printed in Appendices II, VI, VII, VIII.

30. All information as to the movement of men in and out of Sudbury has been gained by a careful study of the Sudbury Records, Watertown Records, Middlesex County Registry of Deeds, *Mass Col. Rcds,* and genealogical publications.
31. Order of Oct., 1643, Sudbury Town Book.
32. Edward Johnson, *Wonder Working Providence* (1654) reprinted in *Original Narratives* (N.Y., 1910), p. 230. Order of May 26, 1646, Sudbury Town Book.
33. *Mass. Col. Rcds,* I, 292.
34. A. Hudson, *History of Sudbury,* p. 62.
35. Orders of 1649, Sudbury Town Book.

CHAPTER VII

1. *Mass. Col. Rcds,* I, 238.
2. One Noyes was Town Clerk of Andover at this time (1638). English genealogists are sure that the Andover family of Noyes was related to the Weyhill family. (Borough of Andover MSS. See Ch. I, pp. 19–20.)
3. Professor Channing and M. Chamberlain emphasize this independent experiment and self-government by Dorchester and other towns in the excellent debate on the origin of Massachusetts towns in the *Proceedings of the Massachusetts Historical Society, 1892* (Boston, 1892), Ch. I, nb. 28, p. 22. John Sly in his *Town Government in Massachusetts* (Cambridge, 1930), pp. 20–21, agrees that the General Court was forced to recognize the system of town government which grew up, by trial and error, in each independent town.
4. E. Johnson, *Wonder Working Providence,* ed. by W. Poole (Andover, 1867), p. 142.
5. Stearns MSS, Sudbury, Mass.
6. Orders of April 13, 1643; December 7, 1647, Sudbury Town Book. See Sudbury map.
7. All quotations on this page: Order of Jan., 1643, Sudbury Town Book.
8. Orders of April 4, 1639; Feb. 1642/3; March 1, 1643/4; March 14, 1653/4; March 13, 1654/5, Sudbury Town Book.
9. Dimensions of house and barn taken from deed to this property: see S. C. Powell, "Seventeenth Century Sudbury, Mass." in *Journal of the Society of Architectural Historians,* XI:50 (March, 1952).
10. *Wat. Rcds,* I, 34 ff.
11. Edmund Rice's purchases can be traced, sale by sale, starting with an exchange of land sanctioned in May, 1644.
12. Order of May 26, 1646, Sudbury Town Book.
13. Order of June, 1644, Sudbury Town Book. These were the first selectmen.
14. Order of Nov. 26, 1645, Sudbury Town Book.
15. Order of Feb. 1639/40, Sudbury Town Book.
16. Only once, in 1648, did the clerk write "constable" for "marshall" in the Town Book. By this substitution of terms, we can be sure that Sudbury did mean J. How to fulfill the office of an English constable.
17. Order of Feb. 24, 1642/3, Sudbury Town Book.
18. *Mass. Col. Rcds.* II, 14. *Wat. Rcds,* I, 44. By 1654 this procedure became clear in Sudbury, for the marshal was ordered to report to the selectmen.
19. The Watertown records for the period have many instances of misdeeds and fines.
20. Order of March, 1644, Sudbury Town Book.
21. Order of March, 1644, Sudbury Town Book. Robert Darvell was one of the field surveyors.
22. Order of June 25, 1644, Sudbury Town Book.
23. Order of Feb. 1647/8, signed by H. Griffin, J. Ruddock, W. Haines, E. Goodnow, and W. Pelham, Sudbury Town Book.

24. See Appendix II.

25. See Appendix VI.

26. *Winthrop's Journal,* II, 19, 24.

27. *Ibid.,* II, 24.

28. Order of March, 1641, Sudbury Town Book.

29. Surrey: heavy work: 18d./day; mowing: 15d./day. Ordinary agricultural work: 18d./ day; servant: £5/year: *Vict. Cty. Hist. of Surrey,* (London, 1907), IV, 432. Sussex wages in 1620: agricultural work: 1s./day; carpenter: 18d./day: *Vict. Cty. Hist. Sussex* (London, 1907), II, 198. See orders of Parliament to J.P.s to set wage level of Suffolk in 1630: *Cal. S.P. Domestic, 1629–1631* (London, 1858), p. 544.

30. Griffin's salary started at 10s./year (1643), went up to £1 (1644), £2½ (1648) and leveled off at £4/year in 1651.

31. Order of 1643, Sudbury Town Book. Average salary in Bay towns, £55/year: J. B. Felt, *Ecclesiastical History of New England* (Boston, 1855–1862), p. 3. Brown's salary rose to £60 in 1653.

32. Order of August, 1643, Sudbury Town Book: calves "prized" worth 15s. each, shoats 6s. 8d. each, and goats 6s. each.

33. Order of June, 1645, Sudbury Town Book.

34. Order of Nov. 1647, Sudbury Town Book. Watertown land, nearer the markets, was more valuable: plowed land: 20s./acre; unplowed land: 10s./acre; all meadow: 20s./ acre: 1647. *Wat. Rcds,* I, 14.

35. *Wat. Rcds,* I, 7.

36. Assume 80 acres, his proportion on the original meadow allotment, divided into the total of 570 acres, estimated, in four general fields, worth £80; 48 acres of meadow, worth £17; assume the upland was "fenced but not broke up," worth £7. His will, 1657, shows even less land: "40 acres of upland, 20 acres of meadow and lands in Watertown" none of the land given a value: Middlesex Court Probate Records, MSS, I, 112–114.

37. Berkhamsted Churchwardens' Accounts (MSS): Taxes of 1637, 1630.

38. Granted 20 acres meadow, 27 acres upland; estimated — 20 acres in open fields.

39. Order of May, 1646, Sudbury Town Book.

40. Order of 1649, Sudbury Town Book.

41. Vincent B. Redstone, *The Ship Money Return for the County of Suffolk, 1639–1640* (Ipswich, 1904), pp. 9–10. The levy on Suffolk was the same in each of the ship-money taxes for 1635–1639. The largest amount levied in Framlingham was paid by T. Alexander, who had over sixty acres, who was assessed at £1/10. F. Ireland, who bought Danforth's property, was assessed at 7s. in 1640.

42. In 1655: Papers in Cases Before Cty Court of Mdsx, 1649–1663 (MSS), p. 198.

43. Orders of 1644–45, Nov. 16, 1650, July 5, 1652, Sudbury Town Book.

44. Order of Sept. 26, 1643, Sudbury Town Book.

45. Order of Jan. 1642; Order of May 28, 1655, Sudbury Town Book.

46. Order of Feb. 7, 1649/50, Sudbury Town Book. The tax for this was £12.

47. In 1655, 50s. was voted for the "ailing Mrs. Hunt." Sudbury Town Book.

48. Order of Jan. 4, 1655/6, Sudbury Town Book.

49. Quoted in *A Brief History of the Town of Sudbury, Mass.* (Federal Writers Project) (Sudbury, 1939), p. 32.

50. The Watertown clerk, on the other hand, recorded tax assessments and town income and expenses. For example, see *Wat. Rcds,* I, 40 ff.

51. Order of Feb. 1648, Sudbury Town Book.

52. Mdsx Cty Court Rcds, 1651–1652 (MSS). Order of Jan. 5, 1651/2 in Sudbury Town Book.

53. Order of Sept. 1654, Sudbury Town Book.

54. Cited in A. Hudson, *History of Sudbury*, p. 97. Edmund Rice was a deacon. Edward Johnson, in *Wonder Working Providence*, counted, in his 1650 survey, "80 souls in church membership and a population of not above 50 or 60 families" (p. 142). No separate church records have been found for Sudbury prior to 1700.

55. Described in 1640. In England the vicar and some church members made a yearly perambulation or walk around the property of their parish church, or glebe land.

56. Order of 1643, Sudbury Town Book.

57. Order of 1643, Sudbury Town Book.

58. Order of Feb. 1643, Sudbury Town Book.

59. Order of Jan. 1646, Sudbury Town Book.

60. Chilton L. Powell, *English Domestic Relations (1487–1653)* (New York, 1917), p. 51 ff.

61. *Mass. Col. Rcds*, II, 245.

62. *Mass. Col. Rcds*, I, 357.

63. *Ibid.*, I, 328; II, 35, 99, 147, 245.

64. H. Ainsworth, *Annotations* (Amsterdam ? 1616–1621).

65. W. Perkins, *Works* (Cambridge, 1608), 3 vols. Listed in the inventory of P. Noyes: Mdsx Cty Probate Records, I (MSS), 112–114.

66. S. Ward, *Jethro's Justice of the Peace* (London, 1621), pp. 2–3.

67. *The Works of William Perkins* (London, 1631), II, 148–149.

68. Case of Oct. 20, 1645, Sudbury Town Book.

69. Order of March 30, 1646, Sudbury Town Book.

70. Orders of April 24, 1648; Feb. 9, 1648/9; Dec. 9, 1649, Sudbury Town Book.

71. Order of March, 1650, Sudbury Town Book.

72. Order of May, 1650, Sudbury Town Book.

73. Papers in Cases Before the Cty Court of Mdsx, 1649–1663 (MSS), pp. 65–66.

74. *Ibid.*, p. 31.

75. In 1638–1639: *Mass. Col. Rcds*, I, 238.

76. *Ibid.*, I, 271.

77. *Ibid.*, I, 291, 296.

78. *Ibid.*, II, 124.

79. *Ibid.*, I, 345; II, 97.

80. *Ibid.*, I, 328; II, 35, 99, 147, 245; III, 130.

81. *Ibid.*, I, 173–174. Every male, 16 and over: 20d./year, plus 1d. for each 20s. of land and estate; 3s. 4d. if earnings over 18d./day.

82. Order of May 28, 1655, Sudbury Town Book.

83. Louis Morton, "The End of Formalized Warfare," *American Heritage*, VI:5 (August, 1955), 12 ff.

84. See contemporary comments of Capt. John Underhill, "The Pequod War," printed in R. M. Dorson, ed., *America Begins* (New York, 1950).

85. *Mass. Col. Rcds*, I, 188, 293, 327–328; II, 28, 47.

86. *Ibid.*, II, 23–26.

87. *Ibid.*, II, 2, 8, 47, 122–124. Orders of Mar. 9, 1646, Mar. 19, 1649, Feb. 7, 1649/50.

88. *Ibid.*, II, 36.

CHAPTER VIII

1. For details, see Appendix I.

2. "Cambridge University Graduates in New England," *Proceedings of the Colonial Society of Massachusetts*, XXV.

3. From Brown's will and inventory: Mdsx Ct. Probate Rcds (MSS), V, 84. Total value £713.

4. Edward Johnson states that Brown attended this Synod: *Wonder Working Providence*, p. 117.

5. H. Foote, ed., *The Cambridge Platform of 1648* (Cambridge, 1949).
6. *Mass. Col. Rcds*, III, 240.
7. Letter printed in L. Shattuck, *History of Concord* (Concord, 1890), p. 155. Bulkley's solution was "to make the church doors narrower," that is, to restrict church membership to those who could be trusted.
8. Grant copied in Sudbury Town Book, December 1649.
9. For land details, see Appendices.
10. P. Noyes was granted 14 more acres of meadow in Jan. 1651.
11. Order of 1651, Sudbury Town Book.
12. Hudson, *History of Sudbury*, p. 63.
13. Order of October, 1651, Sudbury Town Book.
14. Order of Jan. 1649, Sudbury Town Book.
15. Order of Nov., 1651, Sudbury Town Book.
16. Order of Jan. 1652, Sudbury Town Book.
17. Order of August, 1652, Sudbury Town Book.
18. Order of December, 1652, Sudbury Town Book. The contract, with all architectural details, is fully transcribed in S. C. Powell, "Seventeenth Century Sudbury, Mass.," *loc. cit.*, p. 142.
19. Order of December, 1652, Sudbury Town Book.
20. Order to raise building: October, 1653, Sudbury Town Book.
21. All details from clerk's minutes of this Jan. 1654 meeting. Smith was from old Sudbury: see Appendix I.
22. See map, Figure 19. None of the men had been granted meadow strips, or plots of upland in Sudbury. Ward left for Marlborough with Ruddock and Edmund Rice and was given thirty-one acres in the new town.
23. Order of Jan. 10, 1654, Sudbury Town Book.
24. Order of June 9, 1655, Sudbury Town Book.
25. Order of Sept. 1655, Sudbury Town Book.
26. Order of November 1643, signed at the Jan. 1655 meeting by all the selectmen but Edmund Rice and Thomas Noyes, Sudbury Town Book.
27. Order of Jan. 15, 1655/6, Sudbury Town Book.
28. This quotation and all other quotations and detailed references to the land quarrel in Sudbury, unless otherwise noted, are from Commonwealth of Massachusetts, Dept. of Archives, MSS Relating to Sudbury.
29. Order of Jan. 22, 1654/5, Sudbury Town Book.
30. *Ibid.* It is interesting to note that two women, Jane Goodnow and Mary Loker, who had meadow strips, were allowed to vote with the men.
31. Order of Mar. 28, 1654/5, Sudbury Town Book.
32. *Mass. Col. Rcds*, IV, 379–380. Committee of Thomas Danforth (son of Nicholas Danforth), John Sherman, and Major Willard.
33. Letter of Charges, Mass. Archives. Fifth Commandment: Honor thy father and thy mother; Ninth Commandment: Thou shalt not bear false witness against thy neighbor.
34. Cited in the minutes of the investigation, Mass. Archives. Edmund Goodnow had been reduced to swine warden!
35. Petition of 1656: printed in Hudson, *History of Sudbury*, p. 160.
36. See his will, 1657: Mdsx Cty, Probate Rcds, I, 112–114. He left a gift of £1 to "our Reverend Pastor, Mr. Brown."

CHAPTER IX

1. *Mass. Col. Rcds*, III, 403, 406–409, 421.
2. *Colonial Records of Marlborough, Mass.* (Boston, 1909), pp. 7–10. Referred to hereafter as *C.R.M.*

3. *C.R.M.*, pp. 6–7.
4. Compare Appendix VII with the Marlborough grant-list, Appendix VIII.
5. *C.R.M.*, p. 9.
6. *Ibid.*, p. 10. See Marlborough grant-list, Appendix VIII.
7. *Ibid.*, p. 9.
8. *Ibid.*, p. 11.
9. *Proc. Mass. Hist. Soc., 2nd ser.*, IV, p. 300 *et seq.*, "Diary of Reverend William Brimsmead."
10. *C.R.M.*, p. 26. Order of December 25, 1663.
11. *Ibid.*, p. 19: Order of 1662.

<h3 style="text-align:center">CHAPTER X</h3>

1. See "The Theory of the Village Community" in A. S. Eisenstadt, *Charles McLean Andrews* (New York, 1956), p. 18.
2. Personal letter to author from Hilda Grieve, Senior Assistant Archivist, Essex Record Office, Chelmsford, England.
3. Susie Ames, *Studies of the Virginia Eastern Shore in the Seventeenth Century* (Richmond, 1940).
4. Commonwealth of Mass., Dept. of Archives, MSS Relating to Sudbury.
5. *Mass. Col. Rcds*, IV, 379–380.
6. One or two references are made to "freemen," and there is one mention of "A Society of Proprietors" in Sudbury. But the chief local source of governmental power throughout the seventeenth century seems to have been "the inhabitants of the town." Orders of Jan. 16, Jan. 18, Feb. 5, 1694.
7. Warren C. Ault, *The Self-Directing Activities of Village Communities in Mediaeval England* (Boston University, 1952).
8. Orders of Feb. 21, 1665/6, March 2, 1662/3, March 12, 1666, March 26, 1676/7, Aug. 27, 1683, Oct. 5, 1683, March 16, 1684, Feb. 16, 1685, March 15, 1686/7, Sudbury Town Book.
9. Stearns MSS.
10. Order of March 11, 1677/8. The town hired Mr. Sherman; the "Town and church of Sudbury" agreed to the action: Order of Dec. 30, 1678; Dec. 26, 1686; May 23, 1688, Sudbury Town Book.
11. Order: "the last of February, 1647/8," Sudbury Town Book.
12. Orders of Jan. 5, 1662/3; March 12, 1666; Feb. 21, 1665/6; Feb. 14, 1680/1; May 20, 1695, Sudbury Town Book.
13. Order of Sept. 29, 1679, Sudbury Town Book.
14. Order of Dec. 17, 1694, Sudbury Town Book. The selectmen tried with particular fervor to collect information on each man's real and personal estate. They said that anyone who refused to bring in such data "shall by the selectmen be rated, Will and Doome"!
15. Order of April 30, 1683, Sudbury Town Book. Hedley had brought his wife and child "without leave first obtained contrary to a Town order" of Feb. 21, 1665.
16. Order of Jan. 16, 1694, Sudbury Town Book.
17. Order of Jan. 18, 1694, Sudbury Town Book, has an intriguing phrase, "for his services at the General Court under the Revolushun Government." Does it mean Andros's regime or one which followed it?
18. William Caudill, *Effects of Social and Cultural Systems in Reactions to Stress* (Social Science Research Council, Pamphlet 14, 1958), pp. 1, 12–14.
19. Bernard Bailyn, *The N.E. Merchants*, p. 168 ff.

Appendices

Sudbury Settlers, 1639-1641

NAME	PLACE OF ORIGIN	REFERENCE
Thomas Axtell wife: yes age: 23 came: 1642	Berkhamsted, Herts	Parish Register, cited in New England Historical and Genealogical Register, 53/227
"Widow" Bassumthyte	?	No information in sources listed.
Andrew Belcher wife: Eliz. Danforth m. 1639 age: ?	London, England son of Thomas Belcher, clothmaker	W. H. Whitmore, in N.E.R., July 1873, cites records.
John Bent wife: yes child: 4 sons 1 d.	Penton Grafton, Hants Weyhill Parish	Parish Register Psngr List, Banks, *Plnters*, 195.
Richard Bildcome	"Sutton mansfield, Wilts" now Sutton Mandeville	Psngr List, Banks, *Plntrs*, 195.
Thomas Bisbig (Beesbeech) wife: yes child: 4 servts: 2	land in Hedcorn, Fritten-don, Kent. Sailed from Sandwich S. E. Morison, "A yeoman"	Will, cited in Hudson, 52. Psngr list, Banks, *Plntrs*, 116; Articles: N.E.R. 67/33; 75/224; 79/108
John Blandford	Sutton Mandeville, Wilts	Psngr list, Banks, *Plntrs*, 195.
Mr. Edmund Brown wife: yes came: 1638, prob. with T. Lechford	Bap. Lavenham, Suffolk, 1606 (son Edm. Brown of this parish). Artillery Election sermon, 1666	F. L. Weis, *The Colonial Clergy*, p. 42. Will: bequest to Samuel Goffe, Cambr., son of Thomas Gough, London; Power of Attny to Jonath. Goffe, East Bergholdt, Sflk. Kins-man, "John Brown of Bury St. Edmunds, Suffolk": Middlesex Probate, 5/87.
Thomas Brown	Bury St. Edmunds, Suffolk?	N.E.R. 60/357; no real proof, but perhaps a rel. of Rev. Edm. Brown: cf G. Brown, *Descendants of Thomas Brown*, pp. 3–6.
William Brown	Bury St. Edmunds, Suffolk? Rel. of Abraham Brown, Hawkedon, Suffolk, who went to Watertown	Hudson, 35; N.E.R. 39/71; Banks, *Win.Flt.*, 264.

APPENDIX I *(cont.)*

NAME	PLACE OF ORIGIN	REFERENCE
Thomas Buckmaster	?	No information in sources listed.
Thomas Cakebread wife: Sarah	Hatfield Broad Oak, Essex	Psngr list, Banks, *Plntrs,* 68.
Henry Curtis carpenter, wheelwright m. Mary, d. of Nich. Guy, of Watertown sons: Ephraim John Joseph	London? b. 1608	will of sister, Joan Parker, of London, ment: N.E.R. 61/393; also cf: N.E.R. 32/337; 61/258; F. H. Curtiss, *A Gen. of the Curtis Family,* p. xxvi.
Robert Darvell	land in Northchurch, Herts, adjacent to Berkhamsted. officer of Berkhamsted; on tax lists there	will, cited, Pope, 131. Berkhamsted Chwdns Accts, 1600–1645.
Robert Davis	Penton Grafton, Hants Weyhill Parish	Parish Register; Psngr list, Banks, *Plntrs,* 195
Hugh Drury carpenter	?	"Family tradition": Cutter, IV, 2282: No work done: N.E.R. 1–104; Hudson, 52.
Thomas Flyn	?	was this the Concord Thomas Flint ? (from Matlock, Derby): cf: J. L. Bass, *The Flint Gen.,* pp. 106; N.E.R. 18/60.
Robert Fordham came: 1640	Sacombe, Herts, b. 1603 Cambr. Univ. B.A. 1625 M.A. 1629 Vicar: Flamstead, Herts, 1628–1638	article, citing rcds: N.E.R. 57/297ff; Chas. Chauncy, vicar of Ware, 4 mi. SE of Ware: cf N.E.R. 55/298; Am. Gen: 13/67
John Freeman came:1635 m. Eliz. Noyes, d. of Peter & Eliz. Noyes	Origin unknown b. c. 1600 d. c. 1648(?) m. c. 1648(?)	G. Gilbert, *Ancestry of Ezra Holton;* A J. Freeman ment. will of Wm. Read, Bocking, Essex, 1646: N.E.R. 50/124–125; A Freeman ment. in will of J. Bradstreet, Gislingham, Sflk, 1559: N.E.R. 65/71.
John George	?	A George ment. in Probate, Marston-Sicca, Gloucest., Eng. 1602. A J. George of Charlestown, Mass. b. 1677; N.E.R. 59/244.

APPENDIX I *(cont.)*

NAME	PLACE OF ORIGIN	REFERENCE
Edmund Goodnow wife: yes chld: 2 sons	Donhead St. Andrew, Wilts Churchwarden	cited, Archd. of Wilts, Act Book, 1636, 1637. (MSS) Psngr list, Banks, *Plntrs,* 196.
John Goodnow wife: yes chld: 2 d.s	Semley, Wilts	Psngr list, Banks, *Plntrs,* 196.
Thomas Goodnow wife: yes chld: 1 son sister	Shaftesbury, Dorset	Psngr list, Banks, *Plntrs,* 196.
Hugh Griffin wife: Elizabeth	Stepney, Middlesex (London)	Banks MSS; T. Coyler Ferguson, *Stepney Par.* *Reg., Marr.s 1568–1696,* p. 257: Jan. 1637–1638, Hugh Griffyn of Limehouse, brewer svt, m. Eliz. Hands. (Limehouse adj. to Stepney); Hudson.
John Grout wife: Mary, d. 1641 m. Sarah Cakebread, 1642 d. Thomas Cakebread	? (Derby ?) b. 1616, d. 1697	E. B. Jones, *Capt. John* *Grout* claims: desc. Sir Rich. Grout, Walton, Derby. No proof.
Thomas Haines	Sutton Mandeville, Wilts	Psngr list, Banks, *Plntrs,* 195.
Walter Haines linen weaver wife: yes chld: 2 s, 2 d. svts: 3	Sutton Mandeville, Wilts: owned house & outbuild- ings in Shaftesbury, Dorset. (N.E.R. 47/72)	Psngr list, Banks, *Plntrs,* 195; will of Alice Hayme, of Semley, Wilts, cited N.E.R. 39/263–264.
John How wife: Mary	?	D. W. Howe, Howe *Gen.:* no proof of Eng. back- ground, or when or how came: on Savage tip that J. How from Hodinhall, Warwick, searched par. reg. of that area — no results.
William How	?	Possibly the Wm. How of Concord: b. Eng. 1629, came 1635: wife: Mary Farmer, d. 1676, Concord. (MSS of Fred. L. Evans: nb: Abraham How of Roxbury was son of Rbt. How, Hatfield Broad Oak, Essex: cf. D. W. Howe, *Howe Gen.,* pp. 153–157.)

APPENDIX I *(cont.)*

NAME	PLACE OF ORIGIN	REFERENCE
Thomas Hoyte	?	
Robert Hunt	Sudborough, Northants	a Rbt. Hunt will, Charlestown, 1640 says "late of Sudborough, N. hants," N.E.R. 30/80–81; also N.E.R. 56/182; see T. Wyman, *The Gen. & Estates of Charlestown*, p. 528.
"Wid" Hunt	same origin?	No information in sources listed.
Solomon Johnson	?	Eng. origin not known: N.E.R. 66/233 ff; Not in Canterbury, Kent Par. Reg.
Thomas Joslyn wife: yes chld: 5	Roxwell, Essex	article, citing Par. Reg., rcds, etc: N.E.R. 71/227–257.
Edmund Kerley William Kerley	Ashmore, Dorset	Psngr list, Banks, *Plntrs*, 196; article N.E.R. 60/357; 60/20.
Peter King Thomas King	Shaftesbury, Dorset	N.E.R. 49/509; Banks, *Dict.*, 30; Pope. some Kings ment. in Shaftesbury law suit as burgesses. (SCP MSS files.)
John Knight maltster	?	No information in sources listed.
Henry Loker John Loker	Bures St. Mary, Essex	will of father, Henry L., quoted, M. L. Holman, *Ancestry of Col. John Harrington Stevens*, pp. 142–143.
John Maynard	Cambridge, Cambridge-shire	ment., no proof: N.E.R. 53/151; *Cambridgeshire Par. Reg. Marr.s*, I, 15; St. Edwards, Cambr: 28 July 1627, John Maynard, of Bassingbourn marr. Eliz. Aston, licet. Hudson, p. 47 says J. Maynard m. when came with 8-yr old son; remar. '46.
John Moore	? Sailed from London	Psngr list, Banks, *Plntrs*, 141; Hudson, p. 51.

APPENDIX I *(cont.)*

NAME	PLACE OF ORIGIN	REFERENCE
George Munnings wife: yes chld: 2 d.s	Rattlesden, Suffolk	Par. Reg., psngr list, Banks, *Plntrs*, 119.
Richard Newton	?	Nothing known: Ermina Leonard, *Newton Gen.*, p. 1.
Peter Noyes wife: Eliz. d. 1625 chld: 3 s., 3 d. svts: 4 sons: Thomas, b. 1623 Peter, b. 1630 Joseph, b. 1632 daught: Elizabeth, b. 1625 Abigail, b. 1628	Penton Grafton Weyhill Parish	Parish Register. Court-Baron Roll, Manor of Ramridge Psngr list, Banks, *Plntrs* invoice of "carryers": N.E.R. 32/410.
William Parker wife: Eliz. chld: 2	? rem. to Boston, 1648, then L.I., 1650	only Bond, *Gen. . . . of Watertown*, p. 868.
John Parmenter, Sr. John Parmenter, Jr. tailors	b. Little Yeldham, Essex c. 1588. Later, Bures St. Mary, Essex	G. Gilbert, *The Ancestry of Ezra Holton*
Mr. Herbert Pelham wife: Anna, d. 1637 chld: Anthony, Xtn. 1621 Martha, Xtn. 1622 d. 1624 Eliz., Xtn. 1624	Boston, Lincs. later, Bury St. Mary, Essex	articles, cites Par. Reg., records: N.B. Colket in *Am. Gen.* 71/139: *The Par. Reg. of Boston, Lincs*, II.
Mr. William Pelham	Boston, Lincs. Cambr. Univ. B.A. ret. to Eng. c. 1648	*Ibid.,* see Chap. VI, p. 134.
Brian Pendleton wife: Eleanor, d. ca. 1688 chld: Nicholas, Xtn. 1619 Mary James, b. ca. 1627	m. at St. Martins, Birmingham, 1619; res. St. Sepulcher's without Newgate, London	Noyes, Libby, Davis, *Me. & N.H. Gen. Dict.*, p. 537. G. Gilbert, *Ancestors of D. Freeman Britton*
Thomas Plympton	Goodworth Clatford, Hants	Banks MSS; was servant of Peter Noyes, op. cit.
Henry Prentiss wife: Elizabeth	Stewkley, Bucks?	Wm. K. Prentice, *Eight Generations,* p. 9: finds a H. Prentiss, m. Eliz. White; d. Anne, 1638; d. Eliz., 1640 in Stewk. Par. Reg; Hudson, p. 48 says Prentiss had wife, Eliz., who d. 1643. No real proof.

APPENDIX I *(cont.)*

NAME	PLACE OF ORIGIN	REFERENCE
Thomas Reed	Colchester, Essex	son of Thomas Reed, of same city: will cited, N.E.R. 21/369.
John Rediat (Riddet)	Sutton Mandeville, Wilts	Psngr list, Banks, *Plntrs*, 195.
Edmund Rice wife: yes chld: 9 came betw. Mar. 1638–Sept. 1639	prob. b. Sudbury, Suffolk m. at Bury St. Edmunds, 1618. rem. to Berkhamsted, Herts, 1626	Work on Eng. rcds by Mrs. W. Dodge; Berkhamsted Chwnds' Accts, 1600–1645.
John Ruddock	Trowbridge, Wilts	Banks MSS.
John Rutter	Penton Grafton, Wilts Weyhill Parish	Parish Register; psngr list, Banks, *Plntrs*, 195.
Richard Sanger	Semley, Wilts	Psngr list, Banks, *Plntrs*, 195.
John Smith wife: yes	Sudbury, Suffolk	full explanation, article, N.E.R. 56/182.
John Stone	Nayland, Suffolk	His father, Gregory, form. of Great Bromley, Essex. J. G. Bartlett, *G. Stone Gen.*, 10, 65–67.
Joseph Taintor	Upton Grey, Hants	Psngr list, Banks, *Plntrs*, 195.
John Toll	?	No information in sources listed.
Nathaniel Treadaway wife: Sufferana Haynes chld: Jonathan, b. 1640, d. 1710 Mary, b. 1642 Elizabeth, b. 1646 James, Lydia, Josiah, Doborch	perhaps Wiltshire	G. Gilbert, *Ancestry of Ezra Holton*
William Ward	?	After much work, C. M. Ward gives up hunt – thinks prob. E. Anglia: *Ward Gen.*, intro.
John Waterman	Penton Grafton, Hants Weyhill Parish	Weyhill Rectory MSS Noyes's invoice, printed, N.E.R. 32/410
Philemon Whale	Bures St. Mary, Essex bap. Chickney, Essex	will of bro. John cited, N.E.R. 63/280

APPENDIX I *(cont.)*

NAME	PLACE OF ORIGIN	REFERENCE
Anthony White	sailed from Ipswich, Suffolk	Psngr list, Banks, *Plntrs*, 122.
Thomas White	?	No information in sources listed
"Goodman" Witherall	poss. Maidstone, Kent	Psngr list gives Maidstone family: N.E.R. 75/218
John Wood	?	No information in sources listed
John Woodward	prob. sailed with father, Richard Woodward, from Ipswich, Suffolk, 1634	Psngr list, Banks, *Plntrs*, 117–118.
Edward Wright	son of Dorothy Wright, wid.	will cited in Pope, 516; explanation and refutation
Edward Wright (Concord) same ?	land in Castle Bromwick, Warwick	of false claims in Mary W. Ferris, *Dawes-Gates Anc. Lines*, 679–685.

REFERENCES: General

Printed

C. E. Banks, *The Planters of the Commonwealth* (Boston, 1930)
   Topographical Dictionary of 2885 English Emigrants to New England, 1620–1650 (Phila., 1937).
   The Winthrop Fleet (Boston, 1930)
W. R. Cutter, *Genealogical and Personal Memoirs Relating to the Families of Boston and Eastern Massachusetts* (N.Y., 1908), 4 vols.
S. G. Drake, *Founders of New England* (Boston, 1860).
J. C. Hotten, ed. *Original List of Persons of Quality . . . and Others Who Went From Great Britain to the American Plantations, 1600–1700* (London, 1874).
D. Jacobus, comp., *Index to Genealogical Periodicals* (New Haven, 1932).
C. H. Pope, *The Pioneers of Massachusetts* (Boston, 1900)

The American Genealogist and New Haven Genealogist (New Haven,   ) Vols. 1–28.
New England Historical and Genealogical Register (Boston, 1847–   ) Vols. 1–104.

Manuscript

Banks MSS: Collections of the New England Historical and Genealogical Society.
Winnifred L. Dodge library: "Deering File," "General File."
Middlesex County Court Records (See General Bibliography)
Sudbury, Massachusetts, Town Book(s), 1638–1700.
N. C. Tyack, "Emigration From East Anglia to New England, 1600–1660" (Univ. London thesis 1951)

Special Works and Genealogies

J. G. Bartlett, *The Gregory Stone Genealogy* (Boston, 1918)
J. L. Bass, *The Flint Genealogy* (Philadelphia, 1912)

172   PURITAN VILLAGE

H. Bond, *Genealogy . . . of the Early Settlers of Watertown, Mass.* (Boston, 1860)

G. Brown, *The Descendants of Thomas Brown of Concord* (Concord, 1901)

Cambridgeshire Parish Registers and Marriages (London, 1907), Vol. I

F. H. Curtis, *A Genealogy of the Curtis Family* (Boston, 1903)

Mary W. Ferris, *The Dawes-Gates Ancestral Lines* (Chicago, 1931)

T. C. Furgueson, *Stepney Parish Registers and Marriages, 1568–1696* (London, 1891).

G. Gilbert, ed. "The Ancestry of Ezra Holton of Northfield, Mass. and Soperton, Ont., 1785–1824" (Mimeographed, Victoria, B.C., 1953)

Mary L. Holman, *The Ancestry of Col. John Harrington Stevens* (Concord, 1948)

Winnifred H. Lovering-Holman, *The Stevens Miller Ancestry* (Concord, 1953), II

D. W. Howe, *The Howe Genealogy* (Boston, 1929)

A. S. Hudson, *The History of Sudbury, Mass.* (Sudbury, 1889)

E. B. Jones, *Captain John Grout* (Waterloo, Iowa, 1922)

E. Leonard, *The Newton Genealogy* (de Pere, Wisc., 1915)

The Parish Registry of Boston, Lincs (Lincs. Record Society, Par. Regist. Sect., Vol. III, Herncastle, 1915), II

W. K. Prentiss, *Eight Generations* (Princeton, 1947)

A. H. Ward, *A Genealogical History of the Rice Family* (Boston, 1858)
The Ward Family (Boston, 1851)

F. L. Weis, *The Colonial Clergy* (Lancaster, 1936)

T. Wyman, *The Genealogy and Estates of Charlestown* (Boston, 1879)

APPENDIX II

Weyhill Parish Landholders

1601-1639

NAME	COPYHOLD ACRES	COTTAGES HELD	RAMRIDGE JURY	ANDOVER OUT-HUNDRED JURY	CHURCHWARDEN	OVERSEER OF POOR	SURVEYOR OF WAYS	TOTAL POSTS HELD
Ramridge Hall								
(W. Noyes,	240	5h	5	6	4	1	1	17
T. Drake)		0	0	0	0	0	0	0
Blissimore Hall	105							
P. Gale, Sr.	73	1	2	0	0	0	1	3
P. *Noyes*	61	3	3	0	2	0	0	5
R. Bent	45	?	2	4	1	5	4	16
J. Bent								
(son of R. Bent)	"		0	0	1	1	1	3
W. Cole	45	1	3	0	2	1	1	7
R. Fuller	45		4	5	2	4	1	16
W. Bachelor	45	1	0	0	0	0	0	0
J. Buckley	45		0	0	0	0	0	0
E. Cole	38	1	3	7	3	1	1	15
G. Tarrant	30	1	6	4	0	0	3	13
P. Bendall	30	1	3	0	1	2	0	6
R. Tarrant	30		0	5	3	1	0	9
T. Tarrant								
(son of R. Tarrant)	"		1	0	1	1	0	3
S. Tarrant	"(?)		0	0	0	0	0	0
T. Gosselin	30	1	1	0	0	0	0	1
W. Davis	"	1h	0	0	0	0	0	0
W. Fuller	30	1	4	0	2	4	3	13
H. Tarrant	30	1	0	0	0	0	0	0
J. Tarrant	30	1	0	0	0	0	1	1
W. Noyes, Jr.	30	1	0	0	0	0	0	0
J. Noyes	30	1	0	0	0	0	0	0
Agnes Bendall	30	1	0	0	0	0	0	0
Wid. Pewsey	30	1	0	0	0	0	0	0
"Mr. Lewis"	30	1	0	0	0	0	0	0
R. Wale	21	1	5	0	1	2	2	10
John Buckley	21	1	5	0	3	3	0	11
P. Limpas	15	1	4	0	1	1	0	6
R. & T. Buckley	15		0	0	0	0	0	0
P. Whale	15	1h	0	0	0	0	0	0
W. Limpas	15	1h	0	0	0	0	0	0
N. Skeate	15	1h	0	0	0	0	0	0
J. Barnes	15	1h	0	0	0	0	0	0
W. Brown, Sr.	15	1h	0	0	0	0	0	0

APPENDIX II *(cont.)*

NAME	COPYHOLD ACRES	COTTAGES HELD	RAMRIDGE JURY	ANDOVER OUT-HUNDRED JURY	CHURCHWARDEN	OVERSEER OF POOR	SURVEYOR OF WAYS	TOTAL POSTS HELD
H. Tunke, Sr.	12	1	5	3	1	2	4	15
J. Guyatt	12	1h	0	0	0	0	0	0
T. Crouch	12	1h	0	0	1	1	2	4
J. Morrant	7½		0	0	0	0	0	0
R. Grace	7	1	4	1	4	2	3	14
G. Wale	?		4	0	0	1	0	5
J. Grace	6	1h	0	0	1	0	0	1
J. Hurst	6	1	0	0	0	0	0	0
P. Tarrant	0		1	3	1	0	0	5
P. Grace	0		1	0	0	0	0	1
Gregory Wale	0		1	0	0	0	0	1
J. Limpas	0		0	0	0	4	0	4
J. Davis	0		0	0	0	0	3	3
J. Mansfield	0		0	0	1	0	0	1
R. Cole	0		0	0	2	2	0	4
W. Smith	0		0	0	1	1	0	2
H. Cole	0		0	0	0	1	0	1
W. Streake	0		0	0	0	0	1	1
H. Noyes	0		0	0	0	0	1	1
J. Wale	0		0	0	1	1	1	3
P. Mercer	0		0	0	0	0	1	1
Richard Tarrant	0		1	0	0	1	3	5
J. Webb	0		0	0	1	2	0	3
P. Wale	0		0	0	1	1	0	2
J. Mundy	0		0	0	1	1	1	3
J. Bevies	0		0	0	0	1	0	1
W. Streete	0		0	0	0	0	1	1
J. Pewsey	0		0	0	0	1	0	1
R. Knight	0		0	0	0	0	2	2
E. Tugg	0		0	0	0	1	1	2
J. Dowling	0		0	0	0	0	1	1
R. Burger	0		0	0	1	0	2	3
J. Smith	0		0	0	1	1	1	3
P. Bachelor	0		0	0	2	4	0	6
T. Gyatt	0		0	0	0	1	0	1
J. Baker	0		0	0	0	0	3	3
P. Bendall	0		0	0	1	2	0	3
W. Gosling	0		0	0	0	0	1	1
W. Washlea	0		0	0	0	0	1	1
G. Wall	0		0	0	1	0	0	1
T. Noyes	0		0	0	0	1	0	1
E. Joye	0		0	0	1	1	0	2
W. Washboard	0		0	0	1	0	0	1

APPENDIX II *(cont.)*

NAME	COPYHOLD ACRES	COTTAGES HELD	RAMRIDGE JURY	ANDOVER OUT-HUNDRED JURY	CHURCHWARDEN	OVERSEER OF POOR	SURVEYOR OF WAYS	TOTAL POSTS HELD
R. Davis	0		0	0	0	0	1	1
D. Tarrant	0		0	0	0	0	2	2
W. Matthew	0		0	0	1	0	0	1
N. Cole	0		0	0	1	1	0	2
R. Jackman	0		0	0	0	1	0	1
Totals: 84	1318	33						

Key: h — hearth listed (tax); "— indicates inheritance; emigrants in italics.

Weyhill Parish Landholders
1693 *Rate List*

NAME	CHURCH RATE	EST. ACRES	HEARTHS
Ramridge Hall (T. Drake)	16/10	240	5
Blissimore Hall (W. Thomas)	7/0	105	
A. Biley	6/0	90	
T. Knowles	4/6	67	
"Mr. Russell"	4/0	60	
R. Steavens	4/0	60	4
— Poynters	4/0	60	2
P. Noyes	3/0	45	
R. Tarrant	3/0	45	1
Wid. Tarrant	2/0	30	
Wid. Davis	2/0	30	
J. Noyes	2/0	30	1
Wid. Iremonger	2/0	30	
R. Bendal	2/0	30	
P. Bachelor	2/0	30	
J. Mundy	1/9	27	
A. Grace, J. Grace	1/8½	23	1
Wid. Bunkley	1/6	22	1
J. Guyat	1/6	22	
Church Glebe		18½	
W. Limpas	1/2	17	
W. Thomas	1/0	15	
W. Brown, Sr.	1/0	15	
W. Brown, Jr.	1/0	15	
P. Wale	1/0	15	

APPENDIX II *(cont.)*

NAME	CHURCH RATE	EST. ACRES	HEARTHS
G. Rumbold	1/0	15	
Rev. Sanderson		11.5	5
T. Crouch	0/10	11	1
J. Barnes	2/0	12	1
Wid. Wale	0/9	10	
S. Tarrant	0/6	7	3
T. Wales	0/6	7	1
J. Hust	0/4½	5.2	
D. Cops	0/4	5	
P. Coopers	0/4	5	
R. Fuller	0/4	5	
S. Osgood	0/4	5	
W. Beach	0/4	5	
T. Dalby	0/3	4	
H. Gale	0/2	2.2	
J. Barnes, Jr.	0/2	2.2	
J. Helliar	0/2	2.2	
P. Bendal	0/2	2.2	
H. Green	0/2	2.2	
W. Hayes	0/2	2.2	
M. Tarrant	0/2	2.2	
P. Gale	0	0	2
Totals: 48	£4/0/08	1280 acres	28

APPENDIX III

Amounts of Land Held in Parish of Berkhamsted According to Rate Lists

(Land listed in acres)

NAME	1613		1617		1622	1627	1633	1637
	Ara-ble	Meadow	Ara-ble	Meadow				
Mr. Murrey	–	–	–	–	–	160	240	240
Sir P. Cary	–	–	–	–	–	114	–	–
Mr. J. Hudnoll	103	0	–	–	2	–	3	–
Reverend Newman	35	0	92	0	84	94	64	65
Mr. A. Blount	91	5	100	6	119	–	–	–
Mr. Wethered	0	0	100	2	102	92	102	103
Mr. Barker	48	4	92	4	96	28	40	88
J. Climson	30	3	30	3	43	54	52	–
O. Haynes	48	5	50	7	48	52	52	52
M. Dean	40	0	40	0	–	–	–	72
Mr. Baghot	–	–	–	–	–	40	–	–
Mr. Rogers	0	0	0	0	0	40	40	–
Mr. Grower	20	0	6	0	9	40	–	–
W. Pitkin	23	2	23	2	39	39	196	204
S. Dagnoll	0	0	0	0	24	36	112	38
Mr. Hunt	0	0	0	0	30	30	28	12
S. Besouth	0	0	25	1½	24	24	18	–
F. Clymson	0	0	30	3	0	–	–	–
T. Clymson	0	0	21	2½	20	–	–	–
E. Hopkins	18	4	19	3	19	–	–	–
Mr. Kellet	0	0	0	0	0	16	114	50
R. Speed	10	1	18	1	0	–	–	–
J. Surman	0	0	16	0	16	16	16	21
R. Darvell	0	0	0	0	22	15	15	19
N. Broakes	0	0	0	0	0	22	14	–
R. Lawrence	14	0	4	0	4	4	4	3
W. Hill	3	1	3	1	14	12	16	10
J. Shermantine	12	4	0	1½	2	2	2	3
E. How	9	3	12	0	12	12	12	–
J. Grene	0	0	0	0	9	12	–	–
J. Redwood	0	0	0	0	0	12	–	–
T. Bachellor (& wid.)	0	0	0	0	12	12	16	12
R. Grover	0	0	0	0	0	4	12	–
N. Payne	0	0	0	0	12	12	10	10
R. Clark	10	2	15	½	2	2	2	–
G. Dover	0	0	0	0	10	10	30	40
H. Axtill	10	1	12	1	19	–	–	–
W. Lake	0	0	0	0	2	10	20	20
H. Shermantine	10	0	0	0	0	–	–	–
W. Axtell	2	1	7	3	7	9	24	24
T. Eggleton	5	1	8	0	8	9	12	10

APPENDIX III *(cont.)*

NAME	1613		1617		1622	1627	1633	1637
	Arable	Meadow	Arable	Meadow				
T. Reynolds	8	o	1	o	1	9	9	12
T. Stevens & wid.	o	o	o	o	8	8	6	3
J. Pitchfork	o	o	o	o	o	6	6	6
R. Newman	o	o	o	o	6	6	26	67
W. Mead	o	o	o	o	6	6	6	9
E. Darvell	o	o	o	o	o	6	6	–
J. Robinson	o	o	o	o	6	6	6	–
R. Partridge	o	o	o	o	16	12	–	–
W. Goodridge	o	o	o	o	2	5	22	71
R. Benning	o	o	o	o	o	4	10	12
E. Rice	–	–	–	–	–	3	15	15
R. Renolds	o	o	2	1½	3	3	3	12
H. Field	o	o	2	1	3	–	–	–
R. Finch	o	o	o	½	o	–	–	–
T. Wethered	o	o	12	o	12	14	12	12
H. Sheppherd	o	o	3	o	o	–	–	–
Wid. Pope	o	o	1	o	o	–	–	–
T. Trip	o	o	3	2	o	–	–	–
C. Wilkinson	o	o	2	o	2	2	–	–
A. Jaques	o	o	9	o	2	–	–	–
R. How	o	o	10	o	3	3	3	3
R. Chambers	o	o	1½	o	1½	1½	1½	2
J. Collins	o	o	1½	o	1½	–	–	–
J. Blake	o	o	2	o	6	–	–	–
N. Ewer	o	o	o	o	10	–	–	–
T. Lawrence	o	o	o	o	2	3	–	–
Mr. Seth	–	–	–	–	–	–	28	28
Mr. Conquist	–	–	–	–	–	–	16	12
Mrs. Wethered	–	–	–	–	–	–	96	–
W. Henson	–	–	–	–	–	–	12	12
Mr. Sear	–	–	–	–	–	–	9	8
E. How	–	–	–	–	–	–	2	3
N. Beming	–	–	–	–	–	–	1	12
J. Grommet	–	–	–	–	–	–	8	–
R. South	–	–	–	–	–	7	7	–
R. Suttridge	–	–	–	–		–	16	4
T. Smith	–	–	–	–	–	–	3	–
J. Davey	–	–	–	–	–	–	3	3
R. Hill	–	–	–	–	–	–	3	4
W. How	–	–	–	–	–	–	2	2
R. Simmes	–	–	–	–	–	–	2	–
W. Oliver	–	–	–	–	–	–	2	2
E. Marse	–	–	–	–	–	–	3	3
W. Faunch	–	–	–	–	–	–	2	2
W. Cook, Sr.	–	–	–	–	–	–	?	=
W. Cook, Jr.	–	–	–	–	–	–	2	1½

APPENDIX III *(cont.)*

NAME	1613 Arable	1613 Meadow	1617 Arable	1617 Meadow	1622	1627	1633	1637
G. Bailey	–	–	–	–	–	–	3	–
F. Griffin	–	–	–	–	–	–	3	–
J. Haines	–	–	–	–	–	–	2	15
W. Babb	–	–	–	–	–	–	2	3
R. Percival	–	–	–	–	–	–	2	2
G. Percival	–	–	–	–	–	–	2	2
J. Percival	–	–	–	–	–	–	2	2
T. Hadden	–	–	–	–	–	–	2	3
J. Baldwin	–	–	–	–	–	–	2	2
R. Child	–	–	–	–	–	–	2	2
Wid. Bailey	–	–	–	–	–	–	2	2
R. Clark	–	–	–	–	–	–	2	$2\frac{1}{2}$
W. Andrew	–	–	–	–	–	–	2	2
N. Mores	–	–	–	–	–	–	4	4
J. Egleton	–	–	–	–	–	–	6	–
T. Godman	–	–	–	–	–	–	2	2
R. Davey	–	–	–	–	–	–	12	–
J. Adams	–	–	–	–	–	–	3	3
T. Adams	–	–	–	–	–	–	3	3
R. Ward, Sr.	–	–	–	–	–	–	4	2
R. Ward, Jr.	–	–	–	–	–	–	2	2
W. Martin	–	–	–	–	–	–	3	2
R. Baker	–	–	–	–	–	–	2	$1\frac{1}{2}$
R. Bilbe	–	–	–	–	–	–	2	2
J. Buckmaster	–	–	–	–	–	–	3	–
Wid. South	–	–	–	–	–	–	3	3
W. Bennett	–	–	–	–	–	–	2	2
J. England	–	–	–	–	–	–	2	–
T. Presson	–	–	–	–	–	–	2	2
T. Hawes	–	–	–	–	–	–	3	7
T. Nash	–	–	–	–	–	–	6	6
J. Benning	–	–	–	–	–	–	4	7
James Benning	–	–	–	–	–	–	4	–
R. Benning	–	–	–	–	–	–	8	8
W. Glenester	–	–	–	–	–	–	4	4
T. Hunt	–	–	–	–	–	–	4	–
J. Hall	–	–	–	–	–	–	4	4
J. Day	–	–	–	–	–	–	4	8
J. Williams	–	–	–	–	–	–	6	3
J. Verney	–	–	–	–	–	–	6	6
G. Verney	–	–	–	–	–	–	6	–
R. Almond	–	–	–	–	–	–	10	–
J. Kim	–	–	–	–	–	–	6	–
T. Hudnall	–	–	–	–	–	–	6	6
T. Burgess	–	–	–	–	–	–	2	2
T. Dagnall	–	–	–	–	–	–	2	4

APPENDIX III *(cont.)*

NAME	1613		1617		1622	1627	1633	1637
	Arable	Meadow	Arable	Meadow				
W. Oxley	–	–	–	–	–	–	3	2
R. Oxley	–	–	–	–	–	–	2	10
N. Partridge	–	–	–	–	–	–	6	–
W. Phillips	–	–	–	–	–	–	8	9
J. Keene	–	–	–	–	–	–	2	6
J. Baker	–	–	–	–	–	–	3	6
R. Fansome	–	–	–	–	–	–	3	–
Philemon Whale	–	–	–	–	–	–	2	3
R. Stone	–	–	–	–	–	–	2	2
T. Randall	–	–	–	–	–	–	2	2
W. Clerk	–	–	–	–	–	–	3	–
N. Payne	–	–	–	–	–	–	2	3
Wid. Payne	–	–	–	–	–	–	2	–
Wid. Chambers	–	–	–	–	–	–	2	2
D. Webb	–	–	–	–	–	–	2	2
R. Andrew	–	–	–	–	–	–	2	3
T. Cooper	–	–	–	–	–	–	2	2
Wid. R. Chambers	–	–	–	–	–	–	2	–
W. Winkfield	–	–	–	–	–	–	2	2
Wid. Grover	–	–	–	–	–	–	2	–
S. Stanley, Jr.	–	–	–	–	–	–	2	4
C. Gill	–	–	–	–	–	–	2	2
Wid. Fordam	–	–	–	–	–	–	3	3
Wid. Mores	–	–	–	–	–	–	3	–
L. Willcox	–	–	–	–	–	–	2	1½
M. How	–	–	–	–	–	–	2	2
H. Funk	–	–	–	–	–	–	2	2
J. Pope	–	–	–	–	–	–	2	3
R. Pettit	–	–	–	–	–	–	2	3
E. Munn	–	–	–	–	–	–	2	–
F. Russell	–	–	–	–	–	–	2	2
R. Dell, Jr.	–	–	–	–	–	–	45	–
W. Pitkin, Jr.	–	–	–	–	–	–	0	12
T. Newman	–	–	–	–	–	–	–	4
T. Bishop	–	–	–	–	–	–	–	3
T. Dagnall, Jr.	–	–	–	–	–	–	–	2
T. Seeley	–	–	–	–	–	–	–	2
R. Benning	–	–	–	–	–	–	–	4
N. Oxley	–	–	–	–	–	–	–	2
N. Handcock	–	–	–	–	–	–	–	2
"Flood the Welchman"	–	–	–	–	–	–	–	2
C. Johnson	–	–	–	–	–	–	–	2
W. Axtell, Jr.	–	–	–	–	–	–	–	2
W. Hanse	–	–	–	–	–	–	–	2
W. Keper	–	–	–	–	–	–	–	6
W. Johnson	–	–	–	–	–	–	–	2

APPENDIX III *(cont.)*

NAME	1613		1617		1622	1627	1633	1637
	Arable	Meadow	Arable	Meadow				
Wid. Burr	–	–	–	–	–	–	–	2
G. Coole	–	–	–	–	–	–	–	8
G. Piddleton	–	–	–	–	–	–	–	2
J. Stone	–	–	–	–	–	–	–	2
J. Sheesman	–	–	–	–	–	–	–	3
J. Greenbricker	–	–	–	–	–	–	–	1½
J. Lucas	–	–	–	–	–	–	–	15
S. Burgis	–	–	–	–	–	–	–	3
H. Harding	–	–	–	–	–	–	–	8
H. Bemond	–	–	–	–	–	–	–	1½
H. Griffin	–	–	–	–	–	–	–	1½
J. Rolfe	–	–	–	–	–	–	–	1½
J. Gibb	–	–	–	–	–	–	–	1½
J. Hudnoll	–	–	–	–	–	–	–	1½
J. Kinrose	–	–	–	–	–	–	–	1½
S. Watkins	–	–	–	–	–	–	–	2
W. Putnam	–	–	–	–	–	–	–	4
G. Harris	–	–	..	–	–	–	–	1½
C. Willinson	–	–	–	–	–	–	–	2
J. Toy	–		–	–	–	–	–	8
J. Abbot	–	–	–	–	–	–	–	6
T. Johnson	–	–	–	–	–	–	–	4
Totals:	549a. arable, 37a. meadow		673a. arable, 54a. meadow		900	1138½	1823	1743

NORTHCHURCH

NAME	1613		1617		1622	1627	1633	1637
W. Baldwin	0	0	72	8	160	160	160	160
W. Edline	72	8	72	2	–	–	80	–
J. Orice	0	0	30	3	40	48	40	40
J. Hopkins, D.D.	40	2	–	2	2	2	2	2
H. Putnam	0	0	0	0	0	30	30	30
J. How	0	0	7	3	20	20	–	–
T. Hill	0	0	8	½	9	9	13	13
Mr. Madox	8	0	0	0	–	–	–	–
H. Sear	0	2	30	2	2	2	3	3
W. Wellek	0	0	0	0	1	2	2	2
H. Hudnall	2	0	0	0	0	–	–	–
F. Bussell	0	0	0	0	2	2	–	–
J. Brewer	2	0	0	0	–	–	–	–
T. Dabenye	0	2	0	2	2	1	–	–
J. Dabney	0	1	0	0	0	7	9	9
T. Hunt	1	0	0	0	–	–	–	–
J. Climson	0	0	0	0	30	30	30	30

APPENDIX III *(cont.)*

NAME	1613		1617		1622	1627	1633	1637
	Ara-ble	Meadow	Ara-ble	Meadow				
W. Wylett	0	0	0	1½	1	10	10	80
T. Bate	0	0	0	½	1	–	–	–
R. Madox	–	–	18	0	0	–	–	–
T. White	–	–	–	–	–	–	40	40
R. Smith	–	–	–	–	–	–	3	3
H. Dagnall	–	–	–	–	–	–	3	3
Totals:	125	15	237	24½	270	323	425	415

FRESDEN

NAME	Ara-ble	Meadow	Ara-ble	Meadow	1622	1627	1633	1637
J. How Hollybush	20	0	30	0	30	30	30	24
M. Youngs	0	0	2	0	18	18	79	107
W. Grouer	12	0	12	0	–	–	–	–
T. Seyster	12	0	–	–	–	–	–	–
M. Chembers	0	0	0	0	16	10	9	–
N. Downes	0	0	0	0	0	10	10	10
W. Haussey	10	0	10	0	–	–	–	–
T. Babb	0	0	0	0	0	6	60	60
W. Babb	0	0	0	0	6	4	2	–
W. Norkett	0	0	0	0	4	2	–	–
R. How	0	0	0	0	3	4	5	5
J. Fenn	2½	0	2	0	3	4	–	–
R. Davye	0	0	0	0	4	4	4	–
J. How de Corner	0	0	2	0	2	2	2	2
R. Andrer	0	0	0	0	0	2	–	–
R. Lawrence	0	0	0	0	0	2	–	–
I. Thorne	0	0	3	0	2	2	2	2
W. Playter	0	0	0	0	2	2	2	2
R. How	0	0	0	0	6	1	–	–
P. Pix	2	0	0	0	0	–	–	–
R. Godfrey	2	0	0	0	0	–	–	–
H. Taylor	2	0	2	0	2	1	–	–
R. Petit	2	0	0	0	0	–	–	–
M. Young	2	0	2	0	0	–	–	–
E. Gourney	2	0	2	0	0	–	–	–
T. Coke	–	–	–	–	–	1½	–	–
W. Cook	–	–	–	–	–	3	3	–
W. Wood	–	–	–	–	–	–	3	–
J. Cook	–	–	–	–	–	–	3	3
T. Bailey	–	–	–	–	–	–	3	2
Wid. Bates	1	–	0	–	0	–	–	–
J. Coke	0	–	0	–	0	2	2	2
L. Willcock	–	–	–	–	–	–	–	3
T. Gourney	1	–	1	–	–	–	–	–
J. Woodward	0	–	0	–	0	1	1	1
J. Burgess	1	–	1	–	0	–	–	–

APPENDIX III *(cont.)*

NAME	1613		1617		1622	1627	1633	1637
	Arable	Meadow	Arable	Meadow				
R. Rose	1	–	1	–	–	–	–	–
R. Bugberd	½	–	0	–	0	–	–	–
P. Seebrook	½	–	0	–	0	–	–	–
T. Gourney	0	–	½	–	2	–	–	–
R. Ransom	0	–	16	–	0	–	–	–
R. Dean	0	–	0	–	0	0	0	40
J. Trip	–	–	–	–	–	–	–	3
J. Alle	–	–	–	–	–	–	–	10
Totals:	73½ arable; 0 meadow		76½ arable; 0 meadow		104	111½	217	329

"THE PARK TENANTS"

NAME	1613		1617		1622	1627	1633	1637
	Arable	Meadow	Arable	Meadow				
J. Rolfe	–	–	–	–	–	–	60	60
C. Knight	–	–	–	–	–	–	100	100
F. Gadsden	–	–	–	–	–	–	6	60
J. Crane	–	–	–	–	–	–	10	10
J. Alee	–	–	–	–	–	–	10	10
T. Whitney	–	–	–	–	–	–	10	10
C. Wheeler	–	–	–	–	–	–	20	–
T. Lucas	–	–	–	–	–	–	10	–
R. Deane	–	–	–	–	–	–	79	79
W. Hoe	–	–	–	–	–	–	18	18
W. Whelpey	–	–	–	–	–	–	10	10
T. Hill	–	–	–	–	–	–	–	9
H. Dagnall	–	–	–	–	–	–	–	3
J. Fenn	–	–	–	–	–	–	–	4
Totals:							333	383

APPENDIX IV

Relation of Property to Governing Posts in Berkhamsted, Herts

(From data on 30 elections, 1600–1638)

NAME	MAXIMUM ACREAGE HELD AT ANY	ONE PARISH TAX	BAILIFF (MAYOR)	CHIEF BURGESS	CHURCHWARDEN	SIDEMAN	OVERSEER OF POOR	STONEWARDEN	TOWN CLERK	TOTAL POSTS HELD
Mr. Murrey	240	0	No	0	0	0	0	0	0	0
W. Pitkin	204	1	Yes	3	3	2	0	0	0	10
Mr. Blount	119	1	Yes	0	0	0	0	0	0	2
Sir Philip Cary	114	0	No	0	0	0	0	0	0	0
Mr. Kellet	114	0	Yes	0	0	1	0	0	0	2
S. Dagnoll	112	2	Yes	0	0	0	0	0	0	3
Mr. Hudnoll	103	0	No	0	1	0	1	0	0	2
Mr. Barker	96	0	Yes	0	0	2	0	0	0	3
Reverend Newman	94	1	Yes	1	0	2	0	0	0	5
Mr. Wethered	103	0	Yes	0	0	1	0	0	0	2
M. Dean	72	0	No	0	0	0	0	0	0	0
W. Goodrich	71	0	No	0	0	0	0	0	0	0
Ralph Newman	67	0	No	0	0	1	0	0	0	1
J. Climson	54	0	No	1	0	1	0	0	0	2
O. Haynes	52	1	Yes	3	1	1	0	0	0	7
Mr. Baghot	40	0	No	0	0	0	0	0	0	0
G. Dover	40	0	No	0	0	0	0	0	0	0
Mr. Rogers	40	0	No	0	0	0	0	0	0	0
Mr. Grower	40	0	No	0	0	0	0	0	0	0
Mr. Hunt	30	0	Yes	0	0	1	0	0	0	2
F. Clymson	30	0	No	0	0	0	0	0	0	0
Mr. Seth	28	0	No	0	0	0	0	0	0	0
S. Besouth	26	1	Yes	3	2	1	0	0	0	8
*W. Axtell	24	1	Yes	2	3	0	0	1	1	9

APPENDIX IV *(cont.)*

NAME	MAXIMUM ACREAGE HELD AT ANY ONE PARISH TAX	BAILIFF (MAYOR)	CHIEF BURGESS	CHURCHWARDEN	SIDEMAN	OVERSEER OF POOR	STONEWARDEN	TOWN CLERK	TOTAL POSTS HELD
R. Darvell	22	o	Yes	1	o	o	o	o	2
N. Broakes	22	o	No	o	o	o	o	o	o
J. Surman	21	o	No	o	o	o	o	o	o
W. Lake	20	1	Yes	2	1	o	o	o	5
T. Clymson	20	o	No	o	o	o	o	o	o
H. Axtell	19	o	No	o	o	o	o	o	o
E. Hopkins	19	o	No	o	o	o	o	o	o
S. Speed	18	o	No	o	o	o	o	o	o
W. Hill	16	1	Yes	3	2	o	o	o	7
T. Bachellor	16	o	No	o	o	1	1	o	2
Mr. Conquist	16	o	No	o	o	o	o	o	o
R. Suttridge	16	o	No	o	o	o	o	o	o
R. Partridge	16	o	No	1	o	1	o	o	2
E. Rice	15	o	No	o	o	o	o	o	o
R. Clark	15	o	No	o	o	o	o	o	o
T. Wethered	14	o	No	o	o	o	o	o	o
R. Lawrence	14	o	No	o	o	o	o	o	o
T. Eggleton	12	o	No	2	2	2	o	o	6

(160 additional names: all with 12 acres or less: none served in more than two church posts during the entire period. Most of them: no posts)

NORTHCHURCH: No landholders served in parish or borough posts.

FRESDEN: Only 4 landholders served in a maximum of 2 church posts; no borough posts.

(*Father of emigrant.)

Suffolk Churchwardens' Oath, 1638

The Oath of the Churchwardens and Swornemen:

You shall swear that after due consideration had of these Articles given you now in charge, that you will diligently inquire and true presentment make of all and every such person of or within your parish, which you shall know to have committed any offence, or omitted any duty mentioned in the sd Articles, or which are publicly defamed or vehemently suspected of any such offence or negligence. So help you God, by the Contents of the Holy Gospel.

Answer distinctly and severally to every Article:

I: *Concerning Religion and Doctrine.*

1. Whether there be any abiding in, or resorting to your parish that have, or do maintain or defend any heresies, errors, or false opinion, contrary to the faith of Christ, and the Holy Scripture?

2. Whether there be in the parish, sixteen years old and up, any who absent themselves from church, chapel or oratory on Sundays or on Holy Days, and other days appointed, at Morning and Evening prayers?

   Whether there be any persons that come late to church, or depart before the divine service and the sermon be ended? Whether there be any who persuade others to forbear and abstain from coming to church, or to hear the service, or receive communion, according to His Majesty's Law?

3. Whether are any suspected to have been present at any unlawful assemblies, meetings, under pretense of exercise of religion? Or are there any that doth affirm that such meetings are lawful?

4. Whether there be any that deny the King's authority and supremacy in Ecclesiastical matters?

5. Whether there be any in the parish commonly reputed to be ill-affected in matters of religion professed in our Church? Or are there any taken to be recusant, papist, or refusing to repair to church to hear the divine services, or receive Holy Communion, or disobedient to His Highness' Laws?

6. Whether there be any in the parish who has repeated any sermon, or expounded any scripture in any private house, or in any assembly, or meeting of people whatsoever?

7. Whether there be any in the parish who doth impunge any of the 39 Articles of Religion, agreed on 1562 A.D. and established in the Church of England? And is the Declaration which the King prefixed before those Thirty-Nine Articles concerning the settling of questions late in difference, duely observed by all in your parish, according to the King's command?

8. Is there any in the parish that hath, or doth sell, publish, or dispose any superstitious, seditious, schismatical books, libels, writings touching religion, the state of Ecclesiastical government of this Kingdom? If so, then present their names, qualities, and conditions, or If you have heard of any.

II: *Concerning Public Prayer, Administrations of the Holy Sacrament.*

1. Whether there be any in the parish who has spoken or declared anything in derogation or depraving of the form of God's worship, as observed in the Church of England, and the administration of the sacraments, rites, ceremonies set forth in the Book of Common Prayer by the King, authorized and confirmed? Do any preach, or speak, or declare that it contains anything which is not agreeable to the Holy Scripture?

2. Whether there be any in the parish who have caused, procured, or maintained any minister to say common or public prayer, or to administer the Sacrament of Baptism, or the Lord's Supper, otherwise, or in any other manner, than is mentioned in the Book of Common Prayer? Or has any interrupted, hindered, or disturbed the minister while he doth read the divine service, and administer the sacraments, or interrupted him in his sermon?

3. Whether is the Sacrament of Baptism rightly and duly administered, according to the Book of Common Prayer, with all the rites and ceremonies prescribed, without adding or altering any part of any prayer, or interrogatories? Is the sign of the Cross used every time, and the Surplice worn in the administration of it?

4. Whether the administration of the Sacrament of Baptism is deferred longer than the next Sunday, or Holy Day, following the child's birth?

5. Whether the Sacrament of Baptism has been refused to be administered to any child born in or out of wedlock, their birth being made known to the Minister and offered to him to be baptized? Have there been any children died unbaptized?

6. Whether the parents of any child to be baptized, admitted to be Godfathers, Godmothers, or have there been more Godfathers, or Godmothers than is required, viz: two Godfathers and two Godmothers, but only one Godfather for a female?

7. Whether there have been any child baptized in any private houses, by any lay persons, or midwife, or popish priest, or by any other Minister, without urgent occasion, when the child is in danger of death? If so, and the child lived, was the child later baptized in church?

8. Whether the Sacrament of the Lord's Supper has been duly and reverently administered unto any, or received by any communicant within the parish that did unreverently sit, or stand, or lean, or that did not devoutly and humbly kneel on their knees, in plain and open view without collusion or hypocrisy?

9. Whether the Sacrament of the Lord's Supper be administered every month, so that all parishioners over age sixteen have had it at least three times a year, one of these being at Easter?

10. Have you any excommunicate persons or schismaticks, common and notorious depravers of the religion and government of this realm, without

unfeigned sorrow shown for their wickedness, who hath been admitted to Holy Communion and received it?

11. Hath any of the parish been debarred from receiving Holy Communion without just cause, and without instigation, presently given to the Ordinary, that is, the Bishop of the Diocese, Chancellor, or Commisary? And if so, by whom?

12. Have the children born to any popish recusant, or begotten by them, been publicly baptized in your parish, or where were they baptized, by whom?

From: Articles to Be Inquired of in the Ordinary Visitation of the Right Worshipful Mr. Doctor Pearson, Archdeacon of Suffolk, A.D. 1638 (London, 1638). Only half of these articles are reproduced here, with slight changes in phraseology for clarity.

APPENDIX VI

Early Sudbury Settlers: Land and Town Offices

1638-1655

NAME (*MARRIED IN 1640)	ACREAGE IN ENGLAND	ACREAGE IN WATERTOWN	SUDBURY: MEADOW	SUDBURY: UPLAND	SELECTMAN	DEPUTY TO GEN. COURT	CONSTABLE	FENCE VIEWER	JUDGE OF SMALL CAUSES	SURVEYOR OF HIGHWAY	INVOICE TAKER	TIMBER KEEPER	SWINE WARDEN	MILITARY POST	NEW LOT GRANTED 1655	TOTAL POSTS
Edmund Brown*	?	0	74	38	Minister											
B. Pendleton	?	92	57	76	6	0	0	0	0	0	0	0	0	0	Yes	6
T. Cakebread*	?	66	50	124	Miller									Ens	Yes	1
W. Pelham	?	0	50	0	2	0	0	0	1	0	0	0	0	Capt	Yes	4
P. Noyes*	116	111	48	73	14	2	1	3	4	2	0	0	0	S. Arm	Yes	26
E. Goodnow*	?	0	43½	30	13	3	0	1	3	2	2	3	3	Ens	Yes	30
J. Knight	?	394	38½	61	0	0	0	0	0	0	0	0	0	–	No	0
E. Rice*	15	0	33½	54	11	5	0	1	3	1	1	0	0	–	Yes	22
G. Munnings*	?	109	28	10	1	0	0	0	0	0	0	0	0	–	No	1
W. Ward	?	0	25	20	11	1	0	3	2	0	2	1	1	–	Yes	21
W. Haines*	?	0	23½	57	14	5	0	1	2	3	1	2	0	–	Yes	28
T. Brown	?	0	23	25	0	0	0	0	0	0	0	0	0	–	No	0
T. Noyes	0	0	22	0	2	0	1	1	0	2	1	0	0	–	Yes	7
R. Darvell	22	68	20½	27	1	0	0	4	0	2	1	0	0	–	Yes	8
R. Be(a)st	?	0	19	0	0	0	0	0	0	0	0	0	0	–	Yes	0
A. Belcher*	?	–	18½	19	0	0	0	0	0	0	0	0	0	–	No	0
J. Goodnow*	?	0	14	17	3	0	2	3	0	1	0	0	0	Drum	Yes	10
J. Bent	45	0	11½	29	2	0	0	0	1	2	0	1	0	–	Yes	6
J. Wood	?	0	10½	4	1	0	0	1	0	0	0	0	0	–	Yes	2
S. Johnson*	?	0	10	11	0	0	0	1	0	0	0	0	0	–	Yes	0
A. Buckmaster	?	0	10	0	0	0	0	0	0	0	0	0	0	–	No	0
"Wid" Hunt	?	0	10	14½	0	0	0	0	0	0	0	0	0	–	No	0

APPENDIX VI *(cont.)*

NAME (*MARRIED IN 1640)	ACREAGE IN ENGLAND	ACREAGE IN WATERTOWN	SUDBURY: MEADOW	SUDBURY: UPLAND	SELECTMAN	DEPUTY TO GEN. COURT	CONSTABLE	FENCE VIEWER	JUDGE OF SMALL CAUSES	SURVEYOR OF HIGHWAY	INVOICE TAKER	TIMBER KEEPER	SWINE WARDEN	MILITARY POST	NEW LOT GRANTED 1655	TOTAL POSTS
A. White	?	0	9½	10½	0	0	0	0	0	0	0	0	0	—	No	0
H. Griffin*	?	0	8	20	1	1	8	4	Clerk	1	9	0	0	—	Yes	39
T. Haines	?	0	8	0	0	0	0	0	0	0	0	0	0	—	No	0
J. Parmenter, Sr.	?	0	8	27	8	0	0	4	0	0	1	0	0	—	Yes	13
J. Parmenter, Jr.	?	0	8	9	0	0	1	3	0	0	0	0	0	—	Yes	4
J. Ruddock	?	0	7½	18½	6	0	0	5	0	0	1	0	0	—	Yes	12
J. How*	?	0	7½	8	1	0	4	1	0	0	1	1	0	—	Yes	8
J. Stone	?	0	6½	9	0	0	1	0	0	0	0	0	0	—	Yes	1
R. Newton	?	0	6	6½	0	0	0	1	0	0	0	0	0	—	Yes	1
T. Goodnow*	?	0	6	8½	0	0	0	1	0	1	0	0	0	—	Yes	2
"Wid" Rice	0	0	6	8½	0	0	0	0	0	0	0	0	0	—	No	0
G. Witherell	?	0	0	0	0	0	0	0	0	0	0	0	0	—	No	0
J. Blandford	0	0	5¾	17	0	0	1	3	0	1	0	0	0	—	Yes	5
H. Prentiss*	?	0	5½	12	0	0	0	0	0	0	0	0	0	—	No	0
H. Loker	?	0	5	8	1	0	0	1	0	0	0	0	0	—	Yes	2
W. Brown	?	0	4	0	1	1	0	1	0	1	1	0	0	—	Yes	5
T. Flyn	?	0	4	4½	1	0	0	0	0	0	0	0	0	—	No	1
J. Freeman	?	0	4	13	1	0	0	2	0	0	1	0	0	—	Yes	4
R. Hunt	?	0	4	0	0	0	0	0	0	0	0	0	0	—	No	0
H. Curtis*	?	60	3	4	0	0	0	0	0	0	0	0	0	—	Yes	0
J. Maynard	?	0	2½	9	2	0	1	4	0	0	1	0	0	—	Yes	8
J. Taintor	?	24	2½	0	0	0	0	0	0	0	0	0	0	—	No	0
W. Parker*	?	7	1½	0	0	0	0	0	0	0	0	0	0	—	No	0
J. Loker	?	0	1	6½	0	0	0	0	0	0	0	0	0	—	No	0

APPENDIX VII

Sudbury New Grants, 1658
130-*Acre Farm Allotments to Men Not On*
Original Land Grant List

	SELECTMAN	DEPUTY TO GEN. CT.	CONSTABLE	FENCE VIEWER	JUDGE, SMALL CAUSES	SURVEYOR OF ROADS	INVOICE TAKER	TIMBER KEEPER	SWINE WARDEN	MILITARY POST	TOTAL POSTS
W. Kerley, Jr.	0	0	0	0	0	1	0	0	0	0	1
T. Rice*	1	0	1	1	0	0	0	0	0	0	3
R. Davis, died 1655	0	0	0	0	0	0	0	0	0	0	0
John Haines	0	0	0	0	0	0	0	0	0	0	0
P. Whale	1	0	0	0	0	1	0	0	0	0	2
J. Ward	0	0	0	0	0	0	0	0	0	0	0
P. King*	1	0	1	1	0	0	0	0	0	0	3
J. Smith	0	0	0	0	0	0	0	0	0	0	0
H. Rice	1	0	1	1	0	0	2	0	0	0	5
J. Rediat*	0	0	0	0	0	0	0	0	0	0	0
W. Kerley, Sr.*	1	0	0	0	0	1	1	0	0	0	3
J. Moore	3	0	1	4	0	6	1	0	0	0	15
J. Woodward	0	0	0	1	0	0	0	0	0	0	1
J. Grout	2	0	1	0	0	3	0	0	0	0	6
T. Plimpton	1	0	0	3	0	0	0	0	0	0	4
H. Pelham	0	0	0	0	0	0	0	0	0	0	0
J. Haines	1	0	0	0	0	0	0	0	0	0	1
T. King*	2	0	0	5	0	1	0	0	0	0	8
J. Rutter*	1	0	1	2	0	0	0	0	0	0	4

(*) Received Marlborough grant in 1660.

APPENDIX VIII

Marlborough, Massachusetts
Land Grants and Town Offices (1660-1665)

(Total: 6 elections)

	VOTE IN SUDBURY	SUDBURY MEADOW (ACRES)	SUDBURY UPLAND (ACRES)	GRANTED FARM IN SUDBURY?	MARLBOROUGH — UPLAND	MARLBOROUGH — MEADOW	SELECTMAN	CONSTABLE	CLERK	TIMBER KEEPER	HIGHWAY SUPERVISOR	TOTAL POSTS
E. Rice*	No	47	164	Yes	50	25	5	0	0	0	0	5
W. Ward*	No	25	65	Yes	50	25	6	0	0	1	0	7
J. Ruddock*	No	17	35	Yes	50	25	6	0	5	2	1	14
T. King*	No	3	6	Yes	39½	20	6	2	0	1	1	10
T. Rice	No	0	0	Yes	35	17	0	0	0	0	0	0
Edw. Rice*	No	0	0	Yes	35	17	0	0	0	0	0	0
T. Goodnow*	No	10	28	Yes	32	16	2	0	0	0	2	4
"Minister"	–	–	–	–	30	15	–	–	–	–	–	–
W. Kerley*	–	2	18	Yes	30	15	1	0	0	0	3	4
J. Johnson*	–	0	0	No	30	15	1	0	0	0	0	1
R. Newton*	No	9	15	Yes	30	15	0	0	0	0	0	0
J. How, Sr.*	No	11	19	Yes	30	15	4	0	0	0	0	4
J. Woods, Jr.*	No	28	49	Yes	30	15	3	0	0	0	0	3
P. Bent*	No	0	0	No	30	15	0	0	0	0	0	0
J. Rutter	No	0	9	Yes	30	15	0	0	0	0	0	0
"Blacksmith"	–	–	–	–	30	15	–	–	–	–	–	–
Ab. How	–	0	0	No	25	12	0	0	0	0	0	0
B. Rice	–	0	0	No	24	12	0	0	0	0	0	0
S. Johnson*	–	16	37	Yes	23	11	4	3	0	0	0	7
J. Maynard, Jr.*	–	0	0	No	23	11	0	0	0	0	0	0
Jos. Rice	–	0	0	No	22	11	0	0	0	0	0	0

APPENDIX VIII (cont.)

	VOTE IN SUDBURY	SUDBURY MEADOW (ACRES)	SUDBURY UPLAND (ACRES)	GRANTED FARM IN SUDBURY?	MARLBOROUGH — UPLAND	MARLBOROUGH — MEADOW	SELECTMAN	CONSTABLE	CLERK	TIMBER KEEPER	HIGHWAY SUPERVISOR	TOTAL POSTS
P. King	No	0	0	No	22	11	0	0	0	0	0	0
J. Rediat*	No	0	12	Yes	22	11	0	0	0	0	0	0
Ob. Ward	–	0	0	No	21	10	0	0	0	0	0	0
Sam. Rice	–	0	0	No	21	10	0	0	0	0	0	0
A. Belcher	–	18½	36	No	20	10	0	0	0	0	0	0
J. Bellows	–	0	0	No	20	10	0	0	0	0	0	0
T. Goodnow, Jr.*	–	0	0	No	20	10	0	0	0	0	0	0
H. Kerley	–	0	0	No	19½	10	0	0	0	0	0	0
Rich. Ward	–	0	0	No	18	9	0	0	0	0	0	0
J. Barrett	–	0	0	No	18	9	0	0	0	0	0	0
Jos. Holmes	–	0	0	No	18	9	0	0	0	0	0	0
C. Baynster*	–	0	0	No	16	8	0	0	0	0	0	0
J. How, Jr.	–	0	0	No	16	8	0	0	0	0	0	0
Rich. Barnes	–	0	0	No	16	8	0	0	0	0	0	0
Sam. How	–	0	0	No	16	8	0	0	0	0	0	0
J. Newton	–	0	0	No	16	8	0	0	0	0	0	0
H. Axtell	–	0	0	No	16	8	0	0	0	0	0	0

(*) Signed First Petition for Marlborough Settlement.

(Yes) Received 130-acre farm in W. Sudbury, 1658. (No) — did not.

"No" those recorded as voting against the limitation of Sudbury commons.

Bibliography and Index

Notes on Manuscripts - England

This is arranged as a general guide to any student wishing to make precise searches for emigrants in specific areas of England. It should be used in conjunction with the excellent bibliography in W. E. Notestein, *The English People on the Eve of Colonization, 1603–1630*, pp. 267–279 and the notes in B. Bailyn's bibliography, *The New England Merchants of the Seventeenth Century*, pp. 230–239, both of which cover the important printed materials. One should also consult the general list of record societies and the bibliography of special local studies in W. E. Tate, *The Parish Chest*.

The student should be prepared to do much transcription of difficult documents and considerable traveling. The lists in the National Register of Archives, P.R.O. Building, London are invaluable, and the student should consult the MSS collections at the Public Record Office and the British Museum, London, before going out to the county, church, and borough record offices or depositories.

GENERAL

Assize Records

These are stored at the P.R.O., London. Consult M. S. Giuseppi, *A Guide to the MSS Preserved in the P.R.O.* (London, 1923).

Midland Circuit
Counties of Derby, Leicester, Lincoln, Northants, Nottingham, Rutland, and Warwick. Very little for the seventeenth century. No Indictment Books; no Deposition Books; no Minute Books or Miscellaneous Records.

Norfolk Circuit
Counties of Bedford, Bucks, Cambridge, Huntington, Norfolk, and Suffolk.
Little for the seventeenth century. Only Indictment and Subsidiary Documents, 1653–1695.

Southeastern Circuit
This now includes the old Home and Northern circuits, in which were Essex, Hertford, and Kent.
Very little for the seventeenth century. Miscellaneous Cause Books, 1673–1768; no Minute Books; no Agenda Books; no Gaol Books; no Books of Indictments or Depositions; no Books of Pleadings or Presentments; no Record Books; no Process Books; no Instruction Books; no Entry Books; no Certificate Books; no Estreat Books.

Church Records

The church manuscripts are often extremely difficult to read but can be very rewarding if they deal with specific emigrants. Both the diocesan and archidiaconal records should be consulted, even though they may be stored in different depositories and often have overlapping jurisdictions. For convenience, this list is arranged alphabetically by diocese, but deals only with the areas concerned in this study. The full list is entitled "Survey of Ecclesiastical Archives" (typescript report for The Pilgrim Trust, 1951) and may be found at the British Museum; P.R.O.; National Register of Archives; University Library, Cambridge; Bodleian Library, Oxford.

DIOCESE OF CANTERBURY

Present area: Kent, east of Medway; archdeaconries: Canterbury, Maidstone.

Archives: in London and Canterbury; diocesan and archdeacons' at the Canterbury Diocesan Registry, Christ Church Gate; also the Chapter Library; provincial: at the Registrar, Vicar-General's Office in Westminster; or in the Faculty Office Record Room and Vicar-General's Room in Morton Tower, Lambeth Palace; a few in Lambeth Palace Library.

Archbishop's Records:

Administrative:
Registers, 51 vols. from 1279–1896.
Subscription Books: 17th–18th cent.
Convocation Records, Lower House Proceedings, 1589, 1640.
Estates: several hundred court rolls, etc.

Registrar's Working Papers:
Letter Book: one vol. in 17th cent.
Precedent Book: 32 vols., 16th–18th cent.
Citation Register: from late 16th cent.

Court Papers:
Many vols. from 1632 on.
Marriage licenses: from 1600 on.
Court of Arches: a quantity of various dates.

Consistory Court:
Act Books: from 14th–18th cent.
Probate: 16th–17th cent.
Court Papers: from 1587 on.
Deposition Books: 42 vols., 15th–18th cent.
Excommunication Books: 10 vols., 1597–1684.
Faculty Papers: 17th–19th cent.
Registry of Marriages: 1568 on.
Prohibitions in causes of subtractions of tithes: 1573–1728.

Archdeacons' Courts:
Testamentary, Register of Admin: 1636 on.
Registers of Administers' Accounts: 1605–1740.
Inventories: 1569–1604.
Caveats: 1628–1649.
Registers of Depositions in Testamentary Cases: 1555–1649.
Registers of Guardians: 1631–1762.
Inventories: 43 boxes, 1596–1647; 1660 on.
Registers of same: 1597–1638.
Wills: 327 boxes, 1555–1646.
Registers of same: 1459–1641.

Visitation Records:
Visitation Books: 30 vols., 1569–1717.
Call books: 150 vols., 1594–1855.
Citations and Inhibitions: many vols., various dates.
Mandates for Citations to Visitations: 1601–1640.
Parish Register Transcripts: 504 boxes, 1603–1812.
Visitation Papers from 1604 on.

Metropolical of Archbishop Laud: 1634–1636.
> In House of Lords, MSS. Also printed in *Hist. MSS. Comm. Rept. IV* (1874), pp. 124–159.

Archives of Archdeacons

Registrar's Working Papers:
> Precedent Books: 21 vols., 17th–18th cent.

Court Records:
> Act Books: 76 vols., 1476–1709.
> Probate: 1487–1645.
> Court Papers: 53 boxes, 1581–1646.
> Testamentary Records, Administers' Accounts, 1603–1650.
> Inventories: 1571–1842. Registers of same.
> Wills: 235 boxes, 1559–1650. Copies of many.

Visitation Records:
> Visitation Books: 1490–1900.
> Parish Register Transcripts: 1563–1812.

In the Archives of the Dean and Chapter of Canterbury, there are many volumes of Registers of Temporalities, court rolls, bailiffs' accounts from the thirteenth to the sixteenth century, rentals, and court papers. At the Vicar-General's Office, Morton Tower, Lambeth Palace Library, there are the Archives of Peculiar and Exempt Jurisdictions, containing administration records, court records, 1676–1863, and visitation books, 1637–1642.

DIOCESE OF CHELMSFORD

Area: Counties of Essex, Kent north of Thames River, small area in south Cambridgeshire; archdeaconries: Essex and Colchester for 17th cent.

Archives: Diocesan Record Office is part of the Essex Record Office, County Hall, Chelmsford, Essex. Excellent research facilities — see below.

Bishop of London's Commissary in Essex and Herts:

Court Records:
> Act Books, 1619–1642.
> Libri Officiorum, 1616–1642.
> Deposition Books, 1618–1642.

Visitation Records:
> Visitation Books: 1633–1639.
> Act Books: 1633–1639.

Archives of Archdeacons: Essex:

Court Books:
> Act Books: 1595–1640.
> Instance Books: 1629–1637.
> Deposition Books: 1626–1642.
> Excommunication Books: 1590–1602.
> Misc. Court Papers: 1621–1633.

Visitation Records:
> Visitation Books: 1580–1641.

Archdeaconry of Colchester:

Registrar's Papers:
> Probate: 1626–1628.

Court Records:
    Act Books: 1569–1641.
    Instance Books: 1588–1640.
    Deposition Books: 1625–1641.
    Visitation Books: 1597–1612.

DIOCESE OF COVENTRY

Area: Three quarters of Warwick; archdeaconries: currently Coventry and Warwick.

Archives: Diocesan Registry of Coventry — but no pertinent records for 17th cent.

DIOCESE OF ELY

Present Area: Cambridge, Isle of Ely, Huntington, three deaneries in West Norfolk; archdeaconries: Hunts, Wisbech, formerly Bedford (19th cent.), and Sudbury.

Archives: Custody of Legal Secretary of the Bishop in London and of the Diocesan Registrar in the Diocesan Registry Office in Ely.

Bishop's Records:

Consistory Court:
    Many vols., 1579–19th cent.
    Caveats: 1577–1715.
    Wills: 17th cent., with index to wills, 17th–19th cent.

Visitation Records:
    Visitation Books: 1506–19th cent.
    Parish Register Transcripts: many vols., 16th–19th cent.
    Libri Compertorum, 1506–19th cent.

Registrar's Working Papers:
    Precedent Books: 15th–17th cent.
    Registers of Marriages: 1562–1918.

Archives of Archdeacons; Huntington

Court Records:
    Act Book: 1614–1615.
    Parish Register Transcripts: 1604–1625.
    Terriers: 1564–1763.
    Misc. Letters: 1514–1933.

Archdeaconry of Ely: nothing for 17th cent.

DIOCESE OF LONDON

Present Area: the city of London, city of Westminster, Middlesex County, boroughs of the county of London north of the Thames; archdeaconries: London, Middlesex, Hampstead, and formerly Essex, Colchester and St. Albans.

Archives: Bishop's Registrars at the Diocesan Registry and Diocesan Muniment Room in St. Paul's Cathedral; other records at Fulham Palace; records of Archdeacon of London at Morton Tower, Lambeth Palace.

Bishop's Administrative Records:

    Bishop's Books: 1622–1628.
    Ordination Records, Registries: 1578–1628.
    Lecturers' and Preachers' Certificates: 1545–1694.
    Letters Patent: 1545–1694.
    Resignation Deeds: 1640–1662.

Subscription Books: 1627–1786.
Colonial Letters and Papers: boxes of these from America, Canada, Newfoundland, West Indies.
Schools and colleges, reports: 17th–19th cent.

Registrar's Working Papers:
Index to Bishop's Books: to 1829.
Index of Ordinations: 1601–1674.

Court Papers:
Sundry Papers, 1602–1704.
Marriage License Allegations: 1597–1942.

Visitation Records:
Visitation Books: 1598–1637.
Articles of Inquiry and Presentment: 1633–1640.
Parish Register Transcripts: 1629–1631; 1638–1726.

Archdeaconry Archives:

None for London, 1600–1640.
None for Middlesex; 1600–1640.

In the Archives of the Dean and Chapter of St. Paul's Cathedral, in the Library of St. Paul's, there are many administrative records, bailiffs' accounts for various properties, court rolls, rentals, etc. 16th–17th cent.

DIOCESE OF NORWICH

Present Area: Norfolk; Deanery of Lothingland in Suffolk; archdeaconries: Norwich, Norfolk, Lynn; formerly, Suffolk (1126–1914) and Sudbury (1126–1837)

Archives: Diocesan Registrar at Old Palace Chapel, Norfolk; Archdeaconry Records in custody of Archdeaconry of Norwich and Deputy Registrar of Norfolk and Lynn, City Muniment Room in the Castle, under the City Librarian.

Bishop's Administrative Records:

Institution Books, Registers: 1299–1648.
Ordination Books: 1531–1619; 1672–1708.
Subscription Books: 1637–1920.
Fee Books: 1634–1636; 1638; 1645–1648.
Formula Books: 17th–18th cent.

Consistory Court:
Act Books: 1508–1639
Book of Citations: 1637 on.
Book of Depositions: 1499–1788.
Interrogatories: 17th cent.
Libels and Allegations, depos.: 1620–1724.
Personal Answers: 1624–1742.
Testamentary Papers: various, from 1560.

Visitation Records:
Visitation Books: 1555–1636.
Consignation Books: 16th–17th cent.

Archives of Archdeacons:

Court Records:
Act Books, 40 vols., 1557–1785.
Deposition Books: 1608–1611.

Libels: 1611–1617.
Testamentary Papers, Inventories: 17th–18th cent.
Terriers: 17th–19th cent.

Visitation Records:
Visitation Books: 36 vols., 1560–1664.
Churchwardens' Presentments: 17th cent. (a few)
Parish Register Transcripts: 1598–1900.

Archives of the Dean and Chapter of Norwich:

Administrative:
Registers: 14th–16th cent.
Charters and Deeds: 50 boxes, 13th cent. on
Ledger Books: 1538–1860.

Court Records:
Court Books: 30 vols., 16th–17th cent.
Court Rolls: 750 rolls, 13th–17th cent.
Rentals and Surveys: 13th–17th cent.

DIOCESE OF PETERBOROUGH

Present Area: Northants, Rutland; archdeaconries: Northants, Oakham (1875)

Archives: Diocesan Registry and Knight's Chamber, in custody of Diocesan Registrar and Secretary to the Bishop at Peterborough; Dean and Chapter Archives at Chapter Office and Cathedral Library.

Bishop's Administrative Records:

Institution Books: 1541–1648.
Ordination Books: 1570–1687.
Exchequer Quietus Rolls: 1601, 1664.

Registrar's Working Papers:
Probates, Grants of Letters of Administration: 1621–1630.
Precedent Books: 16th–18th cent.

Court Records:
Act Books: 74 vols., 1570–1720.
Instance Books: 63 vols., 1570–1689.
Court Papers: 1550–19th cent.

Visitation Records:
Visitation Books: 24 vols., 1561–1720.

Archives of the Archdeacons: Northampton

Administration Records:
Registers of Inductions: 1598–1695.

Court Records:
Court Books: 1533–1857.

Visitation Records:
Visitation Books: 1599–present.

The archives of the Dean and Chapter of Peterborough contain sundry papers of the period, court rolls, bailiff's accounts of chapter property.

DIOCESE OF ST. EDMUNDSBURY AND IPSWICH

Present Area: The diocese was founded in 1914; area: Suffolk; archdeaconries: Suffolk and Sudbury.

Archives: older MSS at West Suffolk Record Office, Bury St. Edmunds, Suffolk; some also at Central Library, Ipswich; Town Hall Muniment Room; and East Suffolk County Muniment Room, Ipswich.

Archives of the Archdeacons: Suffolk (Ipswich Archives)

Administrative Records:
Induction Register: 1526–1629.

Court Papers:
Act Books: 1667 on.
Book of Depositions: 11 vols., 1615, 1616, 1632, 1640 etc.

Visitation Records:
Visitation Books: from 1664 on.

Archives of Archdeacons: Sudbury (Bury St. Edmunds Archives)

Administrative Records:
Induction Books: 1537–1813.

Registrar's Working Papers:
Precedent Book: 10 vols., 17th–19th cent.
Sundry Papers: 17th–18th cent.

Court Records:
Act Books: 1673 on.
Court Papers: 1677 on.

Visitation Records:
Visitation Books: late 18th cent.
Parish Register Transcript: 1560–1853.

DIOCESE OF WILTSHIRE

Area: Wiltshire and Dorset; archdeaconries of Sarum (Salisbury), Wilts, Dorset.

Archives: Diocesan Registry, the Close, Salisbury, Wilts.

Bishop's Administrative Records:

Bishop's Registers: 1598–1645.

Consistory Court:
Act Books: 1623–1773.
Deposition Books: 1551–1687.
Testamentary Records: 17th cent.

Visitation Records:
Visitation Books: 1698 on.
Parish Register Transcripts: 1605 on.

Archives of Archdeacons: Sarum.

Court Records:
Act Books: 1572 on.
Books of Depositions: 1580 on.

Visitation Records:
Visitation Books: 1670 on.
Churchwardens' Presentments: 17th cent.

Archives of Archdeacons: Wiltshire

Court Records:
Act Books: 1601 on.
Deposition Books: 1605, 1608, 1612.
Court Papers: late 17th cent.

Visitation Records:
    Visitation Books: 1586 on.

No manuscripts for Archdeaconry of Dorset remain for the 17th century.

Present Area: Most of Hampshire, Channel Isles; archdeaconries: Winchester, Basing-stoke (founded 1927), Surrey.

Archives: Bishop's archives at Diocesan Registry in Winchester, also the Diocesan Muniment Room, the Castle, Winchester; also some at the Consistory Court, the Cathedral, Winchester; archdeaconry archives in Archdeacon's Registry and Chapter Clerk's Office, 31 Southgate St., Winchester, and some with Hants Record Office, the Castle, Winchester.

Bishop's Administrative Records:

    Bishop's Registers: 29 vols., 1323–1684.
    Terriers: 350 documents from 1616 on.
    Papers: 7 cases of these, various dates.

    Registrar's Working Papers:
        Registrar's Accounts: 17th–18th cent.

    Consistory Court:
        Act Books: 1540–1678.
        Testamentary Records, Inventories: 17th–19th cent.
        Papers: 17th–19th cent.

    Visitation Records:
        Visitation Books: 50 vols., 1517–1701.

Archives of Archdeacons: Winchester (at Hants Record Office)

    Administrative Records:
        Induction Mandates: 1635–1700.
        Procurations, Gifts: 1632, 1635, 1640, 1641.

    No Court or Visitation Records.

The Archives of the Basingstoke Archdeaconry have only recent MSS; the Archives of the Dean and Chapter of Winchester, at the Cathedral Library or Hants Record Office have many charters, deeds, registers, court books and rolls, bailiffs' accounts for the sixteenth to eighteenth centuries.

SPECIFIC AREAS

The Open-Field Area (Rural)

There is a possibility that J. Maynard emigrated from Basingbourn, or from the borough of Cambridge. The parish of Basingbourn yielded no church records. But views of frank-pledge, with court-baron rolls 1626–1644 of the Manor of Bassingbourn Richmond, the nineteenth-century act of enclosure, and an award map of 1806 are deposited at the Cambridge County Archives, Shire Hall, Cambridge. No J. Maynard was cited in the court-baron rolls, however, and since the Cambridge quarter sessions records do not begin before 1661, no further work could be done on county records. (See borough section for Cambridge.)

DORSET

William Kerley and family came from the parish of Ashmore. While there are no parish records extant, both Kerley and his village were cited in the Wiltshire Archdeacon's records at the Diocesan Registry in Salisbury. The general parish and village background was gleaned from Edward Watson, *Ashmore, History of the Parish* (Gloucester, 1890).

HAMPSHIRE

Since emigrants came from Goodworth Clatford, Weyhill, and Upton Grey, an inquiry as to parish records was made, with positive response from Goodworth Clatford (Parish Register, 1538–1735) and from Weyhill. The rector at Weyhill has extensive manuscripts in his possession, including the Churchwardens' Accounts, 1600–1640, and the Muniment Room of Queen's College, Oxford, yielded the Manor of Ramridge court-baron rolls, 1600–1640, plus additional MSS deeds and miscellaneous material. The Hampshire Record Office, at the Castle, Winchester, has local documents for these parishes, including a detailed open-field map, c. 1725, for Goodworth Clatford. The Record Office has church court documents and quarter sessions rolls for the period, which were searched for any cases involving the emigrants or their parishes. Other students would find useful John R. Williams, *The Early Churchwardens' Accounts of Hants* (London, 1913).

HERTFORDSHIRE

The Reverend Robert Fordham, a friend of Edmund Brown, had been born in Sacombe and had had a vicarage at Flamstead, but since he was merely a brief visitor in Sudbury, no serious search was made for local documents, other than consultation of W. Le Handy, comp. *Herts County Records, Vol. 5: Calendar To The Sessions Books, 1619–1657* (Hertford, 1905–   ) for pertinent material. The main area of interest was Berkhamsted, listed under the boroughs, below.

NORTHANTS

There is questionable evidence that Robert Hunt and family came from Sudborough, and since there were no parish records for the period, serious work in this county was deferred to attention to those areas where the emigrants' activities were well documented. As Notestein has pointed out, the Northants quarter sessions have little for this period. Students should consult the Northants Record Society, Lamport Hall, Northants.

WARWICK

The evidence for the claim that Edward Wright came from Castle Bromwick, Warwick is not certain, and the lack of parish records there complicates the problem. As was true for the Hunt family, Wright played such a minor role in Sudbury that little attention was given to this county, other than careful reading of S. C. Ratcliff, ed. *Warwick County Records*, I, (1935). Students should consult A. C. Wood, Esq., Shire Hall, Warwick.

WILTSHIRE

Emigrants from Donhead St. Andrew, Donhead St. Mary, Semley, and Sutton Mandeville made this an important county to study. The Diocesan Registry in Salisbury yielded important information about these parishes and about specific emigrants, in the court books of the bishop and the archdeacon. There are parish register transcripts for the villages concerned, 1623–1812 at the Diocesan Registry, and the Arundel Collection, Wardour

Castle, Semley has manorial court rolls, reeves' accounts, and surveys for all four villages during the period 1600–1640.

The Wiltshire Record Office, County Hall, Trowbridge, has a very extensive collection of records for this period, including official records and private muniments deposited there, and a short list may be obtained from the archivist. Most important, the quarter sessions are well documented for this period, including great rolls, 1603 onward; process books of indictments, 1661–1851; minute books, 1574–1944; order books, 1641–1897. One may also consult B. Howard Cunningham, *Records of the County of Wilts, Being Extracts From the Quarter Session Great Rolls of the 17th Cent.* (Devizes, 1932) and the Hist. MSS Commiss., *Rpt. on MSS in Var. Colls., Vol. I, Counties of Wilts and Worcester* (London, 1901).

The Incorporated Boroughs

ANDOVER, Hants

Since Peter Noyes, of Weyhill, had property near Andover, sold his land in Weyhill to an Andover merchant, and had relatives in the borough, the records of Andover were searched. There are extensive manuscripts in the Borough Archives, Town Hall, for the period, including: transcript of the charter of 1599, town council minutes, 1573–1574 and 1642–1835; town rentals, scattered entries for the seventeenth century; town account books, 1598–1605, 1605–1612, 1618–1632, 1632–1637, 1638–1651; town charities, account books, 1646–1697; town court books, 1656–1835; views of frankpledge, 1591–1626, 1657–1689; hundred court rolls (Andover in-hundred and Andover out-hundred), intermittently in the seventeenth century; plus many deeds and miscellaneous documents for the period.

BERKHAMSTED, Herts

Although there is an active local historical society in the borough, there are few parish records of the seventeenth century remaining, and the most valuable record is the Churchwardens' Account Book at the British Museum, now transcribed, 1600–1645. There are some borough records extant, including a court book for the last half of the seventeenth century, but one had best consult the chairman of the historical society and J. Cobb, *Two Lectures on the History of Berkhamsted* (London, 1883), which has a transcript of the borough charter and extracts from manorial rolls.

BOSTON, Lincs

Both Herbert and William Pelham came from Boston, and there is a considerable amount of printed material on men from this city which can be found in the bibliography of S. E. Morison, *Builders of the Bay Colony*. The Town Clerk of the borough of Boston has the charters, as well as the Town Book, which runs from the time of Elizabeth to 1637. A study of this "Assembly Book," 1622–1637 was disappointing.

BURY ST. EDMUNDS, Suffolk

Since it is questionable whether Thomas and William Brown came from this borough, not much could be done, seeing that there are very few local MSS dealing with Bury St. Edmunds in the period 1600–1640. But the Bury and West Suffolk Record Office, at Bury, has a borough assembly book, 1664–1669; court of record book, 1650–1750; town clerk's letters, 1610–1631; Chamberlains' Accounts, 1607–1632; inquests before the coroner, 1620–1688; various trade regulations of the seventeenth century and court-leet rolls, as well as a common field book, dated 1700.

CAMBRIDGE, Cambs

Although there are charters for the borough, and a number of documents relating to the period 1600–1640 at the Guildhall, City of Cambridge, the search for evidence of J. Maynard was disappointing.

COLCHESTER, Essex

Thomas Reed emigrated from this borough, but was a minor figure in Sudbury. General records at the Essex Record Office, including their general and special indexes, were consulted, but nothing was found for the emigrant T. Reed.

IPSWICH, Suffolk

Various emigrants sailed from Ipswich, but there are no records indicating that a Sudbury townsman lived in the borough. In addition to the fact that the East Suffolk Record Office is located in Ipswich, there are various borough records in print: the charter in R. Canning, transl. *The Principal Charters Which Have Been Granted to the Corporation of Ipswich in Suffolk* (London, 1754); records of the common council, 1620–1634 in W. H. Richardson, ed., N. Bacon, *The Annals of Ipswich* (1654) (Ipswich, 1884); and borough customs in Mary Bateson, ed., *Borough Customs* (London, 1904), Vols. I, II.

LONDON

Andrew Belcher, Hugh Griffin, and Brian Pendleton all functioned in London, and there are massive amounts of records for the period remaining. The student should go to the Guildhall Library, London, for specific borough MSS, and consult the indexes at the P.R.O. and the British Museum.

SHAFTESBURY, Dorset

Since Thomas Goodnow, a Sudbury selectman, had lived in Shaftesbury, it was disappointing to learn from the Town Clerk that there are no MSS in the borough for the period 1600–1640. The student can, however, consult C. H. Mayor, *Municipal Records of Shaston* (Shaftesbury, 1889) for the charter, rent rolls, 1600–1650; list of the mayors, 1600–1640; and litigation over the rights of the borough, 1604–1634. There are full church records for Shaftesbury in the Diocesan Registry, Salisbury, Wilts.

SUDBURY, Suffolk

The Reverend Edmund Brown and, according to one genealogist, John Smith, came from Sudbury. The All Saints Church parish register remains for 1563–1651, the St. Peter's register from 1593 on, and the register of St. Gregory's starts in 1653, but the account books for the three parishes are missing for the early period. St. Gregory's Church has Churchwardens' Accounts from 1662 to 1829, and St. Peter's has similar records from 1675 on.

Since many important emigrants to New England came from the borough, and since some, like the Ruggles and the Welds, functioned as borough officers, it is fortunate that the Town Clerk has extensive MSS for the borough for this period. The Elizabethan charter is there, together with others; "The Town Clarks Book of Sudbury in the County of Suffolk, 1600–1640," the court books, the book of the court of orders and decrees, 1658 onward; admissions of freedom, 1656 onward; sessions of the peace books; customs of the borough, 16th cent.; and many misc. deeds and documents. The "Burgi de Sudbury, Liber Quintus, 17 Oct. 16 Jacobi I (1622)–2 Sept. Caroli I (1637)" has been transcribed and typed.

TROWBRIDGE, Wilts

Since John Ruddock lived in Trowbridge, it was very disappointing to learn from the Town Clerk that no seventeenth-century borough documents remain. There is one marriage register, 1639–1812, in a private collection, but, in general one must consult the MSS at the Wiltshire Record Office, at the County Hall in Trowbridge.

The Enclosed-Farm Area

ESSEX

Any student tracing emigrants from Essex can use the excellent facilities of the Essex Record Office, County Hall, Chelmsford. Not only does the office have a staff of trained archivists, but also, to quote its own report, it contains "over a million official, ecclesiastical, estate and family archives, dating from the 12th century." Of great importance to the student unfamiliar with English documents is the fact that "guidance in elementary palaeography and methods of research can be given to beginners during the evening opening," and "special facilities may be extended to advanced, post-graduate or training college students."

There are printed E.R.O. publications such as *Guide to the Essex Record Office,* Parts I, II (1946–1948), *Catalogue of Maps in the E.R.O., 1566–1865* (1947), as well as E. J. Erith, *Essex Parish Records, 1240–1894* (London, 1950), and typed Indexes and Calendars to the various collections at the office.

For this study, the general records consulted were: Essex assize records, quarter session rolls, calendar of county records, sessions records, Vol. 18, all for the period 1600–1640. Also: Archdeaconry of Essex, Act Books, 1620–1640; Books of Depositions, 1626–1642; Archdeaconry of Colchester, Act Books, 1620–1640; Book of Depositions, 1625–1636; Special Visitation, 1633; and Bishop Laud's Commissioners, Act Books, 1620–1640.

Specific areas which produced emigrants to Sudbury were searched, as follows: Bures St. Mary, no MSS for the period 1600–1640 extant; Great Bromley, parish registers, 1558–1735; register of marriages, 1559–1731; Churchwardens' Accounts, 1626–1640; Hatfield Broad Oak: parish registers, 1662 on; no churchwardens' or other vestry records, 1600–1640; Manor of Barrington, court rolls, 1609–1637; Walker map of Matching Barnes, 1609; Roxwell, parish registers: baptismal, 1558–1665; burial: 1559–1647; marriages: 1559–1665; no churchwardens' or vestry records, 1600–1640.

KENT

Thomas Beesbeech had land in Hedcorn, Frittendon and "Goodman" Witherall probably came from Maidstone, but both settlers were hardly ever mentioned in the Sudbury records. Consequently, little work was done other than genealogical research, but the student can consult the County Record Office, County Hall, Maidstone, Kent.

MIDDLESEX

There was only one reference to H. Griffin's marriage in the Stepney Parish Register, but since he did not appear in the London records consulted, no further search was made in the Middlesex records. There are, as Notestein points out, voluminous Middlesex quarter sessions records, but they deal principally with London matters.

SUFFOLK

There are two record offices for Suffolk, the Bury and West Suffolk Record Office at Bury St. Edmunds, and the Ipswich and East Suffolk Record Office at Ipswich.

At the Bury office, the following manuscripts were consulted: for Nayland, evidence of titles and wills, 1600–1640; for Rattlesden, title deeds and court-baron rolls, 17th century.

Of considerable use was J. R. Olorenshaw, *Notes on the Parish and Church of Rattlesden* (Peterborough, 1900), which includes reports and documents of the overseers of the poor, 1620–1638.

The Ipswich Record Office yielded the very valuable Framlingham Churchwardens' Accounts, 1629–1639, and the Suffolk Quarter Sessions Record Book, 1639–1651. The detailed account book of Reverend Richard Golty, rector of Framlingham, for the period 1628–1642 is still in private hands, and there are excerpts from the Framlingham court rolls, 1625–1635 in Richard Green, *History of Framlingham* (London, 1884).

As a final note, students might well consult the Victoria County History Committee at the Public Record Office, London, or the Chairman of the Institute of Historical Research, University of London, for further information on documents. The S. C. Powell collection of 2000 photostats of documents made for this study, with many typed transcripts, is available on special request to the author.

Notes on Manuscripts – New England

Since the bibliographies in standard works such as H. L. Osgood, *The American Colonies in the Seventeenth Century* (New York, 1904–1907), Charles M. Andrews, *The Colonial Period of American History* (New Haven, 1934–1938), and Oscar Handlin, *et al.*, *Harvard Guide to American History* (Cambridge, 1954) give the necessary information on general material in print, and the notes in B. Bailyn, *New England Merchants*, pp. 231–239 bring these up to date, this section will deal only with manuscript material necessary for this study.

The Massachusetts State Archives, documents relating to Sudbury, 1650–1700, were invaluable, as were the Middlesex County Court, Papers in Cases, 1649–1663; Depositions, 1650–1700; Registry of Deeds, 1650–1700; Probate Records, Vol. I.

In Sudbury itself, the Town Clerk has an unbroken series of Town Books, 1639–present, a typed transcript of the first book, 1639–1700, and the Goodnow Library contains the Dr. Alfred Stearns collection of MSS pertaining to early Sudbury, together with several early paintings. The town has started a local history society, which promises to add to the collections.

General

Records of the Governor and Company of the Massachusetts Bay in New England, ed. by
    N. B. Shurtleff (Boston, 1863). Vols. I, II, III.
Winthrop Papers (Mass. Hist. Soc., 1943). Vols. I, II, III.
Massachusetts Historical Society, Collections, 3rd Series.
Records of the Town Proceedings, Watertown (Watertown, 1894).
Colonial Records of Marlborough, Mass. (Boston, 1909)
Colonial Society of Massachusetts, Transactions: Vol. 25

Special Studies

Charles F. Adams, *The Genesis of the Massachusetts Town* (Cambridge, 1892)
Henry Ainsworth, *Annotations* (Amsterdam ? 1616–1621)
Warren O. Ault, *The Self-Directing Activities of Village Communities in Mediaeval England* (Boston Univ., 1952)
Harrold Ayres, *The Great Trail of New England* (Boston, 1940)
Bernard Bailyn, *The New England Merchants in the Seventeenth Century* (Cambridge, 1955)

P. Bidwell, F. Falconer, *History of Agriculture in the Northern U.S., 1620–1860.* (Washington, 1925)

John Booth, *Nicholas Danforth and His Neighbors* (Framingham, Mass. Historical Society, 1935).

N. C. Brett-James, *The Growth of Stuart London* (London, 1935)

Mildred Campbell, *The English Yeoman* (New Haven, 1942)

R. H. Clutterbuck, *Notes On The Parishes of Fyfield, Kimpton, Penton Mewsey, Weyhill, and Wherwell* (Salisbury, 1898)

J. Cobb, *Two Lectures on the History and Antiquities of Berkhamsted* (London, 1883)

John Cotton, *An Exposition upon the Thirteenth Chapter of the Revelation* (London, 1656)

Charles M. Ellis, *History of Roxbury Town* (Boston, 1847)

F. G. Emmison, *Court Rolls of the Manor of Ramsden Crays, 1559–1935* (Essex Record Office)

J. B. Felt, *The Ecclesiastical History of New England* (Boston, 1855–1862)

H. W. Foote, ed., *The Cambridge Platform of 1648* (Cambridge, 1949)

John E. Foster, ed., *Diary of Samuel Newton* (Cambridge, 1890)

Alan French, *Charles I and the Puritan Upheaval* (Boston, 1955)

A. Garvan, "The Protestant Plain Style Before 1630," *Journal of the Society of Architectural Historians,* October, 1950

J. W. Gough, *Fundamental Law in English Constitutional History* (Oxford, 1955)

Norman Gras, *The Economic and Social History of an English Village* (Crawley, Hants) (Cambridge, 1930)

Howard L. Gray, *English Field Systems* (Harvard History Series, Vol. 22. Cambridge, 1915)

Alice S. Green, *Town Life in the Fifteenth Century* (London, 1894)

R. Green, *The History of Framlingham* (London, 1884)

C. G. Grimwood and S. A. Kay, *History of Sudbury, Suffolk* (Sudbury, 1952)

William Haller, *Liberty and Reformation in the Puritan Revolution* (New York, 1955)

William Haller, Jr., *The Puritan Frontier* (Columbia University, 1951)

W. Le Handy, comp., *Calendar to Herts Sessions Books, 1619–1657* (Hertford, 1905–   )

R. Hawes and R. Loder, *The History of Framlingham* (Woodbridge, 1798)

R. M. Heanley, *The History of Weyhill and Its Ancient Fair* (Winchester, 1922)

F. J. C. Hearnshaw, *Leet Jurisdiction in England* (Southampton, 1908)

G. W. Hill, W. H. Frere, eds., *Memorials of Stepney Parish* (London, 1890)

George Homans, *The English Villagers of the Thirteenth Century* (Cambridge, 1941)

James K. Hosmer, ed., *Winthrop's Journal* (New York, 1908), Vols. I, II.

Mark Howe, *Readings in American Legal History* (Cambridge, 1949)

Alfred S. Hudson, *History of Sudbury, Mass.* (Sudbury, 1889)

Edward Johnson, *Wonder-Working Providence of Sions Savior,* ed. by W. Poole (Andover, 1867)

William Langland, *The Vision of Piers Plowman,* rendered into modern English by Henry Wells (London, 1935)

Cotton Mather, *Magnalia Christi Americana* (Hartford, 1826)

C. H. Mayor, *Municipal Records of Shaston* (Wilts) (Shaftesbury, 1889)

Perry Miller, T. H. Johnson, eds., *The Puritans* (New York, 1938)

Louis Morton, "The End of Formalized Warfare," *American Heritage,* August, 1955

Thomas Morton, *The New English Canaan* (Prince Society edition Boston, 1883)

Samuel E. Morison, *Builders of the Bay Colony* (Boston, 1930)

Wallace Notestein, *The English People on the Eve of Colonization 1602–1630* (New York, 1955)

H. S. Nourse, *Early Records of Lancaster* (Lancaster, 1890)

J. R. Olorenshaw, *Notes on the Parish and Church of Rattlesden* (Peterborough, 1900)

C. S. and S. Orwin, *The Open Fields* (Oxford, 1938)

Wm. Page, ed., *Victoria History of the County of Hampshire* (London, 1911)

Wm. Page, ed., *Victoria County History of Herts* (London, 1908)

J. G. Palfrey, *History of New England* (Boston, 1859), Vol. I, II

William Perkins, *Works* (Cambridge, 1608).

Chilton L. Powell, *English Domestic Relations (1487–1653)* (Columbia University, 1917)

V. P. Redstone, *The Ship-Money Returns for the County of Suffolk* (Ipswich, 1904)

J. E. T. Rogers, *History of Agriculture and Prices in England* (Oxford, 1887), Vol. VI

L. Shattuck, *The History of Concord, Mass.* (Concord, 1890)

Thomas Shepard, *A Defense of the Answer Made Unto Nine Questions Sent From New England Against the Reply Thereto by Mr. John Ball* (London, 1648)

George Slater, *English Peasantry and the Enclosure of Common Fields* (London, 1907)

John Sly, *Town Government in Massachusetts (1620–1930)* (Cambridge, 1930)

C. F. D. Sperling, *A Short History of the Borough of Sudbury* (Sudbury, 1898)

W. E. Tate, *The Parish Chest* (Cambridge, 1946), Vols. I, III

John Underhill, "The Pequot War" in *America Begins* (New York, 1950)

S. Ward, *Jethro's Justice of the Peace* (London, 1621)

Edward Watson, Ashmore, *History of the Parish* (Gloucester, 1890)

Sidney and Beatrice Webb, *English Local Government* (London, 1906)

William B. Willcox, *Gloucestershire, a Study in Local Government, 1590–1640* (New Haven, 1940)

Ola Winslow, *Meetinghouse Hill* (New York, 1952)

Alexander Young, ed., *Chronicles of Massachusetts Bay* (Cambridge, 1846)